PETER GABRIEL

PETER GABRIEL

An Authorized Biography

SPENCER BRIGHT

SIDGWICK & JACKSON
LONDON

For Ian Annett, 1953–78

'Over the nakedness of truth – the diaphanous cloak of fantasy.'
Eça de Queirós.

First published in Great Britain in February 1988 by
Sidgwick & Jackson Limited

First reprint March 1988
Second reprint April 1988

ISBN 0-283-99498-3

Typeset by Hewer Text Composition Services, Edinburgh
Printed by Adlard & Son Limited
Letchworth, Herts SG6 1JS
for Sidgwick & Jackson Limited
1 Tavistock Chambers, Bloomsbury Way,
London WC1A 2SG

CONTENTS

ACKNOWLEDGEMENTS

This book would not have been possible without the help of the following: Paul Vaughan Phillips for research, transcriptions and insight; Norma Bishop; Carol Willis Impey; Sheryl Gordon; Peter Thomspon; Chris Welch; Jerry Gilbert; Sinclair Salisbury; Anthony Hentschel; Sandy Campbell; Michelle Attanasio; Kgalushi Koka of The Black Peoples Convention; Virgin/Charisma Records – Lee Ellen Newman, Elly Smith, Sian Davies; Barbara Charone; Andrew Collier; Jack Barrie; Brian Gibbons; London Evening Standard Library – Jeff Daish and Jim McShane; Jo-Anne Smith; Kes Owen; Mick Brown; Mike Belben and Smiths Restaurant, Covent Garden; Amanda Gardner; Gordon Coxon (Performance Research); Roy Burchell (Melody Maker); Fiona Foulgar (NME); Geoff and Judy Parkyn of The Genesis Information Service; BBC – Tina Ladwa, Kevin Howlett; Jenny Cathcart; Christine Gorham (MTV UK); Nicholas Treadwell; Belinda Ackerman; Patrick Humphries; Susan Hill, Jane MacAndrew and Juliet Van Oss at Sidgwick and Jackson; Mike Kay, commercial director, British Air Ferries; Jim Reid, assistant manager, Royal Bank of Scotland, Curzon Street, Mayfair; Charterhouse School – Mr Peter Attenborough, Headmaster, and Dr E. H. Zillekens, Archivist; Susie Howard, Rosalind Russell and Peter Holt for their forebearance; The University for Peace, Apartado 199, Escazu, Costa Rica; Dr Daniel Hausermann; Julia Hausermann, Director, Rights and Humanity, 65 Swinton Street, London WC1X 9NT; and Chrissy Iley for not being there when I did not need her.

This book was digitally written on a Commodore Amiga 1000 512k using Word Perfect 4.1 word processing software.

PREFACE

Tony Stratton Smith was concerned that he had inconvenienced me. On the morning of my arrival in Jersey to interview him for this book he started to feel very ill. A doctor had already visited and diagnosed a perforated ulcer.

I arrived at his friend Vera Bampton's large Victorian home overlooking the bay at St Helier, Jersey, just before noon. She was upset and said Tony could not see me and would have to go into hospital. I was ushered into her living room and enjoyed the view of the sea while, unknown to me, an ambulance arrived to carry Strat away.

Before being taken to Jersey's general hospital, Strat asked his financial adviser, Andrew MacHutchon, to take me to lunch. Andrew later visited Strat to report I was well fed, and drunk, and had been deposited back on to the plane. I will allow Andrew his little lie about my sobriety.

Strat was cheered in those last hours with this news, and promised to bring me back out to Jersey a few weeks later so that our postponed interview could take place. From what I have learnt about Strat this was typical. Despite his own discomfort, he was still concerned for others.

I had been trying to get to him for over three months, having missed him when he had last been in London in early December 1986. He finally agreed to see me while he was visiting Vera, a friend who shared his love of racehorses. He arrived in Jersey via Lisbon and Paris from his tax exile home in Las Palmas in the Canary Islands. He had to see his legal and financial advisers and asked Vera to book appointments with her doctor and dentist because he did not trust the local Las Palmas ones.

A few days before my visit I spoke to him briefly on the telephone. He sounded happy. He was proud he had lost 22lbs in weight, although a doctor had told him to ease up because he was dieting too quickly. He said he had an upset stomach, but was sure he would be all right in the next few days. Both of us were looking forward to discussing Peter Gabriel and his long association with Charisma Records.

Strat died just after 2 a.m. on Wednesday 19 March 1987 aged fifty-three, a few hours after surgery had revealed the full extent of his cancer. We do not know whether he was aware of his illness; most of his friends feel it is unlikely. They were thankful his last days were spent not alone in exile, but entertained and finally comforted by trusted business associates and Vera.

In an addendum to the obituary which appeared in *The Times* on 24 March, Peter Gabriel wrote:

Tony Stratton Smith was a rarity in the entertainment business – a man of passion and a crusader.

He believed that rock music could, and should, be more than teenage fashion fodder, and his love for the best of British determined the character of the Charisma label.

The Mad Hatter's Tea Party was his choice of label logo, and there was nowhere else you could find such diverse and eclectic talent as John Betjeman, Vivian Stanshall, Peter Hammill, John Arlott, the Nice, Monty Python, Genesis, Bert Jansch, Dame Edna Everadge and Lindisfarne under one roof.

Despite the competitive nature of the business, he cared more for the quality of the work than the quantity sold, always preferring the difficult challenge of backing outsiders. His artists were supported as family.

His favourite occupations he listed as writing, talking and drinking, and, in each, he could compete with the best.

Strat earned himself a unique place in the worlds of entertainment and sport, a big man with a big heart, I will miss him.

Tony Stratton Smith gave Peter Gabriel invaluable freedom to develop as an artist. He was more of a mentor and a confidante than a record company boss, never forcing Gabriel to change course despite financial and career pressures. It is doubtful whether Peter Gabriel's early career would have followed the same course without his support.

REAL WORLD

Looking out on to the wilderness you can see the sea on the near horizon. The roads leading up to this spot suddenly disappear underground. You become aware that all is not what it seems.

Carefully hidden in the trees are small buildings, little huts really. Some have stairs leading down, others mask ventilation ducts. Beneath you lies another world, the Real World.

As you descend you see what you thought was simply forest and meadows is an illusion. Stairs hug cavern walls, sunlight streams through, natural caves lead into huge underground spaces going in every direction.

Signs point to Minotaur Maze, Ride of Fears, Black Hole, Psyche Drama, Big Dipper Tripper, Hall of Digital Mirrors. It sounds like a fourth dimensional funfair.

Families with children, individuals, groups, and sightseers stroll aimlessly or purposefully. Artists, sculptors, film and video directors, avant garde and pop musicians, psychologists and visionaries have all contributed to the Real World.

You have to go underground, as in Greek mythology, to be initiated, returning to the surface and 'normality'. Those who dare enter the Ride of Fears with its twelve chambers, one for each of our most common phobias. You choose the fear intensity from one to ten. Inside, a computer detects your phobias. They become a holographic reality, crawling over and engulfing you. If you pass through the chamber without pressing the panic button you get a bravery token, if you cannot cope you eject.

You move on, pause briefly with relief, and then gaze down a corridor. In the dim light there are muttering figures stretching into the distance. They are lifelike sculptures that gradually disappear into walls studded with countless glistening razor blades.

The door behind locks, it has no handle, it starts to move, pushing you forward down a corridor barely wider than a person. You must avoid getting lacerated as it gets narrower and narrower. You breath in to try

and make yourself as thin as possible, but it is no use, you brush against
a razor, your brain registering pain before the actual touch . . . only to
find the blades are made out of rubber. In front is the exit.

You see an old fashioned crossroads signpost. You choose Hall of
Digital Mirrors for comic relief. You enter a bare room with mirrors on
all four walls and the ceiling. You are surrounded by images of yourself.
These are not normal mirrors, but 3D video screens. You can distort
your reflection, change colour, turn into an angel or monster, fly over
the Grand Canyon, through Saturn's rings, or join an adventure with
figures from mythology and science fiction.

You carry on. Throughout this wonderland, despite the sense of space
and activity, there is an underlying calm. For, unlike above-the-surface
theme parks and funfairs, here there are relatively few mechanical
devices, the computer is in control.

> *If you go down to Willow Farm,*
> *To look for butterflies, flutterbyes, gutterflies*
> *Open your eyes, it's full of surprise, everyone lies,*
> *Like the fox on the rocks,*
> *And the musical box.*
> *Oh, there's Mum and Dad, and good and bad,*
> *And everyone's happy to be here.*

'Willow Farm', Gabriel, 1972

Willow Farm, a verse from 'Supper's Ready' on the 1972 Genesis
Foxtrot album, saw the first expression of Peter Gabriel's
formative ideas for the Real World theme park. These ideas have
crept into lyrics and videos throughout his career.

> *You could have a big dipper*
> *going up and down, and around the bends*
> *you could have a bumper car, bumping*
> *this amusement never ends*

'Sledgehammer', Gabriel, 1986

The literal interpretation of this excerpt from 'Sledgehammer',
even if not the connotations, are obvious enough.

Peter Gabriel called Real World "A hybrid mix of university,
holiday camp, theme park and Disneyland. A place where people
can go to test themselves, to challenge themselves and entertain
themselves, ideally transform certain parts of what they are."

As yet this dream world, a place once called Gabrieland,
remains hypothetical.

SABBATICAL

The lettuces were not behaving themselves. They should have been leafy and juicy, but persisted in bolting to seed. The country idyll was not proving as straightforward as Peter Gabriel had imagined.

In the first part of 1975 he had frantically performed a rock epic to ecstatic crowds in America and Europe in his final tour with Genesis.

Over the next year in his small cottage on the edge of the Cotswolds, Gabriel had time to think and retreat into himself. At first he was excited and inspired by his new solitude. But as he started to divide his time between playing the piano distractedly and tending to his vegetables, his wife Jill began to fear for his sanity.

"Actually, it was awful. The first little period was lovely, for moments. But I knew that he would slowly go mad. It seemed a very short period before I was encouraging him, telling him, 'You know you can do it, you have to do it. Don't give it up, or you know you will go mad.'" Peter had lost confidence in his abilities as a musician.

"I could feel this thing with the vegetables becoming quite obsessive. He went into himself very much. He would go to the piano and play for hours. He seemed to be going more and more inward. I felt at that point that it was going to get . . . it seems odd to say, it felt dangerous . . . he needed to come outward."

Gabriel's recollection is not so much of incipient madness as introversion, and a determination to be self-sufficient in vegetables. "I was totally ignorant and enthusiastic, so I planted all my lettuces at the same time," said Peter. "I had the Week of the Thousand Lettuces! And then, after, they just went to seed. My carrots were all eaten by worms. We had some good potatoes, but any fool can grow potatoes – they just grow themselves. Runner beans we did OK."

The preoccupation with vegetables bore out one sentence in Gabriel's farewell press statement on leaving Genesis: "I could not expect the band to tie in their schedules with my bondage to cabbages." But this flippancy masked a deeper dissatisfaction that had developed a year earlier when he first became a father. The group did not want to tie in their schedules to his family crises. Naïvely, he was hurt and angered that they put their careers before all else.

Jill was twenty-two and Peter twenty-four when their daughter Anna-Marie was born on 26 July 1974 at St Mary's Hospital, Paddington. Jill had been warned by her doctor that there might be complications. The doctor feared a breech birth, and advised her that the hospital and not their isolated cottage would be the best place for the birth. Until then Peter and Jill had an image of a perfect Le Boyer birth in the warmth and security of their own home. Instead Jill had to move back from Bath to stay with her parents in Kensington.

At the time Gabriel was in the middle of preparing *The Lamb Lies Down On Broadway*, destined to be his final Genesis album. The group were rehearsing in Hampshire before going off to record in Wales. Despite his work commitments he managed to be present at Anna's birth.

Doctors prevented Anna having a breech birth. But in so doing they had to turn her twice, thus wrapping the umbilical chord around her neck. For a while Anna stopped breathing, and had to be ventilated.

Peter remembered, "Anna nearly died. She caught an infection. I was thinking, 'Get the baby on the breast,' all the natural things. What came out was a green lump that was carried away in silver foil like chicken bones." Jill did not see her baby after the birth, and had to wait until the next day when she could view her in an incubator in the premature baby unit. Anna had inhaled fluid during the birth which caused complications in the lungs. Doctors also suspected that she had meningitis, and gave her spinal injections of antibiotics. Jill also suffered a subsequent infection.

"That night they came to me and told me she might not live," said Jill. "It took me six months to make her alive. I mentally rejected her. Peter was wonderful, but such a soppy dad. He used to say hello to her every day and talk to her through the glass of the premature baby ward."

For Peter Gabriel the pressure was becoming intolerable. "Those first two weeks were really traumatic and the band were incredibly unsympathetic. They were pissed off I wasn't taking the album as seriously as my child.

"Having Anna was an experience that put the rest of my life in shadow. I didn't want to be a production-line rock star any more. It was more important to me that things were right with Jill and Anna than with the record. It built up a lot of bad feeling inside the band."

Genesis were poised for major international stardom when Peter Gabriel left in May 1975, seemingly throwing everyone's career into jeopardy. By that time Anna had fully recovered from her difficult birth. For the first time since they moved to the countryside just outside Bath in March 1974, the family had a chance to properly settle into their cottage. Jill had found the transition more difficult than Peter. She had been a town girl and felt she'd been dumped down in the middle of nowhere.

"I said I'd die leaving London. My family were there, my friends were there. People were always vital. I couldn't stand to be by myself, ever," said Jill. But Peter, coming to terms with fatherhood earlier than he had expected to, was insistent his child should be brought up in the country. Jill was persuaded by that argument, but it took her a year to adjust. She was not helped by the suspicions of the locals.

"I wasn't accepted at first. I was this extraordinary pregnant woman walking around in a long dress in the middle of a community which was full of farming. They had heard rumours, from the previous owner of the house, that this wild multi-coloured-haired pop star was coming to live there. It was as difficult for them to accept me as for me to fit in, in some ways. But in having Anna a mother that lived next door took me on, and I found a way of fitting in, via the children, and being accepted."

In those initial months of retreat after the split with Genesis, the Gabriel family's financial future was uncertain. Peter had enough money to survive the next few years, but not enough to retire on. The cottage was bought with a £16,000 mortgage, and part of that was thanks to a loan from Peter's parents.

Gabriel's sabbatical was a period of necessary contrasts; a flight from the madness of the rock world to the isolation and beauty of the Cotswolds, according to Richard Macphail. He was a school friend from Charterhouse, Genesis' first de facto manager and roadie, then Peter Gabriel's road manager at the start of his solo career. Macphail is now one of Gabriel's closest friends. "He let himself go in a way that he hadn't been able to do before and it was a great release. I was never worried about his mental health. It was just a complete pendulum swing in another direction. He just flopped and let it all hang out," said Macphail.

"He just felt he had the freedom to do all the things he couldn't do while he was in the group and he just did them until he got it out of his system and the music just started coming back. He wrote 'Here Comes The Flood' during that period.

"He was discovering himself as a family man. And I think that that period really provided him with a foundation for him being able to do both now, which was what he was unable to do during Genesis. Coupled with the fact he is now in control of his own career and he's not subject to other people's decisions.

"It was a measure of his commitment to Jill and the family that he was willing to give all that up. He was willing to do something that a lot of people wouldn't do; most people let the family thing go."

The move to the country in spring 1974 was partly prompted by Gabriel's enduring belief that society should be divided into smaller units, on a more human scale. He was initially inspired by an advertisement in a magazine which held out the prospect of an experimental community. "I was looking for purpose and a sense of self. The idea of being self-sufficient and independent appealed to me because I felt I had become dependent on the music business, and the community seemed to be the physical embodiment of some idealism, which I had always been attracted to," said Gabriel. Ironically the community called itself Genesis, though that was not mentioned in the advertisement.

Gabriel was impressed with the fat brochure, the manifesto and the detailed questionnaire that arrived. "It was a mixture of psychological, spiritual, and political new thinking. It would now be described as an attractive yuppie package," said Gabriel.

It included reports on the philosophers, writers and movements that had influenced the instigators of the proposed community. One of the most important was Henry Thoreau who, with Ralph Waldo Emerson, was a leading figure in the Transcendental Club, a romantic and reformist literary movement in New England in the mid-nineteenth century. Thoreau, author of *Walden: or Life in the Woods*, was a progenitor of the hippy ideal of returning to nature. The founders of the Genesis community were also inspired by psychologist B. F. Skinner's 1948 novel, *Walden Two*, based on life in a Utopian community and modelled on his principles of behaviourism and social engineering. They were also impressed with Werner Erhard and his Erhard Seminar Training.

Although interviewed and accepted for the experiment in community living, Gabriel never joined.

"It was being run in a very professional way, unlike most of the community things. They had auditions and they were turning people away in their hundreds. It took a long time to put together and I realized there was no way I could stay in control of my music in the community. It was full of idealism, but full of impracticalities as well. As the year went on I got back into playing music and I began to think, I don't want other people having a vote on whether I can tour, or whether I can afford to make a 24-track record or a 4-track record. I want to be in control of that." The Genesis community never did live up to the promise of that brochure, though trial communities were set up in the United States and Ireland.

The break from the music business had allowed Gabriel to indulge his spiritual and intellectual fantasies. In the few interviews he gave during this sabbatical his ideas were muddled and his confidence low. He joked about the 'Cosmic Cadet Force', a name inspired by the Combined Cadet Force military training at public schools. "Some people are too heavenly to be of earthly use and too earthly to be of heavenly use," he told Chris Welch of *Melody Maker*. Perhaps having been too earthly with Genesis he was now becoming too heavenly alone.

He explored other ways of discovering himself, from trying out bio-feedback machines designed to reduce stress, to reading about the paranormal. He studied the I Ching, valuing the advice of this Chinese oracle. Though for many the I Ching became little more than a parlour game, Gabriel kept it for matters of great importance. He has taken some of his biggest decisions on the toss of a coin.

He went with Jill on a Silva Mind Control course in London inspired by the work of the California-based Mexican Dr Jose Silva. The mind control exercises had them learning how to memorize a hundred different things and promised techniques to unlock the unconscious powers of the mind, including telepathic ways of diagnosing illnesses.

In Bath he took dance, yoga and piano lessons. "I've never quite lived up to my Fred Astaire fantasies . . . I'm not the most natural of movers, but it was something I wanted to know more about."

He was relieved at having severed ties with Genesis. But he

soon realized that he needed to reach out beyond the family and local community. "I think I went through a strange period, I think it's similar to when people retire. Part of the way they relate to the world is through their work. When you suddenly remove that – in my case I had removed it voluntarily – it was quite unsettling.

"I didn't feel I had a base of self-respect from which to launch other projects. I didn't realize I had lanced some of myself too in cutting off from Genesis. In other words, that some of my confidence came from being an active musician who was getting a few strokes. It wasn't all bad, but there was a sense of 'What the hell am I doing?' and 'What purpose is there for me carrying on?' That sounds suicidal, but it wasn't. But then I did a lot of thinking. I think sabbaticals should become a part of everyone's life. People should do the opposite of what they normally do for a while, and see what happens, because you learn a lot. I think I did learn."

Before leaving Genesis, Peter had started writing songs with Martin Hall, a poet and lyricist with a deadpan Black Country wit. It was Gabriel's first collaboration outside of the group, and he developed a close friendship with Hall. "Peter had not only left the band, but he had left London. So he was not living in the same environment either physically, emotionally, intellectually, spiritually or any other way you could think of. It was a total change for him," Martin Hall remembered.

"Having come out of the little cocoon that he had lived in he felt a complete change was better than still being in and around London seeing many of the same people. So he thought, let's go for broke."

In 1974 Charisma Books, an offshoot of Tony Stratton Smith's Charisma Records, had published a book of Hall's poetry. The title poem, 'The Stan Cullis Blues', about a legendary Wolverhampton Wanderers football manager, read:

> *The night Stan Cullis got the sack*
> *Wolverhampton wandered round in circles*
> *Like a disallowed goal*
> *Looking for a friendly linesman.*

Hall and Gabriel had met in 1969, drawn by a common introversion, and artistic and mystical interests. They first thought about working together in 1973 during the recording of the Genesis album *Selling England by the Pound*. "He came round one afternoon because he was quite troubled by his progress. I acted as a sounding board and it helped him finish the lyrics," said Hall.

On the cover of his paperback Hall was described as a "rock poet". Any reader who had failed to notice his songwriting credits was promised they soon would, "for he is currently working on, among other projects, an album with Genesis' leader, Peter Gabriel".

Hall wishes that blurb had never appeared. His and Gabriel's idea of writing an album of songs to be recorded by other artists never materialized. They started their songwriting partnership first at the Gabriels' Notting Hill Gate flat, continuing at the cottage.

Hall and Gabriel were introduced by record producer John Anthony while he worked on *Trespass*, the first Genesis album on the Charisma label. Hall had written songs for Rare Bird, Charisma's first signing and hit act.

"John felt that we would get on and had a lot in common musically, and he was right. We became fairly close friends, but didn't actually work together for quite some time." In October 1973 Jill and Peter were witnesses at Martin's wedding. "Peter was my closest friend at the time," said Martin.

"I suppose it was like a late schoolboy relationship. One of us would say, you must see this film, or must read that book. I remember Peter being very impressed by the Jodorowsky film *El Topo*, which has the flavour of a spaghetti western made by Buñuel. And I think I dragged him to see *Solaris* by Tarkovsky, hopelessly arty, but it was a general creative interchange." Their common reading matter was the essential list for the seeker of truth at that period including *The Tibetan Book of the Dead*, Carlos Casteneda's *Journey to Ixtlan* and books on Zen Buddhism.

"He was able to investigate himself more than hitherto when he got to the cottage," said Hall. "He certainly didn't drink or drug. He believed in what has come to be a somewhat sneered at cliché, the natural high. He was a bit scared of losing control. He was comfortable with the environment that he was in, but he was ill at ease inside himself for a while because he was trying to find out who he was and what he was capable of, because much of his talent, ability, ideas, had, in my view, been repressed within Genesis." The relative isolation of the cottage only encouraged Gabriel's shyness; he became nervous and hesitant in company to such an extent that it appeared he was stammering.

"He'd lived and worked in almost the same environment for a

9

good many years. The band came out of school and onto the road, and it was almost like a divorce, I suppose. In a sense it was the first time that he had stepped out into the world. Inevitably he was nervous at times, but I never had the impression that he would go completely bananas."

Gabriel was trying to improve as a writer. At first he did not want to perform and tried to think of new ways to stage other acts performing his songs. "Underlying it all, of course," said Hall, "was a determination to prove that he could do it without Genesis."

During 1975 Martin Hall and Peter Gabriel worked on about a dozen songs, half of which were completed. The urge to write for Peter Gabriel had been irresistible. "I think lots of art – it seems like a grand word, but I mean painting, music, any sort of creative activity – has some therapeutic value, and it's a means of externalizing thoughts and feelings. So I was doing it regardless, and then I got into the situation that I was in at the beginning of Genesis, of being a songwriter and not wanting to become a performer, and I was having trouble interesting people in my songs. We took the songs to a few publishers."

Gabriel and Hall could at least rely on Charisma to back them. They launched their joint songwriting career with a light-hearted number, 'You Never Know', and chose the lightweight comedian Charlie Drake to record it. Drake was a bizarre contrast to the Olympian Genesis. A buffoon on films and TV, the diminutive Drake was famous for his immortal phrase: "Hello my darlings."

Gabriel, inspired by his love of animation, imagined Drake as a cartoon character. "We thought maybe we should try and get a hit record and sell it as a TV idea. We were looking at idiosyncratic comedians and Charlie Drake seemed like a good choice. I had sketches of this stick-insect type character that would have fitted in." The character was loosely inspired by Jiminy Cricket, and Hall and Gabriel took the idea to George Dunning, the animator and creator of the Beatles' *Yellow Submarine*. He was not impressed enough to support the project.

Drake lived in a mansion block opposite Leicester Square, and Gabriel remembers him spending a lot of time looking out of his window at people walking past. 'You Never Know' was released on 21 November 1975. "When we wrote it we were just trying to find out if we could write a song together," recalled Hall. "It started with me having an exceptionally mundane

10

guitar riff and oddly enough I think Peter maybe came up with the title.

"Looking back it is not really funny. It's not a comedy song in the way you would have expected from Charlie Drake. With hindsight it is just Peter and me showing off."

The record used an unlikely collection of some of the most respected musicians of the day; jazz fusion pianist Keith Tippett, Sandy Denny, Brian Eno and Robert Fripp, with Gabriel producing, and Steve Nye, who went on to produce Roxy Music, mixing.

The punning lyrics were typical of Hall's over-clever play on words. The bouncy up-tempo single had Charlie Drake getting as close as he could to sounding like Peter Gabriel, though he could not resist opening with "hello my darlings". The first verse ran:

> *You never know who the honeycombs*
> *You never know why the hippodromes*
> *You never know where the waterfalls*
> *You never know when the basketballs*

The chorus included the lines:

> *Things on wings are wonderwise, the melon sings.*
> *And butterflies don't want to fall!*
> *Pop an illusion!*
> *Better get the butternut, better let the lily put the lullaby.*

'You Never Know', Hall/Gabriel, 1975

A Charisma press release interpreted the line "pop an illusion" as a send-up of pop stardom, hinting at Peter Gabriel's departure from Genesis. The lyrics were Hall's, and had little significance other than in the way they sounded.

Gabriel took the Charlie Drake single seriously, said Hall. "It was never intended as any kind of lark. Peter actually wanted to do it. It was one of his songs, albeit co-written, and he was going to produce and put the whole thing together with his choice of musicians, and he hadn't done that before." Despite promised heavy TV and radio coverage designed to make 'You Never Know' the Christmas single of 1975, the record, as the music industry says, stiffed.

Only one of Gabriel and Hall's songs, what became the barber shop a capella 'Excuse Me', was ever recorded by Peter Gabriel. "'Excuse Me' was one of several musical fragments he gave me on tape. I would take those bits away and come up with a title or shape a chorus into it somehow. And then we would get back together and work on it overall together where possible. 'Excuse Me' was almost entirely his music and almost entirely my words. I think he changed one line of the words. It was originally called 'I Want To Be Alone'. It seems to be aimed at Genesis, but it wasn't," said Hall.

When Gabriel and Hall wrote they would throw lyrical ideas at each other, praising, criticizing or suggesting improvements. "We finished about half a dozen songs, and probably some of the unfinished bits are better than the finished bits, which is often the way. He had gone through the catharsis of that period and come out the other side as a confident solo songwriter," said Hall.

By Christmas 1975 Gabriel's sabbatical was inexorably leading towards a new recording career. With this in mind he tried to make his songs as different as possible from Genesis'. "A lot of my new stuff is very emotional. Genesis wasn't a platform for personal songs, you couldn't have a good dose of self-pity," he told one interviewer. "I'll probably record an album soon, but there won't be any heavy sell solo career and I'm not going on the road yet because that would defeat a lot of the object I left the band for."

CHILDHOOD

The River Bourne, as it flowed through Deep Pool Farm, brought out Peter Gabriel's boyhood sense of adventure. It presented a challenge that had to be confronted and surmounted.

He would gather branches, twigs, stones and mud and wade into the water. Slowly and determinedly he would construct a dam, raising the level of the water. When it was high enough he would enjoy the fruits of this labour and swim. Occasionally he would light a fire on top of the dam. "That was a nice thing to do, because the water would eventually overflow and gradually push these smouldering embers over into the water."

Once a year he had to face the demolition of his constructions. The Bourne is a tributary of the River Wey which flows into the Thames. Thames Conservancy workers would make their way down the river in a punt hacking down all the weeds and clearing all obstructions, including up to five Gabriel dams. "I was obsessed with dam making and fire making, which a lot of shrinks would relate more to sex. I think if in doubt they always say sex," said Peter.

Deep Pool Farm gave the infant Gabriel space to explore and the freedom to daydream. He would go into the farm buildings with his younger sister Anne and build dens in the hay bales connected by passages.

He was not the most gregarious of playmates, but he had his mischievous moments, like climbing into an oak tree along the main road with a friend and flicking acorns at passing cars. When he was older he enjoyed trying to catch his and Anne's friends in the net of his imagination. One summer, during their teens, their mother held a dance for them. Peter decorated the living room with stems of maize grown for the farm cattle. He stood the maize upright in land drains left lying around by his father who was installing them on the farm. "He constructed a tunnel made out of wood and netting which you had to crawl

13

into to get to the dance. We greeted them at the other end in the room that was made to look like a jungle," said Anne.

"I had this crawl-way so people coming in had to arrive in the room on all fours," Peter remembered. "I used to get fed up at the way people would come in to a party with an act. There was a lot of defence based on fear, but I thought it might effectively loosen things up a little, which it did. We are creatures of habit, and when the habit is broken we are much more awake and responsive; you have got to throw people off their guard before they open up." The original inspiration came from mythology in which mazes were built for initiates to penetrate.

He was known as a pyromaniac when he toured in the early days with Genesis. Instead of stopping in transport cafés the group would buy bread and cheese and stop off in a field for a picnic, sometimes taking their guitars and harmonium. "Even if it was only for half an hour Peter would be off with lots of soggy sticks and things to light a fire," recalled Richard Macphail, his friend and then road manager. "We'd all arrive at the gig stinking of wood smoke."

Peter's boyhood sense of wonder and defiance has not left him. One of his more recent constructions was a hot bath built while on holiday with friends and family. "He got the idea he wanted to make something for the kids on the beach, so he spent all one afternoon digging a huge hole that we filled with water," said Richard Macphail. "Then he made a fire, collecting these great big rocks and heating them in the fire and then putting them in the water. And then, of course, he'd create this hot bath and we'd all say wonderful and we'd get in and splash around for ten minutes and then it was all over. But it's that kind of determination and single-mindedness he has to do his thing. He'd always do his best to drag everyone else into it."

Peter Brian Gabriel was dragged into the world at Woking Hospital, Surrey, on 13 February 1950. "As a little baby he was so happy and utterly contented," remembered his mother Irene.

His father Ralph Gabriel was an electrical engineer working in London who employed a resident bailiff and a tractor driver to handle the day-to-day running of the family dairy farm. The 150-acre Coxhill Farm, near Chobham, in a rare unspoilt part of this over-developed and affluent county, had been in the Gabriel family since 1915.

Ralph Gabriel was brought up in Coxhill, the large country house believed to date from Elizabethan times that the farm

14

took its name from. Its panelled walls and billiard room, formal garden and croquet lawn, inspired some of Peter's later song-writing.

Peter's grandfather died while his parents were on honey-moon, Coxhill was sold, and the proceeds divided up by the family. Ralph and Irene moved into Deep Pool, one of the farm cottages, and Ralph kept the farmland until his own retirement in 1977. The wooden beams in the more modest Deep Pool house date back to the 1620s. It had been added to through the centuries, and was extensively modernized by Ralph Gabriel.

The Gabriel name is believed to have originated in Spain. The family can be traced back to Christopher Gabriel, a plane maker, who was born in Cornwall in 1675. He prospered and founded what became the timber merchants Gabriel, Wade and English. The family wealth derived from imported timber from Scandinavia and Russia used as sleepers for the expanding nineteenth-century railways network. Peter was not the first celebrated Gabriel; in 1866 his ancestor, Sir Thomas Gabriel, became Lord Mayor of London.

Ralph Gabriel is an inventor and DIY enthusiast. He has taken out seven or eight patents on farming and cable TV inventions. But the patents have long since run out and he has never capitalized on them. In the sixties as chief engineer for Rediffusion TV he installed the world's first public fibre optic system, Dial a Programme. He studied at the University of London, and during the war helped develop artificial direction-finding systems for use in training for the RAF. The company he worked for expanded and later built flight simulators, devices that have fascinated Peter. Ralph still works on various ideas in his sophisticated workshop behind the house.

One of his biggest home improvements was the swimming pool Peter helped him construct in the garden in 1964. The Gabriels were ecologically sound even then. Ralph devised an elementary solar heating panel made from a large sheet of aluminium painted black to warm up the pool.

But Peter never shared his father's enthusiasm for the workshop or his mother's love of horses. He was first put on a horse at the age of three, but despite having a natural seat he decided horses were only for girls and by the age of five would have no more to do with them.

His mother's other passion was playing the piano, like her own mother, who sang at one of Sir Henry Wood's Promenade concerts. "My mother played the piano very well. She could play back anything she had heard. She had perfect pitch," said Mrs Gabriel. If her impersonation of her mother was accurate then Peter's grandmother sounded like a stern Edwardian schoolmistress booming "C sharp in the bass, dear!"

Irene was one of five sisters, two of whom studied at the Royal Academy of Music. The family would entertain each other with musical evenings at home, a tradition carried on by Irene Gabriel in her capacity as chair of the Chobham Music Club which holds concerts in its members' homes, including her own.

Irene's father, Colonel Edward Watts Allen, OBE, also sang, though only in an amateur fashion. He was one of eleven children, and left school at the age of eleven to help his impoverished mother when his schoolteacher father died. He started in a printer's shop, went on to help Sir Woodman Burbidge, Chairman of Harrods, set up a training school for shop assistants, and eventually became chairman and managing director of the Civil Service Stores in the Strand. Colonel Watts Allen was a keen athlete, golfer, skier, salmon fisher, bridge player and gambler. He flew with his family to Le Touquet and Monte Carlo to enjoy the casinos. "He was a great fighter in everything. The more the odds were against him, the better he liked it and the better he did. I think Peter has perhaps inherited that," said Mrs Gabriel.

His mother's musical tradition didn't impress Peter. "He was bored with his piano, there was not a strong enough incentive to go on with the lessons," said Mrs Gabriel. Peter showed no interest in music, nor was he interested in any of the other lessons his mother inflicted on him, including French and ballroom dancing, and gave everything up by the age of nine.

He would rather play with his sister Anne, twenty months his junior, with the bailiff David Wilson's children, Juliet, Jane and Jeremy, and tractor driver Bill Punter's children Pat and Sheena.

Anne did everything Peter did not. She persevered with the piano showing musical ability if not technical accomplishment, and loved horses. "I think I was an obnoxious little girl. I liked pleasing everybody and doing what they asked me," she remembered. "I always learnt pieces off by heart."

The two played together well, though Peter did take advantage of his sister's weak bladder. "Wet at both ends, my title used to be. Peter used to sit astride me and tickle me and then say, mummy, mummy look what Anne has done."

Anne got more attention not out of favouritism, but because she took part in more activities. Peter said, "There were times when I would be left to my own devices. My mother and sister were both into riding and pony clubs. This didn't appeal to me, so I would find myself wandering around in a world of my own. That's probably when I started my preoccupation with fantasy." When Peter and Anne played together she would usually follow his lead. "I tended to look up to him for ideas. He was mainly the one who thought up what games to do."

Peter did not always come off unscathed in his explorations. Accompanied by the other children on the farm, he once went to investigate his parents' attic. In the dark Peter inadvertently put his fingers into a live light socket. The tractor driver's daughter Pat, who was wearing gumboots, pulled him down. And a forlorn, white-faced Peter slumped down stairs.

Peter confesses to a very uninhibited sex life up to the age of ten, thanks largely to the presence of the daughters of the tractor driver and bailiff. "That provided much open and liberated and safe sex. I think it was my first experience of sadism because there was one girl who used to love using stinging nettles in strange ways. I leave the rest to your imagination."

"The whole lot of them used to have fun together around the farm. Peter was a bit of a loner, he wasn't the sort that wanted to have people round to play tennis," said Mrs Gabriel.

"I had a very happy and free childhood," said Peter. "My father was an influence in the sense that he was always in his workshop and he used to build things out of nothing. He has a very creative mind. And my mother's piano playing was regularly sinking into my subconscious."

Though Peter and Anne were brought up in the Church of England, their parents were never regular churchgoers until their children left home. "Prayers and bible stories were a part of our lives, but Peter and Anne didn't see it genuinely lived by us," said Mrs Gabriel. Not enamoured of organized religion, Peter was first introduced to other spiritual traditions through his father, whose shelves were full of books on theosophy and Eastern religions. When Peter was in his teens his father took up yoga, which he thanks for his enduring health.

In most other ways the Gabriels were a conventional upper middle-class English family. They behaved formally even among themselves, with voices rarely raised. "It seemed claustrophobic to me in some ways. There was an enormous amount of love and, latterly, an enormous amount of support, but it wasn't always as open as I wanted it to be," said Peter.

Despite being hemmed in emotionally, Peter benefited from

17

adventurous childhood holidays. He went deep-sea fishing in Spain and skiing in Norway. "We went to Norway in 1960 with friends of ours. We were near the Hardanger Glacier, it was miles from anywhere, very remote, and we went for a walk. It was unwalkable in the snow so we went up the railway line and into the tunnel. There was not much room to press against the tunnel wall as a train came past. I think we flatter ourselves it was more dangerous than it was," said Mrs Gabriel.

If he does not stumble into danger, Peter often courts it, pursuing what his mother calls his "obstinate nonsense" against all advice, even as an adult. In the winter of 1976 he went with family and friends to the French alps. "The local ski-professionals gave a floodlit display one evening for the tourists, including some stunts from the ski-jump," said Mrs Gabriel. "When it was all over, my idiot son was determined to have a go over this ski-jump. Time and time again he tried and always took a terrific purler falling backwards and cracking his head. Jill and I could hardly bear to look but the more we begged him to stop, the more determined he was to continue. He wanted to achieve one jump without falling. However, on this occasion, he couldn't manage it, but mercifully didn't break his skull."

Peter's uncompromising nature is chronicled in his first school report in the summer of 1955 from Cable House pre-prep school in Woking. "Peter does his very best and would rather leave a word out than spell it incorrectly." Even at this age he was plagued by doubt about his own ability though teachers noticed his self-confidence growing. One report said he needed to express himself more quickly and clearly. But one thing was clear when he was six, his voice: he sang "very sweetly".

When he was nine Peter went to St Andrew's prep school in Woking. He never liked eating meat and used to leave it at the side of the plate, causing particular problems with a master who used to try and force it down him. Nevertheless, in the Christmas term, 1959, Peter was top of the form. "An excellent term as his place shows. But is he really as worried as he sometimes appears?" questioned headmaster W. T. C. Maynard, who obviously liked his boys to be jolly. The following year he wrote, "Many reports condemn inattention and frivolity: in his case, a little gaiety would not come amiss." Peter must have eventually cheered up. In his final report from St Andrew's in the summer of 1963 the housemaster wrote, "He is thoughtful, kind and unselfish and amusing." And the headmaster wrote, "He will be missed very much."

"Peter was popular, he was liked, but he was a loner, in a way," said Mrs Gabriel. "He did quite well at school. I was surprised to see him often in the first one or two in the form. He was certainly no brilliant academic, no scholarship boy." But, as his father remembers, he always was a conscientious worker.

In his last year at St Andrew's he became a weekday boarder to prepare him for being away from home when he went to public school the following year. That was when his idyllic and relatively isolated life ceased and when he and Anne grew apart. "I think it was hard on him boarding at St Andrew's. He was going to be given the cane after one weekend and I can remember him crying. My parents were upset too," said Anne.

In September 1963 Peter reluctantly continued a family tradition. His father and his father before him had been to the prestigious Charterhouse, fifteen miles away in Godalming. The school was founded in London in 1611 and moved in 1872 to its new gothic home in Surrey. Peter was put in Girdlestone House. Its inmates are known as Duckites because founder Mr Girldestone, who had short legs, reputedly walked like a duck, and because Girdlestoneites was too much of a mouthful.

"It seemed a pleasant school, and it was near here. At that period lads did go to boarding school if you could manage it," said Mrs Gabriel. "It was quite impractical for Peter to live here and commute in the rush hour.

"Peter has always maintained he didn't like Charterhouse. But he never grumbled, he never complained when he was there though I got the feeling he never enjoyed it all that much. It never got to the point where we talked about it and he asked us to take him away from there.

"He grew quickly and went through a heavy stage, though he wasn't fat, and therefore wasn't able to be very quick at sports. If you were not quick at sports it was difficult to be a success. I don't think he shined anywhere.

"I think when we have talked about Charterhouse he thinks it has taught him to stand on his own two feet. I don't feel and I don't think he does think he really would have settled happily into any type of school regime. I don't think it was the school's fault."

"With hindsight we might have chosen another school," said his father. "Had we known what we know now we might have chosen Dartington Hall." Peter's upbringing dictated that he should not complain about disliking school, though clearly Irene and Ralph Gabriel later became aware of his misery.

Fifty years before Peter Gabriel, another new boy, Robert Graves, had similar sentiments later expressed in *Goodbye To All That*. "From my first moment at Charterhouse I suffered an oppression of spirit that I hesitate to recall in its full intensity."

The sixties saw great changes at Charterhouse, though Peter Gabriel was unfortunate to catch some of the last, worst vestiges of the old system. In common with other junior boys he had to be a senior boy's fag, making his bed, occasionally frying him an egg and getting his tuck. Older boys were also allowed to beat the younger ones. "If someone screamed down the corridor, you ran," remembered Philip Kingsley-Jones, a contemporary of Peter Gabriel's in Duckites, and now head of department in a comprehensive school. He felt the depiction of British public schools in Lindsay Anderson's film *If . . .* accurately reflected the pent-up aggression and frustration of the brown-uniformed boys at Charterhouse who called their teachers 'beaks'.

The junior dormitories at Charterhouse consisted of cubicles six-foot square, known as cubes, designed so that each boy could have some privacy. "I hated it. It was terrible. You'd arrive and there would be this huge room with little dormitories divided by hardboard, and you'd hear all these strange voices late at night. It was dark and by a road, so it felt to me like the films of the First World War I had seen: ack ack guns and big flares lighting up the sky, as the car headlights went by on the road outside. And everyone seemed to be nervous and unhappy, and there were some boys crying when I first went there," Peter told writer and photographer Armando Gallo.

"All through the first year I felt miserable. There was this incredible power set-up, you know, with the older boys having fags – the younger boys – to do all their menial duties, clean their shoes, and so on. It was really crazy. I think I was very sensitive at school, everything was a great drama, and many nights I would spend awake trying to get to sleep. The senior boys in the dormitory were allowed to talk, and they would talk about anything, and try to impress the other boys. Cars, girlfriends . . . all sorts of cocky sensationalism."

Peter's housemaster, John Marriott, remembers him as a model student. Part of that clearly entailed not expressing one's emotions. "He was a very pleasant person indeed, not the sort of person who would fling his weight around. He was a perfectionist.

"Quiet people tend to keep things to themselves. I am sure that he was under a bit of pressure to do better.

"I would not think that he was unhappy. Some boys show that they are unhappy, although I think if he had been unhappy he would not have shown it. When I was a schoolboy I would have had a bit more pride than to show I was unhappy.

"One of the most remarkable things about Charterhouse, which is not all that usual, is the friendliness of the boys in talking to teaching staff, they would always chat to you."

Peter's school reports were undistinguished, though he could not completely disguise his dislike for the place. "I think he is just beginning to emerge from the doldrums and there are signs that he envisages putting his spare time to better and more constructive use," wrote Mr Marriott, in the Long Quarter (spring) report for 1966.

Like all boys at the school Peter had to join the CCF, the Combined Cadet Force. He joined the RAF section, and achieved the rank of corporal, according to Mr Marriott, though Peter does not remember winning this accolade. As a corporal his duties would have included teaching younger recruits the syllabus. "Everyone else was keen and the RAF was a cop out. You didn't have to turn up for parade and the RAF always had the dirtiest, sloppiest uniforms," Peter said.

"He was not the sort of chap if you ask him to play football he would say, 'Yippee.' He'd say, 'Of course I will,'" remembered Mr Marriott.

"Basically one's memory was of an extremely pleasant young man. Quiet and gentle and very supportive to the community.

"He was quite able although he did under-perform in a way. When he first came to Charterhouse he did well enough in the lower forms to get promotion. The whole impression was that he was a thoughtful student," Mr Marriott said. Peter's own recollection is that he was anonymous at school, and was never a model member of the community. He was made a monitor in his last term at Charterhouse, more as an afterthought than a sign that the school held him in great esteem.

But what rankled then as much as now was his distaste for the class system perpetuated by public schools. Charterhouse boys were told not to mix with the boys from the town. Peter bore no grudge despite getting beaten up when he was at his pre-prep school, Cable House. "I used to cycle there every day. There would be a gang of us on bicycles, but we were the snotty little middle class boys, and the tough working class kids in the area didn't like us, so they used to ambush us, and fire airguns at us, and throw stones." Once he was caught with a friend and

21

attacked with chains. Their bicycles were broken up and thrown into the mud with their blazers and caps. To counter any future attacks Peter and his friends formed a gang of about fifteen, all cycling back from school together to outnumber the enemy.

At Charterhouse Peter got five 'O' Levels, in Elementary Maths, English, French, Latin and Chemistry. "He took his 'A' Levels for the first time in July 1967, at a fairly youngish age of seventeen-and-a-half, and in many ways he didn't do at all badly," said Mr Marriott.

He got a D in Mathematics, but failed Physics, and Politics and Economics. In 1968 he took two further 'A' Levels, and got an E in British Constitution and E in Economics.

"He was academically the sort of person who needed a little bit more time to master his 'A' Level subjects. I think he was a bit slow on paper and wasn't a terribly good examinee. We reckoned he was capable of achieving university level. I think his parents were fairly ambitious for him and possibly were a little worried what he might end up doing."

He listed his interests as poetry, music, astrology, graphology, tennis and squash. According to schoolfriend Anthony Phillips he was a keen cricketer. "We had house games in cricket which we played once a week. Everyone hated them and we used to try and fix the results so that we could get off as quickly as possible. There was always a couple of guys who would take it seriously and not want to be got out.

"Pete in one of these games was the guy who was upright and straight and refused to do the dirty just because everyone else who was in the wicket was got out. So someone had to knock his stumps over."

Peter was a member of the natural history, debating, jazz and motor societies, and belonged to the Beerbohm (arts) Society and Beveridge (politics/economics) Society of which he was treasurer.

Mr Marriott wrote in his report for the 1964 Cricket Quarter (summer term): "I very much enjoyed his performance on the drums in the House musical evening – it was delightfully spontaneous." Even by his own admission Peter was a terrible drummer, and there seems to be a feeling of relief from Mr Marriott in his report for the winter of 1965: "I am pleased to hear he is thinking of taking up playing an instrument next quarter as variety to his drumming."

"He did enjoy all forms of music. He had a very pleasant natural singing voice, I remember it well. He also drummed and played flute," said Mr Marriott. "He was quiet, but when he got on stage he did lose himself."

"I was all right until I went to Charterhouse," said Peter. "Then I got fat and spotty. I used to think that I didn't have what it took to get the girls, so I should become a rock musician like the Beatles and the Rolling Stones, because they never seemed to have any trouble getting the girls. No, it wasn't quite that simple . . . I wanted the money too!" he told Armando Gallo.

"I started off trying to write songs at about eleven or twelve. The first song I wrote was called 'Sammy the Slug'. Everyone else was writing about girls, and I was writing about slugs, which shows what I was interested in!

"I had this dream when I was eleven, and I saw a fork in the path where I could either be an entertainer or singer, or a farmer. I used to dream very vividly then. Not so much now. Now I get daydreams when I am half awake, but the night time stuff I don't remember so much. But I never thought that I would be a singer, because I didn't think that I could sing. When I was young they thought I had a nice choirboy voice, but when I tried to sing rock songs, it sounded terrible.

"I liked to play drums, because I thought, 'Well, this is where it's all at, where it comes from – rhythm,' and I was given a snare drum by my parents when I was thirteen. Then this friend Andrew Ramage's brother had an old Premier tom-tom which he sold to me for seven pounds and ten shillings. He told me it was a bad drum, but I was determined to get it because it was a real drum. It was like the ones they used in *Six Five Special* on TV, and I thought, 'This is great, it doesn't matter what it sounds like, it'll make a noise when I hit it, I can hit it hard.' The drums provided Peter with an emotional release and kindled his first serious interest in music. His schoolfriends were interested in pop and the beat groups. But true music aficionados were touched by the intensity of American black soul music.

GENESIS

Tiger Ryan, Silly Billy and Ray Fury were waiting for Peter Gabriel and the rest of the crowd as they made their way to the second floor above Burton's tailoring store in Brixton Road. The three wrestlers were bouncers at the Ram Jam Club, a red and blue mirrored venue that put on the greatest acts of the sixties.

Even before the riots of the eighties Brixton had a reputation as a tough area, a long way in spirit from genteel Surrey. Sixteen-year-old Peter Gabriel was on a date with a girl, a million miles from Charterhouse on Sunday evening, 18 September 1966 to see Stax Records' star soul singer, Otis Redding. Such activities were frowned upon by his schoolmasters.

Redding was on his first visit to Britain with his fourteen-piece All-American Band. The Ram Jam Club was hot, steamy, sweaty and bursting at the seams. Its capacity was 800 and 2,000 people tried to cram inside. Fainting girls had to be pulled over the four rows of cinema seats in front of the stage. Peter had difficulty finding the club. "It was very dark, I hadn't been to many clubs, and there were nearly all black faces, so it was an unusual environment for me. But the music was so warm, and he was such a big-hearted performer; you just felt the passion of this man," remembered Peter.

Redding was vigorously punching air on stage for 'Respect', getting crushingly intense for 'I've Been Loving You Too Long', and jumping around on 'Turn Me Loose'. The show had to be halted before The Big O could complete his set. "We had to pull him off because it was dangerous. Backstage after the show he put his arms in a fire bucket of water up to his elbows to cool himself off because he was so hot," remembered John Gunnell, who, with his brother Rik, promoted the Who, Cream, Nina Simone and Ike and Tina Turner at the Ram Jam. They managed Geno Washington and his Ram Jam Band, naming the club after them.

Otis Redding's first British shows did not receive a great deal of attention in the music press. But a letter from Vanessa Taylor of Heywood, Lancashire to *Melody Maker* in October 1966, after seeing Otis in Manchester, echoed Peter's feelings. "I have just seen this incredible man and I still think he was a dream. The feeling, soul, and deep deep sincerity he put into those songs was just too perfect. I did not believe anyone could be so exciting. No one could be as good as Otis."

In the sleeve notes on the 1965 LP *Otis Blue*, Bob Rolontz wrote, "The moving style of Otis Redding is a fusion of blues, pop and gospel. It comes as naturally and normally to him as crying to a baby. His sound is real. It is also personal and individual. Anyone who listens to Otis Redding understands his message. That, perhaps, is the real meaning of soul."

When Alan Smith of the *NME* tried to interview Redding after one of his British dates he found him in a near trance state. "Otis seemed to have worked himself to such a pitch that he found it almost impossible to concentrate on my questions," he wrote.

The teenage Gabriel was moved by the intensity of seeing Redding. "It is still my favourite gig of all time. It was just the way he could generate feeling and excitement, that was an up-tempo memory for me. But the strong, soulful, passionate ballads were also amazing.

"There was an energy there which I think you don't see elsewhere. Springsteen gets close at times, but it's a little more thought out. I think with Otis it was direct from the gut. He was my hero as a singer, definitely, and a lot of that music was part of what drove me to consider music for myself. I was a teenager, very impressionable and very ready to be impressed."

Peter first heard Otis Redding at Record Corner in Godalming with Tony Banks. "We'd sneak there very bravely, because loafing around in cafés and record shops of the town was out and if we were caught we would have been punished. But we would still hang around there and listen to soul records, people like Otis Redding and James Brown."

Peter used to go into the billiards room, the only place where they were allowed to play records in school. "It had this really beaten-up, old Dansette record player in a wooden cabinet. You could only play it for about an hour and a half every day," he told Hugh Fielder of *Sounds*. "I used to take my Otis Redding records in there and turn them up full volume and dance until I was in a frenzied sweat. This ritual gave me an immense feeling of relief."

Tony and Peter, both shy boys, found solace in their friendship and music. Tony's experiences of Charterhouse were similar to Peter's. "I went through periods of being extremely unhappy then. I was shy, and I don't think that adolescence is really made for shy people, and just going to a school like that really aggravated it. I was the sort of person who liked to be on my own a lot, and I could never be tied to rules."

Tony Banks studied classical piano at prep school, but he could never play note-perfect because of his nervousness. A friend introduced him to the Beatles and at one stage he knew 120 Beatles songs by ear. Tony would play the dining hall piano while Peter attempted to sing. "I liked to accompany him as a singer because I always thought he had a good voice," said Tony. "He seemed to put a kind of passion into it. He would do vague impersonations of people like Otis Redding and Nina Simone, which was good, because that was the type of thing I liked."

The fight to get to the dining hall piano was crucial, the combatants racing there once games were finished. As a short cut, instead of going round the passages, Peter would cut through the kitchen and slip through the serving hatch.

Peter's first group was the Milords, who he joined when he was fifteen. Formed out of Charterhouse boys all older than him they were a seven-piece semi-professional outfit playing trad jazz at twenty-first birthday parties and wedding receptions in London, Oxfordshire and Buckinghamshire during the school holidays, earning £15 an appearance.

The group took its name from 'Milord', the Edith Piaf song, which they played at hops. "We used to play in full formal dress, top hats and tails. Peter looked pretty scruffy," said group founder and double bass player John Wilkinson, now a consultant dermatologist in High Wycombe. Their repertoire included 'Sixteen Coal Black Horses' and 'House of the Rising Sun'.

"Peter was a nice enough chap. We started the jazz band and we needed a drummer. His drumming echoed around the house from the dining room where he practised so we asked him to join."

Gabriel failed in his attempts to veer the group more towards rock. But he was given the chance to sing from behind the drums. "He had a reasonable, quite natural voice," said Dr Wilkinson. "He was slightly quiet, but he was younger than the rest of us." Tony Banks and Anthony Phillips also made isolated appearances with the group.

"It was very bad. It was funny because I was definitely right at the back. The drummer of the dance band was a very unspectacular character," Peter said.

Peter left them in the summer of 1966 to become the drummer for the Spoken Word, a semi-professional rhythm and blues group formed at Bryanston School in Dorset. Peter was recommended by a friend of a friend. "Peter rang me up and said he would love to do some drumming. We had no idea he had any ambitions to sing," said Spoken Word's singer David Thomas. Anthony Phillips was also recruited from Charterhouse. Rehearsals were held at Thomas' parents' home at South Warnborough Manor in Hampshire, and they gigged at middle class parties around Surrey and Hampshire. They played a mixture of John Mayall influenced blues and Chuck Berry rock and roll. "We were attracted to the music because it had a poignancy. It was classic rebellion stuff for those days. We were not aware of being middle class. It was just normal for us."

"Peter never sang except once at this Junior Hunt Ball, when he tried to scrape out a number," said Thomas. "The very idea that Pete should be a singer was at the time so peculiar, because I had no idea that he had any aspiration to be a singer. He didn't look like one, he never moved or did anything that could suggest that he might be, but obviously burning at the back of his mind was this ambition to be a singer."

But the group were ambitious enough to travel to London to cut an acetate of the Jimmy Witherspoon blues number, 'Evening', which marked Peter Gabriel's recording debut, albeit on drums. "It was a simple cutting machine which did the thing on the spot from a tape," said Thomas. "We intended taking it around to some people to see if we could get any reaction. But I can't remember anything positive happening."

One of Peter's dining room practice sessions was overheard by a curious Richard Macphail. "I was always interested in anything to do with rock music. On Saturday afternoons we used to commandeer classrooms as rehearsal rooms. You'd suddenly hear this cacophony crashing around the cloisters, and I guess one time I just walked in. I remember someone was playing a saxophone which I thought was pretty amazing. Peter was pretty fat as a teenager, in fact he was quite porky. And he was playing the drums, and I remember his drums sounded like he looked," he said.

Macphail was singer in Anon, another Charterhouse group formed by two younger boys, Anthony Phillips and Rivers Job, veterans of Beatles inspired prep school band The Spiders.

Anon's line-up was completed by Mike Rutherford on bass and Rob Tyrell on drums, and the group played Beatles and Stones numbers. Macphail was dubbed Mick Phail for his attempted Jagger impersonations.

Peter Gabriel was disillusioned as a drummer in Spoken Word. "I wanted to sing the songs I was writing. Then I tried writing with Tony Banks, and he could play piano better than I could. He was a real piano player and I was a thumper, still am, really, but I get by."

During the Easter break of 1966 Richard Macphail visited Tiles Club in Oxford Street and the Marquee in Wardour Street. At Tiles he saw the Alan Price Set and a pop group called the Koobas managed by Tony Stratton Smith, who was to become the first manager of Genesis.

The following term, the Cricket Quarter of 1966, Macphail was asked to leave Charterhouse. The headmaster was dismayed at his neglect of school work in favour of pop music. Inspired by visits to London and displaying his organizational abilities, Macphail planned a school concert as his swansong. "I wanted to try and recreate a sort of club atmosphere. It's quite an interesting thought without any women, but it caught my imagination," he said.

Anthony Phillips asked Peter if Anon's drummer, Rob Tyrell, could borrow Peter's drum kit. "He was very approachable, but quite fastidious, and understandably so, about his drums when he lent them to us. He insisted on coming along and watching."

But Phillips did not suspect Gabriel's real ambition until he came across him in the house dining room. "I remember him standing on a table singing soul songs with Tony Banks playing piano," said Phillips. "It was my first recollection of this other side of him, not just this straight, nice but difficult to know character."

Music satisfied the craving for attention and recognition that lay behind Gabriel's innate shyness. He also displayed entrepreneurial abilities. He made money out of two schemes, dyeing T-shirts with bright colours, and manufacturing felt hats.

"I had this hat of my grandfather's which I used to love the shape of, it looked Cromwellian. There was this great hippy phenomenon happening in London which I wanted to become a part of. Wearing these hats I thought would be a good idea for getting me involved, so I went to various manufacturers to try to get them made up. There was an old guy in Dunn & Co. in Piccadilly who was quite amused by it and took me seriously.

I wanted them in gaudy colours, pinks and purples and yellows and orange.

"Once I had a few made I took them to boutiques in Carnaby Street and King's Road. And flogged some to Emerton and Lambert in the Chelsea Antiques Market, which at the time was frequented by the Stones and the current hipsters of that period. When I came back from school one Saturday and turned on *Juke Box Jury* there was Marianne Faithfull wearing one of my hats, and I nearly wet myself with excitement. She'd stuck a feather into it, and Keith Richard also had one. That was a real thrill, it was some tangible connection with this exciting world.

"I felt really intimidated getting on a train and going to London, going into a shop and trying to persuade these old people it was a good idea. I think it is one of the best things to teach people – to go for it."

Gabriel did not maximize his profits because he gave some away to friends. The T-shirt dyeing business at two shillings a go also failed to make his fortune. "This got me into a certain amount of trouble because they went into the wash with cricket whites, which then came out pink or green."

Music seemed a safer bet, and just before Macphail's beat concert in July 1966 Peter and Tony formed the Garden Wall. They found a drummer, Chris Stewart, and Johnny Trapman on trumpet, but had to poach some members of Anon to complete the group. Anthony Phillips, the most musicianly of them all, agreed to help on guitar, with Rivers Job on bass, as well as playing their own set in Anon with Macphail singing.

At the concert Tony Banks played piano off the stage. "No one knew I was there until the fourth song," he said. They did Percy Sledge's 'When A Man Loves A Woman', and a soul version of Simon and Garfunkel's 'I Am A Rock'. They also did a 12-bar blues which no one could stop because Chris Stewart refused to look up from his drum kit. Peter was wearing one of his hats, a kaftan and beads and crawled around on his hands and knees.

Permission to hold the concert had been granted reluctantly by the masters at Charterhouse. One master insisted that, like a classical concert, there should be no announcements. Macphail inadvertently broke that rule and the master seized his opportunity, halting the show half-way through.

To many pupils the staff seemed fearful of the new mood in the outside world. Mike Rutherford had been prevented from playing at the beat concert because his housemaster thought rock music, in the shape of Rutherford's guitar, could ignite a revolution in Lockites House. Such paranoia was only reenforced on the last day of one term when someone painted a huge ban the bomb symbol on the armoury which housed the CCF rifles.

In November 1966 *The Carthusian*, the school magazine, gave a round-up of Charterhouse groups including the Climax, the Scarlet and Black, and the Garden Wall. It was the first time Gabriel's singing was mentioned in print. "This group, which was formed at the beginning of last Cricket Quarter, claims to be the only true exponent of Soul Music in the school. With a distinctly earthy quality to their work, they gave some spirited performances in last quarter's Charity Beat Concert, Peter Gabriel's vocalizing being a major feature. They practise two or three times a week, but encounter difficulty when the lead and bass guitarists are occupied with Anon . . . Other features of the group are their compositions, which number two to date, and their partiality to improvisation on well-known themes. They claim to be a united group in their capacity as a part-time affair, necessitated by two of them playing with Anon, and like Anon take their music and their playing quality very seriously."

Peter was growing out of his spotty phase and was the first of his fellow musicians to have a regular girlfriend. He met Jill Moore, a pupil at St Catherine's, sister school to Charterhouse, at a party just before Christmas 1966. Girls from St Catherine's were allowed to come to the next school hop in the hippy heyday of summer 1967 where all the regular school pop musicians played once again. Before his performance Peter together with Jill collected a bin liner full of rose petals from surrounding gardens. Peter then sprinkled them over the audience.

The first song Tony and Peter wrote together was 'She Is Beautiful', which underwent several rewrites and a change of title to 'The Serpent' before it appeared on the first Genesis album, *From Genesis To Revelation*. "I used to stay with Peter a lot at weekends when we were writing music," said Tony. "I got to know his family very well, they were very kind to me.

"Music was one thing we had in common. We also used to play squash and tennis, we could talk about rubbish for hours. We had lots of surface similarities and also had lots of differences. I think we complemented each other pretty well. In the early days of Genesis we wrote as a pair a lot of the time."

Ant Phillips and Mike Rutherford took a musical career more seriously than Tony and Peter. They raised twenty guineas to record one of their rhythm and blues compositions, 'Pennsylvania Flickhouse', at a studio in Putney with the rest of Anon. Some months later they were ready to record five new songs, after a brief flirtation with blues influenced by John Mayall and the Bluesbreakers.

Over the Easter holidays of 1967 Ant and Mike hired a studio which was being built in the garage of schoolfriend Brian Roberts' home in Chiswick. Ant phoned Tony to ask him if he would like to come and play keyboards, and he in turn asked if he could bring Peter. The assembled group recorded five Phillips and Rutherford songs and the Banks/Gabriel composition 'She Is Beautiful'. "This was the song that got the most attention, so it gave us encouragement. After that we started writing a lot of songs together. Initially we weren't interested in songwriting as much as playing other stuff and fun interpretations of things," said Tony. Phillips wanted to sing his own songs, but he was persuaded by Tony that Peter had the better voice. What became the first Genesis line-up was now established. Macphail was out, and Gabriel, Banks, Phillips, Rutherford and drummer Chris Stewart were in.

Early that summer Jonathan King, an Old Carthusian, returned to Charterhouse for Old Boys Day. The school was proud of this international celebrity from among their ranks, and King was pleased to bathe in the glory. In 1965 King had scored a major hit while still at Trinity College, Cambridge, with 'Everyone's Gone To The Moon', and was writer, producer and publisher of 'It's Good News Week', a hit for Hedgehoppers Anonymous.

Too nervous to approach King themselves, the group's friend John Alexander did it for them. He asked King to listen to the tape and left it on the back seat of his car.

"I listened to it and I thought, 'This is really good, these are nice little songs,' and I thought the guy had a really nice voice. I was interested in doing more work as a producer because I wanted to become a person in the music industry instead of just another singer. So I called them up and said, 'I think this is fun, let's do something.' They were really amazed to hear from me, completely staggered and overexcited."

"We were by the swimming pool," said Mrs Gabriel. "Tony Banks was here. Peter took a telephone call from Jonathan King and came running out saying, 'We've made it.' He was jumping around for joy when he said he liked their tape."

"I would have to go down to the phone box out of school and

struggle with my coins and the pip box, to try and locate this person from the pop business," said Peter. "At that point, everyone who was involved with the music business was regarded with suspicion, including King." Peter became the group hustler. He had learnt to drive and bought an old London taxi for £50. He put one of his mother's dining room chairs in the front luggage section to accommodate another person.

"Peter was very, very intelligent, and kept bothering me to do something. I liked him, I thought that he was a nice kid and he was intelligent. Terribly nervous, but quite natural. I quite liked Tony, but they were all typical public school boys. They were all very nose in the air. I, of course, was a public school boy, but I had already experienced a couple of years in the pop world, which is very classless, and so as a result I was the ultimate non-snob," said King.

Peter and Tony visited King in London. "We were using the old boy network. And, I think, at that time King seemed quite happy to use the young boy network. He gave us some money to experiment with and told us to produce a demo," said Peter. Excited by a new tape of four songs King signed them to a five-year contract with a further five-year option. It was modified on the intervention of their parents to one year, with a one-year option.

"We were excited just by the fact that anyone was interested in our songs. We would have signed for life at that stage," said Tony. The group thought they had it made and also signed a publishing contract of £40 for four songs.

The next tape of eight new songs was recorded at two studios in Denmark Street, London's old Tin Pan Alley. The songs were more complex and longer. King was not impressed, preferring the earlier ones. "We were really disillusioned because we thought it was better than our first two tapes," said Tony.

In the summer of 1967 Peter and Tony took their 'A' levels. Following Peter's moderate success in the autumn he went to a 'crammer', the prestigious Davies, Laing and Dick tutorial college in Notting Hill to study for two more 'A' levels. Peter had to move out of home for the first time and into a lodging house in Notting Hill full of other students from the crammer. "All thickies, trying to buy their way through the exam system," said Peter. "My parents were very keen for me to go to university. I was not really working very hard, but going along for the ride to keep them happy. I actually found it very interesting because I had a very good politics and economics teacher there."

Peter was offered a place at the London School of Film Technique which satisfied his parents' wishes for further education. Still unsure of his musical career, the idea of eventually becoming a film director appealed to Peter, and he seriously considered taking up the film course.

Tony Banks went to Sussex University outside Brighton where he read Chemistry, later switching to Physics and Philosophy. Ant and Mike were still at Charterhouse.

After receiving the publishers letter expressing Johnathan King's disappointment with their new material Tony and Peter contrived to please him. "Peter and I – it was probably the only time we have ever been calculating at all in our careers, I think – we felt we were losing King, and we felt he was the only contact we had ever had in the business, and so we sat down and thought we would write a song to please him," said Tony. "As he liked the Bee Gees very much we wrote a Bee Gees number, 'Silent Sun', with a Robin Gibb vocal, and he loved it, so we were right back there with him." The song is distinguished for being one of the few songs they ever wrote which included the word 'baby'. It lasted for two minutes and four seconds.

"There have been stories that say that they said to each other, 'Let's write a Bee Gees song because Jonathan likes the Bee Gees,'" said King. "This had nothing to do with it. The whole motivation in the early days was to get them to simplify what they were trying to do. They were writing very nice songs with good lyrics and they were singing well, but their ambitions were too large. They were, after all, only sixteen- or seventeen-year-old kids and they just couldn't play any more than basic chords. So, when they tried to do an elaborate solo and things they just sounded pretentious and awful."

They discussed a name for the group with King. "His first suggestion, which the rest of the band have forgotten although I haven't, was Gabriel's Angels – which appealed to me. Somehow this didn't seem to register with the others," said Peter. "His thinking was that some of the stuff was influenced by hymns, and so this new name suggested an absurd, naïve innocence."

"We were looking for a new sound, and Genesis insinuated that it was the beginning of a new sound, and a new feeling," said King.

The group recorded their first single, 'Silent Sun', in December 1967 at Regent Sound in Denmark Street, with King producing. "Jonathan King told us that we would be on *Top of the Pops* so we all went out and bought new clothes," Peter said.

33

King arranged for a deal with his own record company, Decca, and the single was released on 22 February 1968.

Richard Macphail was working as a messenger on the Stock Exchange. "I must have been the first person to buy the single because I bought it the day it came out and I can't believe anyone else would have done that because no one else knew it existed." The following week Chris Welch, in the *Melody Maker*, gave Genesis their first write-up. "I was a big fan of Chris Welch and his writing and I used to get *Melody Maker* and ring up Peter and Anthony and read things out. His review started 'Dear Jonathan King, producer of Genesis, this recording, sir, is muck . . .' and then he said, 'Zounds man, I am jesting, 'tis sorry sport to poke fun at one of the better sounds of the week,' and said Gabriel's vocals were "Peter Framptonish".

Peter's sister Anne, at boarding school, listened out for the single on her transistor radio. "I was very proud when 'Silent Sun' came out. I remember lying awake listening to Radio Luxembourg with my friends, I thought it was wonderful." And the Duckites were instructed to send requests to radio stations. It was played on the pirate Radio Caroline, and by Kenny Everett on Radio 1, but *Top of the Pops* was still a distant dream. The second single, 'A Winter's Tale', was released on 10 May and sank without trace in spite of winning 'possible hit' status from the *New Musical Express*.

Having received more tapes which he liked, King booked Genesis into Regent Sound in their 1968 summer holidays. Drummer Chris Stewart was replaced by another schoolfriend, John Silver. King came up with the concept for the album *From Genesis To Revelation*, recorded in one day. "It was supposed to be the history of the universe, altogether a very duff concept," said Peter. The group's name had to be left off the album because a group in America claimed the same name. The name was then changed to Revelation, but someone claimed that too. The record was not released until May 1969.

The inner sleeve notes reveal an ethereal sixties mind at work. "Sometimes, before the hard age of flitting teens, shapes are sharper, patterns clearer, ideas more simple and statements more crystal. Sometimes, indeed, wrongly so. Sometimes rightly . . ." it mused. Banks and Phillips were unhappy with King's production, particularly the string arrangements. "I remember storming out of the session, suddenly the whole thing – this dream of a great album – had crumbled," said Phillips, who complained their music had been butchered. But

Peter did not protest as much. "We wanted to see the record out and there's no way we would have rocked the boat," said Phillips. "I think after that Pete was very uncompromising, but when you're getting going you have to compromise." The acoustic guitars, string arrangements and folky harmonies gave the album a dreamy pastoral air, all a long way from the group's soul and rhythm and blues influences. Peter's voice was restrained, and he struggled to get some high notes. He was so exhausted towards the end that he kept taking showers to keep himself awake.

Decca failed to promote the album, and record dealers were confused because it did not have an artist's name on it. According to King it got mistaken in some shops for religious music. *From Genesis To Revelation* was reviewed by Mark Williams in the underground paper *International Times*. "The most noteworthy aspect of the group is that they are all young, from seventeen to twenty, and are therefore only in the early stages of their musical development which is an awe-inspiring thought because the ideas they express on the album are already streets ahead of so many other groups. The album sets out to recall the memories of adolescence in all their fleeting naïvety and it succeeds quite excellently. At times, however, the words border on the pretentious, but then one's teens are often pretentious anyway . . ." Peter's vocals reminded him of Roger Daltrey in *Tommy*. "It was really important to me that we should do well in that paper," said Peter. "It was one of the most exciting moments for me, ever." By the time the album came out they were gradually losing touch with King, and eventually simply drifted apart.

The group were later thankful none of their earliest recordings were hits, partly through embarrassment, and partly because early success could have stunted their future development. Having taken his 'A' levels again, Peter moved out of digs to share a flat first in Boston Place, by St Marylebone Station, and then Bramham Gardens, Earls Court with David Thomas, his old partner in Spoken Word. Tony Banks also moved in with them, and become one of Thomas' best friends.

"The flat was very important for us both. There was the sudden introduction to women and the freedom – to cook your own meal and go out and do what you wanted. It was only a few months, but it seemed like years, that period lives on in my mind," said Tony.

The sense of freedom for Peter at Bramham Gardens was considerable. He walked through the flat with no clothes on one night in an attempt to show he had broken free. Peter later recalled the incident. "It was flower power time. I became very angry with myself. I would get very inhibited and shy and I used to wither inwardly because I felt I couldn't articulate or express what I was feeling in any way. It would really drive me crazy that I didn't have the confidence or assurance to do that, and they would tease me about that. I thought, sod this, I'll show you."

Gabriel shocked his flatmates, including Margaret McBain, later Tony's wife, and some other visitors. "I walked back through the room with nothing on and was ridiculed for quite a while afterwards." Tony Banks, despite being equally shy, joined in the acidic comments.

Though he was not seriously considering a career in acting, Peter tried for a role in the film *If . . .* He passed the first audition, went for a reading and was considered for one of the leading parts. But he told the producers he might not be able to commit himself to the film. "They said, 'Either you go for it, or you don't.' And so I said, 'OK, well I don't.' But it was still exciting, just to get a taste of it."

During the summer of 1969 Tony announced he was leaving to return to Sussex University, but was persuaded to stay by Peter. A week later the roles were reversed when Peter decided to quit. He then agreed to Tony's requests that he stay on condition they try to get some positive reaction to the group and play some gigs. Drummer John Silver had left to go to university and was replaced by John Mayhew, who answered the group's advertisement in *Melody Maker* for a drummer sensitive to bongos and acoustic music. With Mike also considering going back to college, Ant was the only one not to waver in his determination to succeed in music.

The summer was spent rehearsing in different parents' houses. Jonathan King was still sufficiently involved to lend them £300, and with £150 from each set of parents they bought their equipment.

Over the previous two years they had written over 300 songs between them. They would start off with chords, building them on the piano, and then develop the melody. The rhythm and lyrics would come last. Gabriel was the main lyricist, but not the only one. His words perplexed Phillips. "He wrote some pretty eccentric things right from the start," said Phillips. "There was one called 'Masochistic Man' with a line that goes, 'Carve the eglantine with bitter juices of her body.' I didn't understand half the stuff he was on about." Not all Gabriel's lyrics were that obscure. During that period he wrote the words for 'The Knife', which would become the group's first stage favourite among fans. The imagery is unusually violent for him, but it fitted in with what was becoming an established pattern of fancifulness, inspired by mythology, childhood books and poetry.

Peter and Tony took their latest tapes to publishers, who dismissed the songs because they were not potential singles. They visited agents, including John Martin and Ian Smithers at the Marquee Martin Agency. "Martin sat Tony and me down and told us to go back to bricklaying or whatever we were doing before that. The music business was not for us, and we should just forget it," said Peter. "I felt as if a black cloud which had been hovering in the distance had actually come down and engulfed us. It was most unpleasant. The worst of it was that we'd go straight back to the rehearsal room to play this music – this magic that we were convinced could inspire the world. I decided then that I would stay with the band, and forget about film school."

"I would go round with Pete a lot," said Tony. "He would do the talking and I would listen and assess these people. I am no good at communicating, but I was quite good at making judgements on people. You knew if you had people interested or not. To be honest, most people weren't at all interested.

"Peter doesn't mind making a nuisance of himself," said Tony. "It all bounced off him. I would get keyed up and get too impassioned. If I thought the song was great and these people we were playing it to didn't respond, they were such fools. Whereas Pete was more philosophical about it."

"The more Pete progressed in music, the more every aspect of his character became streamlined into that. He seemed to lose the tubbiness. His girlfriend sharpened him up a bit," said Ant. Peter had been the only one with a steady girlfriend. But Ant also harboured affections for Jill, according to Peter. Ant's song 'Visions of Angels', which appeared on their second album, *Trespass*, was said to be inspired by her. "Every time he was trying to see her there was me in the way," said Peter.

"Ant is definitely a gifted musician and writer, but because we are both repressed Englishmen I think we didn't shout at each other, and when he was getting pissed off at me he didn't feel able to express it. There was some sort of darkness which built up which came out in ways that I don't even think he would see or understand to this day, but in my mind that is part of the picture. I think the situation with Jill, Jill initiated, but one of my favourite quotes is 'we seek the teeth to match our wounds'."

37

Jill also affected Peter and Tony's relationship. "He had a girlfriend before I did," said Tony. "And then he was very on and off with Jill in those early days, and Jill and I used to have lots of fights. I have a slightly spiteful side to my nature, and I think I tended to attack her sometimes. When you are on top of people all the time it comes out occasionally. Peter would be more resilient to that. He's a very difficult person to really puncture, in a way, because he always remains quite aloof whereas Jill couldn't."

In September 1969 Genesis were booked for £25 to play their first professional gig, at the home of the Balme family just a few hundred yards from Peter's parents in Chobham. "One of their children had a dance. It wasn't altogether successful because their music wasn't really designed to be danced to," said Mrs Gabriel. "They were out on the porch, it was such a terribly cold night everyone went in to keep warm."

Genesis doggedly kept playing their undanceable set, an attitude they maintained despite further unsuitable bookings. Richard Macphail, returning from a kibbutz in Israel, was impressed with the improvement in the band. "I didn't really have any objective view of what Genesis were like, they were just my mates," said Richard. "Then I wasn't around for a while and I heard them rehearse at Anthony Phillips' house in Guildford, and it suddenly occurred to me that they were really very good, I could compare them to other groups and see they had something. From then on I became an absolute number one fan, convinced how wonderful every note was."

He became their unofficial manager and dogsbody. Ant and Mike felt they needed a base where they could rehearse for hours on end and Richard suggested they move into a cottage owned by his parents. Isolated near woodland between Dorking and Guildford, it had been burgled that summer, and Richard's parents, who intended selling it in the spring, offered the cottage rent free.

In November 1969, they moved in and Richard's father, an executive at Rank Hovis McDougall, gave them an old bread van to help cart their equipment around. "They figured they had nothing to lose," said Richard. "The pressure of their backgrounds, upbringing and education was pretty strong, and they were flying in the face of it. But music was their abiding passion and they felt there was enough of a chance of it to go somewhere." Despite their disapproval, the parents each donated £100 to the cost of buying some basic equipment – the main item being a Hammond organ for Tony Banks.

For the next five months the band rehearsed for up to fifteen hours a day. Richard Macphail ran around for them and cooked. Each weekend they would receive Red Cross parcels from their parents. "Mike used to come back with boxes and boxes of stuff from his mother who was convinced we were going to starve to death," said Richard.

"Peter would be on the phone trying above the din of the others to get people to come down and see us." Visitors included Ken Pitt, then still David Bowie's manager, and agent Pete Saunders of College Entertainments, who got them regular gigs. They were also visited by fledgling agent and manager Marcus Bicknell who in his efforts to become the group's manager found them gigs. "The band strung Marcus along wonderfully. The guy did wonderful things for us. He had a grasp of reality, thank God, and got us leaflets and posters," said Richard.

The band were woefully ignorant of performance for their first proper gig at Brunel University in Uxbridge soon after their move to the cottage. They rehearsed in a circle, but when faced with a stage were not sure how to place themselves, and Mike ended up behind Peter. Ant and Peter argued about whether the loudspeakers and amplifiers should go at the front or the back of the stage. "Peter wanted to put the PA behind, so that he could hear it, but Ant knew that if you put it behind, it would feed back into the microphone," said Mike.

Money was a constant problem, and the band were jubilant when they got £50 for a gig at Twickenham Technical College. Soon after, Richard, who drove the van despite not having a driving licence, crashed into a car and caused exactly £50's worth of damage, wiping their funds right out. Money was so short they had to have committee meetings to work out if they could afford to buy a new set of guitar strings.

Just before Christmas 1969 they were booked in Manchester and Birmingham, regarded as "outer space" because it was so far from their previous catchment area around London.

"Peter had really annoyed everyone by insisting he brought his double mattress along with him, packing it in the van with all the gear," said Richard. "In Birmingham we slept on the floor of the sports club we played in, and in the middle of the night the underground heating came on and it became too hot to touch. We were all trying to get out of this room, throwing our clothes ahead of us to make stepping stones on the floor." After the Manchester gig they were put up in a big house in Buxton and all had to sleep in the same room to keep warm.

39

They received mixed receptions. Often it was negative because people wanted a group they could dance to. "They used to do three twenty-minute sets and nobody would listen while we were cracking away in the corner expecting everyone to sit on the floor in rapt attention," said Macphail.

The tensions in the cottage resulted in occasional outbursts from the inhabitants who tended to bottle things up and then explode. That energy was channelled into the music which became more aggressive. Though their time at the cottage was an enormously creative period, they were also removed from reality, cut off from the world in much the same way they had been at public school. The cottage helped them compose what was to become the next album. Though it bonded them as musicians it gave them a distorted view of performance. They played without time limits, and then found it hard to adapt to the needs of an audience.

Only Peter and Mike had girlfriends, but they were restricted to seeing them at weekends. "Peter felt trapped, stuck down in the cottage and unable to influence things while his beloved was getting out in the world," said Richard. Jill was then at the Guildhall School of Music and Drama and sharing a flat in Swiss Cottage. "He could never come up and join my parties there, or see the performances I was doing, or take part in my life up there," said Jill. "All I wanted to do was be down in the cottage. I was so resentful Mike's girlfriend was there."

"I look on the cottage as the start of the professional group," said Mike Rutherford. "Because that is when we started to do it a hundred per cent of the time. I often think we stopped each other growing up. Normally you leave school and you go off into the world and you have experiences that make you grow up very fast. Because we were locked into this very tight unit it was very insular. We were a good, but also a very bad, influence on each other.

"The cottage was, in a way, very claustrophobic. It wasn't a specially happy time in my memory though musically it was very formative. None of us had a social life. We were actually more interested in music than sex in those days. Girlfriends were squeezed in on odd afternoons off, everything was secondary to the group."

"It was a mistake," said Ant. "We were just too young to know that if you live and work together for five solid months, fifteen hours a day, seven days a week, there's bound to be friction and people are going to suffer because of it. I felt the relationships in the group deteriorated because of the ridiculously extreme conditions under which we put ourselves. The fun element, the easy geniality, was suddenly removed. It was no wonder that various people became disenchanted."

The toil of being on the road was a strain. The group carted all their own equipment up and down the forty steps leading to the cottage, drove to the gigs and set everything up themselves. The bread van was uncomfortable, and for Ant, claustrophobic. "There were no windows in the van. Obviously in the front the guy next to the driver could see. But behind that was this narrow compartment in which four people had to sit. That for 300 miles would kill me."

Tony Banks never enjoyed playing on stage because of his introverted personality. He liked the piano and found it hard to adapt to organ. "Peter had to triumph over the quieter, more retiring side of his personality, deliberately exploit the showman," said Ant. "When we started to play on the road at one stage the introductions for the songs were so bad that Richard, who was always cocky and very confident, was going to come on and do the announcements because Peter didn't talk. Once he switched into this other person he was fine, but at that stage he just couldn't do it. He quickly got it sorted out, and then of course, he was magnificent."

Ant was a perfectionist, and insisted on having his guitars properly tuned in between numbers. That delay, coupled with frequent equipment breakdowns, caused Peter to start improvising stories. "Anthony was very meticulous about things, and he and Mike had twelve-strings. So as a diversionary tactic, because the gaps in between songs were so long, Peter started this repartee, telling ridiculous stories that he made up on the spot," said Richard. Peter dressed on stage in a long black and white cloak he referred to as the bathrobe. He banged the tambourine, occasionally played flute, and to the increasing annoyance of the rest of the band, kicked a bass drum at the front of the stage, frequently out of time.

The group discarded the short, largely acoustic set of their first album and moved towards more epic-length aggressive rock. Though they were lumped under the category of 'progressive rock' Genesis bore little relation to bands like Led Zeppelin, Black Sabbath and Yes, all then breaking through. They admitted 'In The Court of The Crimson King', the classic King Crimson album, was one of their favourite records during the cottage period. And they also were impressed with Family, Procol Harum and Fairport Convention. But Genesis wanted to carve out their own niche, using the 12-string guitar, the busy organ, and the dramatic vocals and frequently surreal imagery of Peter Gabriel. It was a sound that could not be categorized or compared to their contemporaries as the sixties turned into the seventies.

Marcus Bicknell booked them at an odd mixture of places around the southeast starting in February 1970. They played student unions and the Revolution Club in Mayfair, bemusing the suburban trendies who were in town for a bit of disco. They started a six-week residency at Upstairs at Ronnie Scott's in Soho in March, playing literally in front of a handful of people who were usually friends.

On the gig circuit Genesis had met a group called Rare Bird who in February 1970 got into the UK Top 30 with 'Sympathy'. The single proved a massive worldwide hit selling over one-and-a-half million copies. 'Sympathy' was the first release on a new record label, Charisma, set up by former sports journalist Tony Stratton Smith.

Rare Bird had recommended Genesis to their producer, John Anthony, who went to see them Upstairs at Ronnie Scott's. One number, 'Visions of Angels', particularly struck Anthony. "When I first heard Genesis I always thought of William Blake," said Anthony. "I was quite taken with the band because I was interested in classical music, mythology, history and the general Englishness of things. I was genuinely enthralled. They were a very strong band with a commanding presence and an emotive energy.

"I spoke to Peter, which was quite difficult because he was quite shy. In a funny kind of way Jill was talking for him. I got the feeling she was the one who was checking me out as a record company weazel. I think I passed the test. I said, 'I've got to have you for this record company that I work for.' "

The group had drawn up a list of big and little fish in the music business who it would be worth cultivating to further their careers. Marcus Bicknell was a little fish, Tony Stratton Smith was big.

After Anthony saw Genesis at Ronnie Scott's he enthused about them to Stratton Smith. The following Tuesday he managed to drag Strat away from La Chasse, a one-roomed drinking club in Wardour Street and got him to walk the two blocks to Frith Street. "When he really liked something he became very, very quiet," said Anthony. "He soaked it up, his eyes were closed and he heard what I heard. They were signed almost immediately after that."

Stratton Smith, then thirty-six, had struggled in the music business since 1965 as an unsuccessful publisher and pop group manager, first tasting success managing the Nice in 1967. He had been a successful cricket and football journalist, in his mid-twenties working as northern sports editor of the *Daily Sketch* before writing for the *Daily Express*. He wrote numerous sports books and narrowly missed being on the plane that killed the Manchester United football team in Munich in 1958 when he was assigned to another job. In 1964 he went to live in Brazil for a year to write a book on Pele. There he discovered the bossanova rhythm, which marked his musical awakening, and he decided to become a music publisher on returning to England.

Spurred by the demise of the Nice's label, Immediate, frustrated by his dealings with other record companies and inspired by a new group, Van Der Graaf Generator, and in particular their singer and songwriter Peter Hammill, Stratton Smith decided in 1969 to form Charisma Records. Anthony had produced Van Der Graaf for Mercury Records and Stratton Smith asked him to produce Charisma's first signing, Rare Bird. Flushed by beginner's luck when he saw Genesis in 1970, Stratton Smith knew he had the capital to sign more acts.

"It was a long shot and I knew it would take time," Strat told Armando Gallo. "Like all good things, it needed to grow into itself. They were rather like a young classic racehorse – if you work them too hard too early, they'll just burn out. They needed to find their strength.

"I saw them as a band that was still putting together its own language, an album band, and therefore a concert band. A band to whom you had to make a two or three year commitment, whatever it cost. They knew they were doing the right thing with their music, and had great, genuine integrity. In the early days, I knew this, respected it, and indeed I loved them for it."

Within two weeks the group were signed to Charisma and offered a wage of £15 a week. Such was their naïvety that drummer John Mayhew insisted they could manage on £10 a week, and their wage was dropped accordingly. As well as being their record company boss, Strat had also become their de facto manager, an unusual combination in the music business, often leading to a conflict of interests. Their wage meant the group could at last leave the cottage and find digs of their own.

The group continued gigging, becoming an established act at Friars in Aylesbury, a market town forty miles northwest of London in an area similar to their native Surrey. They were paid

£10 for their first gig at Friars by promoter David Stopps. "That's probably what they were worth at the time because they were practically unknown," said Stopps, who upped it to £30 after that because of their good reception. Long after the demise of Friars in the late seventies, Stopps became the manager of Howard Jones.

The band were still left to organize their own gigs. Gabriel's signature is on the contract for those first Friars gigs, proving that he was still the group hustler. Friars featured joss sticks and bubble lightshows, and the audience was seated and earnest, they were not there to dance. Stopps also put on Black Sabbath, Blodwyn Pig, Keith Relf's Renaissance and Atomic Rooster at Friars.

"I suppose Genesis took more of an intellectual approach compared to the other bands," said Stopps. "I was very, very keen to see them succeed, that's why I put them on scores of times." Communal life and a gruelling touring schedule strained all the friendships within the band. But Ant was suffering most because of his stage fright. "We stopped communicating. We had seen too much of each other, so a lot of us stopped talking. I went through two months of extremely unpleasant stuff, being too frightened to talk to the others. My main memory of the gig at Ronnie Scott's was being so nervous at the start, and the relief at the end when we got through. It was like I'd got to the top of Everest," said Ant. "When Pete found out I had been going through bad times he made an attempt in his own slightly stuttering way to help. He would say, 'You must tell them things are wrong.' He seemed to bend over backwards to accommodate me."

The group rehearsed material for their next album at the Angel pub in Godalming in early summer 1970. They had been forced to come off the road for three weeks because Ant had bronchial pneumonia. A year earlier, while doing his 'A' levels, Ant had suffered from glandular fever, and he now considered leaving the band. "I did feel a bit guilty that I was letting them down. I thought, I did love this when I started, maybe all this stuff will pass away. But secretly I knew it wouldn't."

He decided to carry on and after rehearsals and some more gigs went with them into Trident Studios off Wardour Street in June and July 1970 to record *Trespass*, their first Charisma album, produced by John Anthony. Two months in a studio was then regarded as an inordinately long time to spend making a record.

The most influential tracks were 'Stagnation', distinctive for the dreamy, soft, acoustic, 12-string feel, mainly the work of

Phillips and Rutherford, which built into an aggressive sound, richly-textured with organ, flute, and guitars. It set the pattern for their work for the next few years. 'The Knife', mainly the work of Banks and Gabriel, was firmly in the up-tempo progressive rock mould, the violent imagery of Gabriel's lyrics backed by a whole range of military drum beats, electric guitar and swirling organ.

The tension of making the album had affected all the relationships in the group with none of them able to communicate their feelings openly to the others. Ant, unhappy with the album production, felt the strain most and decided to quit the band. But he could not face all of them, and chose his oldest friend, Mike, to pass the message on.

Tony Banks credits Ant as being perhaps the most dominant early member of the group responsible for the musical direction and the introduction of their then unique 12-string guitar. Banks felt the group might not survive Ant's departure. "That was the most difficult period for me," said Tony. "We thought there was a kind of magic in the four of us writing, the original format. I thought once he left we wouldn't be able to do it, and I was almost surprised when we decided to carry on because the group hadn't been that successful at that point and there were other things to do, like my going back to university.

"Richard was very much a friend of Ant's at the time and Richard said there was no way we should stop just because Ant was leaving, and it made me think, here was Ant's friend saying that. Mike and Pete really wanted to carry on.

"We talked about it and I suggested we ought to get a new drummer because if we were going to have a restart we should have a fresh start in that direction as well, maybe the three of us should get together and audition guitarists and drummers." They were all unhappy with John Mayhew's performance on the album; he had problems keeping the correct time, and instead of being the rhythmic lead tended to follow the other instruments.

In September 1970 an advertisement was placed in *Melody Maker*: "Tony Stratton Smith requires drummer sensitive to acoustic music, and acoustic 12-string guitarist." The advertisement was spotted by 19-year-old Phil Collins, drummer in the group Flaming Youth which was then disintegrating. Collins was known at the Marquee Club in Wardour Street where Strat could often be found by the bar with his friend Jack Barrie, managing director of the club. As a schoolboy Collins helped arrange seats at the Marquee so he could get in free. He asked

Strat which of his groups had put in the advertisement. "Strat said he could not get him the job, but he could get him an audition," said Barrie.

Collins spoke to Peter Gabriel and was invited to Deep Pool for the auditions, travelling to Chobham in a Morris Minor with his Flaming Youth guitarist mate Ronnie Caryl. Collins was by his own admission at the other end of the evolutionary scale to the rest of Genesis. He was a gregarious likely lad who had been to grammar and stage school. When he played the Artful Dodger in the West End production of Lionel Bart's musical *Oliver!* he had not acted that much out of character.

"My first impression was, this is a bit of all right," said Collins. "They had a swimming pool and the piano was out on the patio and the drum kits were under these umbrellas. It was very different from what I had been used to, so were the people. Peter was, and he still is, an uhmmer and an aaher."

Collins and a few other drummers were played excerpts from *Trespass*. "For some reason what stuck in my mind was a Crosby, Stills and Nash feeling. I think it was the warmth of the music and some of the harmonies." Collins was then invited to take a dip in the pool while the others were auditioned. He listened to the mistakes other people made and took it coolly when his turn came. He was the third of fifteen drummers Gabriel, Banks and Rutherford listened to. They took their customary vote, with Rutherford against, and Banks and Gabriel for Collins. Peter phoned him that evening to offer him the job.

Collins was given his first week's wage, a £10 note, at the Charisma office and told to take a two-week holiday before playing a note as part of Genesis. They returned to rehearse and write at the Maltings, a run down oasthouse in Farnham, near Peter's parents, and were put up by Captain Rutherford, Mike's father. Phil found himself plunged into an unfamiliar, intense atmosphere with Peter and Tony having arguments and temper tantrums. "I didn't really know what was going on," said Phil. But Phil was approachable, cracked jokes and was not averse to putting his arms around someone. He helped bind the group together. "I was made to feel welcome so I quickly felt at home there."

Banks' role had become more demanding on Ant's departure. He tried to make up for the lack of guitar by playing the electric piano through a fuzzbox. They took on guitarist Mick Barnard at the suggestion of David Stopps, but he was not up to standard and left after a few months.

Trespass was released in October 1970, attracting some favourable press comment, but sold poorly. "One could bring out all the adjectives for this. It is tasteful, subtle and refined, but with enough spunk in the music to prevent the album becoming an over-indulgent wallow in insipidity," was Michael Watts' generous opinion in *Melody Maker*.

The band were still playing gigs as they came up. In their search for a guitarist Peter saw an advertisement in *Melody Maker* in December 1970. "Guitarist/writer seeks receptive musicians determined to strive beyond existing stagnant music forms." Peter phoned and invited Steve Hackett, who advertised regularly, to see them play at the Lyceum in Covent Garden. They met backstage and Peter and Tony arranged to visit Steve at his parents' council flat in Victoria. Two painfully shy people were confronted with yet another similar character. Steve played guitar while his brother John played flute. His interest in songwriting, his recent purchase of a 12-string guitar, and his attempts to play unusual chords got him the job.

"I sensed that Pete was the prime mover in the band, he was the driving force," said Hackett. "If we were at an airport Pete would go to the nearest phone and be on the case." But Peter was also renowned for his lateness and tendency to go missing inbetween breaks, constantly infuriating the band and road manager.

Steve Hackett was disturbed to find that Mike Rutherford, then twenty, was in bed suffering from a stomach ulcer brought on by the tensions of the group. Steve found it painful to play in public for his first six months in Genesis. He was so nervous at his first gig he did not realize the set had ended because he was concentrating so hard on remembering his part.

The Lyceum date had been promoted by father and son, John and Tony Smith. John had arranged the first Beatles tour. Three years later Tony Smith would become Genesis' manager. With their help, Tony Stratton Smith devised the Charisma package tour for January and February 1971 in his first major attempt to push Genesis, Van Der Graaf Generator and Lindisfarne and their new albums. It became known as the 'Six Bob Tour' because all seats were 30p.

"The predominant feeling was very much of a family. But that could include a degree of sibling rivalry," said Peter Hammill. They vied for the top of the bill depending on the strength of their local following.

The first concert at the Lyceum on 24 January was reviewed by

Michael Watts in *Melody Maker*. "It is not too far-fetched to say that at least one of the three bands who appeared at the Lyceum on Sunday will become a major force in the rock world . . . Genesis emerged with the greatest honours and audience acclaim. They are harder and more incisive than the delicacy and refinement of their album would suggest, and their vocalist, Peter Gabriel, frantic in his tambourine shaking, his voice hoarse and urgent, is a focus for all the band's energy."

Despite much toil and friction during the year the band were failing to break through to a wide public. Tony Banks described that period as one of their most difficult. "It was a productive time," said Banks. "When we weren't talking about music Peter and I were as close as we had ever been. But within the music we tended to argue a lot." In the battles between Peter and Tony, Mike could usually side with Tony, while newcomers Phil and Steve avoided taking sides.

In December 1970 Peter and Jill had become engaged and they were married on 17 March, 1971. Jill and Peter could at last live together and moved into a dingy basement flat in Wandsworth. The newlywed Mr and Mrs Gabriel found their time together was interrupted by the group's relentlessly increasing work schedule. "In the first two years of our marriage it was him being away and coming back very late at night, and one night he didn't come back. I was actually standing and waiting at the gate until about two. And suddenly something said in my head, 'He's dead! He's actually been killed!' And I actually came to terms with the idea that he had died. The doorbell rang about five and it was Mike Rutherford, and I said, 'It's OK. I know what's happened.' And he said, 'He's in the car. He's broken his leg. He jumped off stage and broke his leg.'"

Peter took his running jump in June 1971 at Friars, Aylesbury performing 'The Knife' as the finale. "Peter got so carried away that he ran from the back of the stage to the front and leaped into the audience from a great height," remembered David Stopps. "I suppose it was the forerunner of his being carried around the audience, the thing that he does now. Luckily he's adept at it now, he's found a much safer way of doing it by just dropping backwards.

"That first time he leaped headlong like he was going to heaven, or something, a huge leap, and flattened about three people, and unfortunately landed very badly and broke his ankle. It was the end of the set, and I remember him being carried off in absolute agony to the dressing room. We called the ambulance. I remember thinking, 'Oh my God, he really is hurt.' He went to the hospital. It was very badly broken and they put a pin in it. And it's there to this day. Every now and then he gets a twinge and he says, 'Oh that was the old Friars leg.' He wrote a little article for our Friars magazine after that, and he said, 'I shall never forget Friars. I got the best screw I ever had when I did Friars and I shall carry it with me till the day I die.' Peter still insisted on performing odd dates in a wheelchair, using an upturned broom as a crutch. His leg was badly set by the doctors who treated him, and a few weeks later he was sent by his parents to a private specialist who had to rebreak and reset it.

The group by now had a small band of music press journalists who were championing them. Jerry Gilbert of *Sounds* was one of the first to interview them after he gave the *Trespass* album a favourable review. Genesis bore the trademarks of British progressive rock: elongated solos, Gabriel's stabs at playing flute, tambourine and bass drum, and surreal lyrics that hinted at more depth than they contained.

"I was hooked on their music, they were experimental and different," said Gilbert. "Off stage Peter would stutter and stammer. You would have these great pregnant pauses. He was a very nervous person. He used to think in incredible depth when answering a question, however simplistic the question might be. There'd be these long tracks of time before the answer would come, and maybe a regal 'no' at the end. He was very much the spokesman of the band. Nobody pushed themselves forward. There was no natural front man."

For the next album, *Nursery Cryme*, they spent the summer of 1971 at Luxford House, Crowborough in Surrey, Tony Stratton Smith's country home. They found writing difficult; Tony missed Ant's input though there were some songs dating back to before Ant had left.

Gabriel's lyrics for 'The Musical Box' inspired the album title and the cover by Paul Whitehead with a Victorian girl staring menacingly with her croquet mallet swung over her shoulder. On the lawn are several severed heads, the Henry of the song. A manor house and some surreal images are dotted around. The croquet lawn and manor house were inspired by Coxhill, Gabriel's grandfather's house. The song encapsulated the early image of the band. Other songs are more fantastical, like 'The Return of the Giant Hogweed', about a killer weed that threatens to wipe out mankind, and 'The Fountain of Salmacis', drawn from the companion to mythology that Gabriel and Banks possessed.

The songs contained tragedy, lust, and comedy. It was all an attempt to break new lyrical as well as musical ground. Producer John Anthony and Peter experimented with different microphone techniques. It marked the start of Gabriel's never-ending search for studio innovation.

When the album was finished the group felt *Nursery Cryme* showed little creative advance. Though references to Gabriel's childhood experiences could be gleaned in 'Musical Box', the album was full of fey stories with bland observations on life that promised great depth simply because they were obscure. Released in November 1971, *Nursery Cryme*, like *Trespass*, was recorded at Trident Studios.

It was Anthony's last album for the group, to his great disappointment. But his last recording came the following summer with the single 'Happy The Man', recorded at Richard Branson's new studios at the Manor, in Oxfordshire. "I remember Tony turning round and saying, 'I really hate that,' to one lyric. That was the first time I had seen that side of the band. Peter took it all very personally. He hid his light under a bushel because of peer pressure." Anthony certainly never hid his own light. "At that time everything I was doing was worldbeating and better than the Beatles," he said.

Anthony, the Charisma house producer, befriended Peter and Jill more than the rest of the band. He had experimented regularly with LSD, his grandmother had been a spiritualist and he had read up on the subject. One night Anthony went with Jill and Peter to her parents' flat at the Old Barracks in Kensington Palace. They were in a cold room decorated in glaring turquoise and purple at the top of the house. "Jill and I were having a conversation about power and strength and will," said Anthony. "Suddenly I was aware that the whole room's atmosphere had changed. Jill had gone into some sort of trance. Suddenly the windows blew in, followed by extreme cold, followed by this psychic phenomenon.

"Neither Peter, Jill or I were doing drugs or drinking. I realized it was a basic manifestation. I have seen it before, the room was full of cold astral smoke, psychic ether. The thing that scared me was that it started moving in the form of a tourbillion – the great wheel that projects spirits into the astrosphere. It is nothing to do with death. It is a phenomenon that can occur with people with strong psyches. If you go through one there is a good chance that if you come back you will never be the same. It is associated with high spiritual fervour, not a happy frenzy, a very disturbed state of mind.

"Peter didn't know what to do. He grabbed a couple of candlesticks and crossed them and put them over her. Then Jill went into a seizure, thrashing around, rending her clothes, that's when she started speaking in tongues and not making sense." The noise disturbed Jill's sister Sally and her parents who came to see what the fuss was about and comfort Jill.

Anthony thought Jill's one experience with LSD was partly to blame. "She was susceptible to a lot of metaphysical garbage." He also believed Peter's personality had a lot to do with the incident, something about transmitting and receiving psychic energy.

Soon after that Jill received a mysterious note full of ritualistic symbols and dates. "She didn't know where she got it from," said Anthony. "Somebody was trying to frighten her. I read the note several times and I just blew it off, using a lot of knowledge I have regarding ritualized magic." Jill and Peter thought the note might have come from an ex-girlfriend of Anthony's who had dabbled in the occult, but Anthony dismissed the possibility.

"I feel that John is very responsible," said Jill. "Peter and John told me the story afterwards. I have no memory of it, only of coming to and feeling ghastly and frightened. I guess it made me believe that there are other forces, or whatever, both good and evil. I think it is very stupid to dabble in it, and I never have since."

Peter admitted he was extremely frightened. "We saw other faces in each other. It was almost as if something else had come into us and was using us as a meeting point," he said. "The curtain flew wide open, though there was no wind, and the room became ice cold. And I did feel that I saw figures outside, figures in white cloaks, and the lawn I saw them on wasn't the lawn that was outside.

"I was shaking like a leaf and in a cold sweat, and eventually I made a cross with a candlestick and held it up to Jill when she was talking in this voice. She reacted like a wild animal and John and I had to hold her down." The incident inspired 'Supper's Ready', the epic track that takes up the entire second side of *Foxtrot*, the subsequent Genesis album. "I experienced a sense of evil at that point,' said Peter. "I don't know how much of this was going on inside my head and how much was actually happening, but it was an experience I could not forget and was the starting point for a song about the struggle between good and evil."

Nursery Cryme did not sell well in the UK. The group played their first foreign concert in Brussels in January 1972 in front of 200 people and soon after they learnt *Nursery Cryme* was at Number 1 in the Belgium charts. In April they visited Italy for a week's tour where the album got to Number 4.

The British press was not interested in writing about the group, and the public was not too bothered about listening to them. Gabriel followed his instincts, going against his innate reserve, in an attempt to draw attention to himself and the group. He shaved the top of his head in a sort of reverse Mohican. The look was premiered at the dreary Lincoln Festival in May 1971 on a mixed bill that included the Average White Band, Monty Python, Slade and the Beach Boys. His new image was enhanced by heavy black eyeliner, and an Egyptian-style heavy jewelled collar and cuffs. The group's performance and Gabriel's bizarre appearance passed almost unnoticed among the damp 50,000 crowd.

David Stopps tried to boost the flagging interest in the band by organizing a Genesis Convention. Friars was too small, so he hired the Town Hall at Watford, Aylesbury's big neighbour, not famed for being in the vanguard of artistic innovation. "I thought they were getting nowhere. I honestly thought they were going to split up at the time," said Stopps. "Watford was really too big for them, but I wanted to push them forward into some progress."

The advertisement in *Melody Maker* was a classic. 'Home Counties Genesis Freaks Unite, Your Time Has Come To Shine,' it proclaimed, and quoted 'Visions Of Angels': "Visions of Angels all around dance in the sky. Leaving me here forever. Goodbye." Fans came from London and in coaches from Aylesbury. Rosettes with 'Genesis '72' emblazoned on them were given out. They looked like the type that litter gymkhanas, though the idea was to imitate a presidential campaign. The event was also designed to attract press attention, succeeding with Chris Welch, from *Melody Maker*.

"Their music and attitude have changed, improved, and progressed, until they have reached that most exciting time for all groups, when they have not quite cracked the publicity barrier, but are enjoying the much more worthwhile and rewarding acclaim of genuinely appreciative audiences . . ." wrote Welch. "The feeling of excitement of a band that is happening musically, and knows it, is only rarely experienced. That feeling is happening now, with Genesis."

Strat's first choice to produce *Foxtrot* was Bob Potter, who had worked with Bob Dylan. But after a week he decided he did not like Genesis' music and walked out. By now the group were capable of producing themselves, and needed someone mainly to help them edit. David Hitchcock met Strat in the Marquee and was offered the job. He had produced Caravan's 'In The Land Of Grey And Pink' and the experience of putting together seemingly unconnected pieces of music came in useful when Strat hired him for Genesis.

The atmosphere at Island Records' Basing Street Studios was fraught, though not overtly aggressive, according to Hitchcock. The arguments were mainly still between Tony and Peter, who tried to keep the rest of the group out of the studio while he recorded the vocals for 'Supper's Ready'. He felt self-conscious, and also wanted to try out a part he knew Tony would object to because it meant editing his keyboard solo. "Tony was outraged that I'd gone over his sacred solo," said Peter. "However, the rest of the band were really excited by what I'd done and the popular vote was always the deciding factor. These were the absurd manipulating tactics which we were all guilty of – but probably me more than any other."

'Supper's Ready' told the tale of that night at Kensington Palace, building into a universal struggle of good and evil and closing with references to the Book of Revelation. Tony Banks warned it should not be taken too seriously, a response to the endless pleas of fans desperate to know what it all meant. Even though there are lighter moments in the piece, there is little doubt that Peter Gabriel felt the song and his performance on the record were important. "I felt as if I were really singing from my soul, almost like singing for my life," he said.

The album was generally more focused in subject matter than their earlier material. 'Get 'Em Out By Friday' saw the group's first stab at social comment, in this case a ruthless landlord. There was still an excess of florid language and imagery, particularly on the science-fiction inspired 'Watcher of the Skies' by Tony Banks and Mike Rutherford.

The group were due to go off on yet another tour from late September through October 1972 to coincide with the release of *Foxtrot*. But Peter was concerned that they were not getting the attention he felt they deserved in the press. Just before the tour he cycled from his new flat in Notting Hill Gate to the Charisma

53

office in Brewer Street, Soho, for a meeting with press officer Glen Colson and Paul Conroy who ran the Charisma Agency booking the group's dates.

"Peter was really frustrated. The group were getting reasonable money, but I don't think he thought they were going very far," said Conroy. "Glen said to him, 'Well, look, if you're gonna want to get in the music papers, you're gonna have to do something a bit outrageous.' So we dreamed up the idea of getting more theatrical."

Artist Paul Whitehead's cover for the album depicted a woman's body in a red dress with a fox's head standing on ice floating in the sea, with numerous other surreal images including red jacketed horse riders with monstrous faces. Peter found himself a fox's head and borrowed an expensive Ossie Clark red dress from Jill that he ruined. On 28 September at the Stadium, a venue in Dublin used for boxing matches, Peter premiered his new image, going off stage during the instrumental section of 'Musical Box' and returning for the chorus in costume. It became a feature of the tour. The theatrical effects had their desired aim, and for the first time Genesis appeared on the front cover of *Melody Maker* and doubled their earnings overnight from £300 to £600 a show.

Rock theatrics were not original to Genesis. David Bowie and Alice Cooper were starting the trend towards glam rock at the same time. Gabriel said he was trying for a more humorous and surreal approach, and did not want the theatrics to dominate the music. He told the rest of the group he was going to put on the costume. Anything that meant deflecting the attention of the audience away from them suited Mike, Steve and Tony, who preferred anonymity. But it eventually backfired and was a source of resentment for them all. "There was a tendency to put the credit for things like 'Supper's Ready' at Peter's door, which was just ridiculous because it was a group-written piece," said Tony. "It contained a lot of stuff that I wrote in university, so I was just really pissed off. That sort of thing made you feel antagonistic towards the guy himself, which was a shame, because we still got on very well as friends."

Foxtrot was favourably received by the press on its release in October 1972. It went into the album charts at Number 12, Genesis' first real UK success, helped by their new high press profile.

The stage show had now developed a unique character. Pivotal to this were the surreal stories that Peter told in between

54

songs. Regarded by some fans as artistic pointers to the meaning of the songs, the reality was that they were developed to fill in the gaps left by constant equipment breakdowns that afflicted the first part of Genesis' career.

Their first American dates were booked for December. They warmed up in Boston before playing the Philharmonic Hall, since renamed the Avery Fischer Hall, in New York. Strat planned the New York gig as a PR exercise. Playing a prestigious, unusual venue normally used for classical concerts would, he hoped, get them valuable publicity in the States that would not come if they just started slogging around.

The concert was a technical disaster, but received a rave review in *Cashbox* magazine and a favourable response from DJs who had been flown in. Peter's stories proved lifesavers while the various electrical hitches were sorted out, though some of the American audience thought the tales were the product of a sick mind.

An abridged version of this story appeared on the cover of the *Genesis Live* album released in August 1973. After setting the scene on a busy tube train stuck in the middle of a tunnel, Gabriel went on, "The young lady in the green trouser suit got up in the middle of the carriage and slowly started to undo the buttons of her top. Then she peeled it off and dropped it on the floor. She repeated this process with her trousers, her blouse, her little panties and her brassiere. Having taken off her shoes this left her totally naked. She then moved one hand down right in between her legs and began to fiddle about until she caught hold of a strange metal object; this was a zip.

"She then very meticulously proceeded to unzip the zip, through her body, through her breasts, right through the middle of her face and down the back of her spine. Then she lifted her fingers to the crack the zip had left, beginning to work them very slowly and carefully through the crack, separating it and then dividing her body into two neat little pieces, letting it drop on the floor, splat! However, right where she had been standing, there was now a golden shimmering rod, hovering just above the ground.

"Well, the rest of the carriage had been completely silent but this was really too much for a large middle-aged lady who was wearing a green poodle. 'Stop this! It's disgusting!' she cried. The golden rod disappeared, leaving the green trouser suit on a hanger, with a cleaning ticket. On the cleaning ticket was a message. 'Must fly – supper's ready.'"" That should have been the cue for the song to start, but Peter had to improvise some more, taking pictures of the audience with his Kodak Instamatic, before they were ready to go.

In February they played the Rainbow Theatre in Finsbury Park, then London's premiere rock venue, erecting a giant white gauze backdrop. The fox's head was still there for 'Musical Box'. It was later replaced by a rubber mask of an old man. More bizarre costumes followed, including batwings and a multi-coloured cape for 'Watcher of the Skies'.

Peter put on a crown of thorns for 'The Guaranteed Eternal Sanctuary Man'; painted Day-Glo around his eyes to glow in ultra-violet light; wore a daisy headdress for the squeaky 'A flower?' before the start of 'Willow Farm'; and donned a red geometric box headdress and black cape – to represent the anti-christ – for 'Apocalypse in 9/8' on 'Supper's Ready'. The finale to 'Supper's Ready' saw him toss off his headdress and cape to reveal an angelic sparkly white jumpsuit. And on a few occasions he held aloft an ultra-violet tube as he sang the final line of 'Supper's Ready', "Take them to the new Jerusalem".

In a few months Genesis had gone from support act to headliner. Their UK tour in February 1973 was followed by a brief American tour to try to establish a firmer bridgehead on the other side of the Atlantic. They were now established as one of the top British rock attractions. Inspired by the success of their theatrics, they planned more ambitious and expensive extrava-ganzas. After two years of constant touring they took time off over the summer of 1973 to write and record their next album, *Selling England By The Pound*, which was released in October and reached Number 3 in the UK charts.

The group were frustrated with the time it took them to write the album, and had mixed feelings about how it turned out. They were already fragmenting as writers. Tony Banks pre-sented a complete song with 'Firth of Fifth', including the lyrics. Despite the album's technical superiority to their past work, and a far more skilful musicianship, they felt it did not convey their spirit as well as *Foxtrot*. The album did include their first hit single, 'I Know What I Like (In Your Wardrobe)'. It was a favourite with fans for its singalong tune and Gabriel's funny walk, yokel hat and straw between his teeth, and his impersona-tion of a lawnmower.

Their contract with Charisma Records came up for renewal in 1973. They were approached by Chrysalis Records, the most successful of the independent labels. The group felt vulnerable

56

handling negotiations without a manager. They were not convinced Chrysalis believed in them and they stayed with Charisma on a better royalty. Strat advised them there was now too big a conflict of interest between his roles as record company boss and manager.

The group had dropped hints to Tony Smith that he manage them the previous year. But Smith, who had successfully promoted the Who and more recently Led Zeppelin, was not interested in moving into management. He arranged their first headline tour that February and the English tour in October to promote *Selling England By The Pound*. Plans to use inflatables on stage were scrapped because of stringent new fire regulations.

The opening date at Glasgow was cancelled just before the group were due to go on stage because of the danger of electrocution from live equipment that the roadies could not fix. Tony Smith gave them a pep talk on how they needed someone to organize their affairs, and then accepted their renewed offer of the job.

Smith immediately set about putting order into their tour set-ups, and was dismayed to find their mounting debt to Charisma due to losses from touring was approaching a frightening £200,000. The chaos was the same in America to which they returned for a tour culminating in their first West Coast appearance at the Roxy in Los Angeles in December 1973 for six shows. Peter's new costumes included a black jumpsuit, a balaclava with cut out eyes and mouth, and a stick for 'The Battle of Epping Forest', and full Britannia regalia including a trident for 'Dancing with the Moonlit Knight'. The audience reception and reviews in the States were becoming ecstatic. *Selling England By The Pound* became their first album to enter the US charts. At the final Roxy dates Peter dressed as Father Christmas, despite a ninety-degree LA temperature, and took some helium to give him a Mickey Mouse voice at the end of the show to sing the sixties comic song 'They're Coming To Take Me Away Ha-Haaa!' Unfortunately he took too much and was hiccupping for three days afterwards.

They returned to England for three dates at the Drury Lane Theatre in January 1974. Peter's assertion that the theatrics should not dominate the music was looking less convincing. Strapped to a harness he flew through the air for the finale of 'Supper's Ready'. It did not work so well in New York when the wire was caught around his neck. He waved his arms at the operator who was convinced this was part of the performance.

Gabriel narrowly avoided being hanged by freeing himself a moment before the cue to raise the wire.

Later in the year they were voted Top Stage Band in the 1974 *NME* Readers' Poll above the Who and Pink Floyd. Their lives now seemed mapped out for them. Tony Smith took care of business, and the group just had to concern itself with the machinery of rock and roll. Yet another heavy touring schedule was set up for the first part of 1974 to include Europe and eleven weeks in America. But Peter was beginning to feel creatively stifled. He was tired of making music by committee, subjecting all contentious parts to the group's democratic vote. By his own admission he had to become Machiavellian in his machinations to get his own way in the group, often facing opposition from Tony.

Impending parenthood also put pressure on Peter. In March 1974, in a brief break from touring, he and Jill moved into their cottage outside Bath. The group still found it difficult to express their personal worries to each other. Public school inhibitions lingered on and Peter did not reveal his doubts to his colleagues.

In June 1974 the group started rehearsals for their next album at Headley Grange in Surrey. Peter was interviewed by Jerry Gilbert for *Sounds*. "I want to take more of a back seat role," he said. "I hope that there will be opportunities to work with other artists this year." It was the first public indication that Peter was dissatisfied and needed another creative outlet. He had already written some songs with Martin Hall and wanted other people to record them. Later in the same interview he said, "We are going into our new album with a strong feeling that a change is about to take place."

Peter insisted on having a free hand to write the lyrics for the new album, but first he had to argue his case. "I persuaded the band to go for a concept – I really had something in mind, which was *The Lamb* – but we had to go through this democratic procedure of saying, 'Let's all submit ideas and let's work on the best one.' I know I probably was getting difficult and obstinate as I tend to get if I'm put in a corner. We were all unfair manipulators. But Tony Banks and I were better at it than the others. Phil wouldn't come into the arguments, he tended to chicken out."

Phil disagreed. "It's funny how different people survey different things. I was usually on Pete's side. He would be hoping for my support because he felt Mike would be supporting Tony. Peter's a very stubborn, bloody-minded, obstinate person, and very single minded. The more you say black the more he will say white is right.

"We would argue about anything, not just music," said Phil. "We used to collect Green Shield stamps when we pulled up for petrol. When you got twelve books you got a free tea-set or something. Tony was quite intense about his collecting Green Shield stamps, and there used to be almost fistfights as to who got the free Green Shield stamps. On the way to and from gigs there would be three or four fill-ups and you could actually do half a book."

Peter had doubts about his place in the group for some time. "Band politics are always fraught with ego struggles," said Peter. 'So on bad days you are thinking, 'Is this worth it?' and on good days, 'This is wonderful.' My wanting to leave was a slow process." He thought his chance had come with the offer to work in Hollywood.

William Friedkin, who directed *The Exorcist* and *The French Connection*, was in the audience at one of the Christmas 1973 Los Angeles concerts. He thought Peter's surreal stories in between numbers showed film scriptwriting potential and invited Peter to visit him on a Hollywood film set. Six months later, soon after rehearsals had started for *The Lamb*, Friedkin sent Peter a telegram and asked if he was interested in writing a film script. Tony Banks insisted Peter should put the group first.

"I was planning to do it after *The Lamb*, but things got pretty black," said Peter. "*The Exorcist* was an enormous film at that point, so all sorts of doors were opening for Friedkin in Hollywood. He had this idea of bringing in his own team that had never worked in Hollywood. There was a guy called Philippe Druillet who co-founded *Heavy Metal* magazine and delivered it round Paris, and Tangerine Dream. I was to be the ideas man for the script."

When the group learnt of Peter's departure they thought about auditioning for a new singer and started drawing up a shortlist while Peter frantically tried to get Friedkin to guarantee the film project. Friedkin backed away when he realized he could be responsible for splitting the band. Jill was eight months pregnant and Peter was left insecure and out of a job with no obvious means of supporting his new family.

Just a few days after Peter left, Tony Smith told the group he thought he could get Peter back if they wanted him. They did and Peter returned. But Peter was not the only person who felt hemmed in that summer. Mike Rutherford got back together with Anthony Phillips to help him record a solo album. Both Phil Collins and Steve Hackett had already threatened to leave before, but were talked out of it by the other members and Tony Stratton Smith.

Peter felt uncomfortable in run down Headley Grange, a house previously used by Led Zeppelin to write *Houses of the Holy*. Peter was disturbed by rumours it was haunted. There was a cold atmosphere between him and the rest of the group. "The band were rehearsing in one room and Pete was working on the lyrics and melodies in another. There were long periods when the band didn't actually come together," said Steve. "I felt that the tension was really very, very strong. It was the closest I had ever come to going over the brink myself." Steve was also going through the break-up of his first marriage.

Headley Grange was a throwback to the days of Richard Macphail's cottage. There was no telephone in the run-down house and he had to cycle down the hill to the coinbox to talk to Jill.

The rest of the group went along with Peter's insistence that he should write all the lyrics, though their resentment surfaced later. "The story had a lot of faults, but there aren't many books written by committee," said Peter. "I think you need leadership in a lot of artistic work because committees spend a lot of time not being bold and going for compromise solutions. You need singular vision."

Though Peter was clear about the idea, he had few lyrics prepared, a problem that dogged the entire recording of the album. After rehearsals the group moved to Pembrokeshire where they rented a house and a cowshed converted into an ad hoc studio with softboard. Genesis wanted to get away from a normal studio atmosphere and acoustics. Soon after the group moved to Wales, Jill went into hospital in London for the traumatic birth of Anna-Marie on 26 July 1974. Peter had to commute between London and Wales, much to the displeasure of the rest of the band, concerned about the delay in his delivery of the lyrics.

The group have since regretted their unsympathetic attitude. "The band needed a lot of commitment at that point, and he was the first to not be able to do that," said Tony Banks. "I can totally understand that now, but at the time I couldn't, because I didn't have any children, and you don't realize what that does to you. Maybe he just matured quicker for that reason."

In between the fraught moments Peter started experimenting to get different vocal effects. He got producer John Burns to record in a toilet and another cowshed two miles down the road. Peter was still plagued by his perennial voice problems, and could frequently be found standing on his head in the studio control room in the belief it would help. He also came equipped with herbal remedies to stop his voice from going. Peter played Burns some songs he had written on his own.

"I would say, 'Couldn't we use some of these tracks?' but he said politically it wouldn't work out because they wanted to jointly write the music," said Burns.

"*The Lamb* was intended to be like a *Pilgrim's Progress*," said Peter, "an adventure through which one gets a better under-standing of self – the transformation theme. I was trying to give it a street slant, and that was before punk happened. I felt an energy in that direction, and it seemed that prancing around in fairyland was rapidly becoming obsolete."

Rael, the character around which *The Lamb Lies Down On Broadway* revolves, was as far removed from fairyland as possible. He was a streetwise Puerto Rican from the ghettos of the Bronx, and provided a transatlantic antidote to the English-ness of *Selling England By The Pound* and much of Genesis' previous work. Rael was Gabriel's made-up name. It was similar enough to the popular Spanish name Raoul to fit in with the character, but English enough to suggest both reality and fantasy.

At the time Peter was credited with the major contribution on the album. Since then all concerned have stressed their own role in what is Genesis' most controversial and for many most inspiring album.

The lyrics were mainly Peter's, but he felt he was never given enough credit for his contribution to the music as well. He regards his composition 'The Carpet Crawlers' as one of his favourite melodies and the title track's chorus was also his composition with the use of the *On Broadway* theme.

Though Rael was portrayed by Gabriel on stage as a punk wearing leather jacket and jeans, the imagery of the lyrics owes more to the supernatural than subways and sidewalks. Rael's journey through his subconscious to eventual self-discovery includes a confrontation with death, 'The Supernatural Anaes-thetist'; falling in love, 'The Lamia' (which are female demons in classical mythology); and sensual gratification, 'The Colony of Slippermen'. There follows a nasty castration followed by the comical theft of the dismembered organ by a bird, and his final self-realization.

The group were annoyed at Peter's delay in delivering the lyrics. But to him it was still rushed and he was not able to revise the story as much as he would have liked, which explains why some of the lyrics are so obscure. Gabriel has always been unwilling to give a precise explanation of the lyrics. Often there would be no point because much of it did not have a direct meaning other than the interplay, feel and sound of words. The understanding was largely in the feeling of the performance rather than the literal examination of the words.

The bulk of the album was recorded in Wales, but Peter's vocals were put down at Island Studios in Notting Hill, and everyone else was excluded from the studio. Just as the album was nearing completion Steve Hackett severed a tendon and nerve in his thumb when he crushed a wine glass in his hand. It was indicative of the tension that ran throughout the project. He was at a reception after seeing Alex Harvey in concert. "I hadn't realized I'd done it," said Steve. "Funnily enough the same thing happened on the *Bionic Man* TV programme, and he hadn't realized why he had done it, and they had worked out that it was 'an involuntary surge of adrenalin due to stress'."

Steve's accident meant the three-week tour of England billed for the autumn of 1974 promoting the new album had to be cancelled. It turned out to be a blessing because the delays in recording would have left the band under-rehearsed. Steve had completed all his overdubs, so the album was not delayed further.

The Lamb Lies Down On Broadway took five months to complete, turning into a double album because of the surfeit of material, and was released in November 1974. It was called a 'concept' album when the term concept had already become passé.

The Lamb Lies Down On Broadway tour started in America in December 1974. Gabriel spent most of the show wearing the for him uncustomary uniform of leather jacket and trousers. The plot was visualized on three backdrop screens showing 1,000 slides.

Gabriel did not put on his first costume until 'The Lamia', three-quarters of the way through the set. He was covered in a cone-like object bathed in ultra-violet light that was meant to signify the tourbillion, the wheel that catapults beings into the mystical world. 'The Colony of Slippermen' followed, represented on stage by Gabriel in a monstrous, bulbous costume with outsized inflatable genitals. Earlier in the set a dummy of Gabriel had a light shone on it. The prop created the illusion of two Gabriels. However, the roadies played tricks. On one gig the dummy had a banana stuck out of its flies, and on the very last show of the tour the dummy was replaced by a stark naked roadie.

For Jill this was the first time that Peter had exposed his sexuality so strongly on stage. "He was angry, and it was a very powerful performance. He totally opened himself and put himself on the line to the world, but he wasn't in his relationship with me. I would say to him, 'Why can't you be like that for me?' I remember sitting in the audience and feeling completely turned on by this guy who I was married to. But he was not able to be that person outside the stage. And that is what has slowly broken down over the years, being able to take that part of himself into his everyday life."

Soon after *The Lamb Lies Down On Broadway* tour started Gabriel made his final decision to leave the group. He first told Tony Smith when they were in Cleveland, Ohio.

"I was shattered," said Smith. "I was just at the stage where I felt that we were doing something new, and the next time around it would be really good, and here I was left in a situation where there probably wasn't going to be a next time."

The Lamb Lies Down On Broadway shows had accentuated the rift and resentments in the band, projecting Gabriel as the star while the rest of the group were static. Gabriel knew he would not be allowed to exert as much creative control on any subsequent album. And he was finding it hard to cope with the added pressures and responsibilities of fatherhood. Gabriel wanted to leave almost immediately.

"The rest of the band were told a few days later in Canada. Their position was that we had worked eight years to get this far, and now, finally, we were about to make it and I was pulling the carpet out from underneath it all," Gabriel told Hugh Fielder of *Sounds*.

"I felt terrible, but I knew that I'd made up my mind, and I can be really obstinate. I wanted a career where I had the opportunity to take on other projects but the band had this army-like attitude. There was no room to be flexible – if you were in the band you were in it 100 per cent, or you were out.

"I had no idea of what I wanted to do, but I knew I was sick of rock, the business, and everything about it. I just wanted to get out." The pressure for Peter to stay from the rest of the group became intense. Tony Stratton Smith even tried to intervene, offering Gabriel extra cash which was refused, but when word of that got around everyone wanted a share.

Eventually Gabriel was persuaded that if he completed the tour of Europe, due to take them through six months to May 1975, there was a good chance the band could pay off their huge debts. He agreed, though when he left the debt was still around £160,000.

"I spent a long time trying to persuade him at various times to reconsider," said Tony Banks. 'Not so much during that tour as afterwards. I didn't want him to leave, I still thought we were a good creative unit. I knew in my mind that there was going to be a problem when he left with the public and the press. I was wrong about that. There was a degree of unfairness, I thought, that we had built up a thing together and he was the only one who was going to walk away with the chance of a career, I thought the band would fail. It seemed such a big thing at the time, but now I think everyone has to have the freedom to come and go in a band. At that point, at the back of my mind, I did think about leaving myself and doing a solo record."

Steve Hackett started planning a solo career that led to his *Voyage of the Acolyte* album before leaving Genesis, and Phil Collins considered forsaking Genesis for his jazz-rock band Brand X. But Tony Stratton Smith showed great faith in the ability of the rest of the band to continue without Gabriel. In the end they agreed to work on a new album and try to hold back from announcing Gabriel's departure publicly until as late as possible.

Gabriel played his last gig with Genesis at St Etienne in France in May 1975. He was cheated of an emotional fanfare because St Etienne was meant to be the penultimate date of the tour, but after that appearance the final date was cancelled.

"I had a big lump in my throat when we did the last gigs in France. A big chapter in my life was coming to an end, and I couldn't tell anyone. We had a policy of doing no interviews throughout that tour.

"I felt a real sham, I couldn't tell people what was going on. But I'd made an agreement, because I felt so guilty, that I would keep quiet about it until the band had time to sort themselves out."

News of Gabriel's departure eventually leaked out in the *NME* in July 1975, seven months after Gabriel had made his decision. The rumours were at first denied by Charisma Records. By then Gabriel had retreated to Bath, and Genesis were writing their next album, *A Trick of the Tail*, destined to be more successful than their previous records with Gabriel. They searched for a new singer to replace Gabriel, but when no one suitable was found thought they might as well try Phil Collins and get a drummer to replace him.

Six weeks after the rumour first appeared in print, Genesis finally admitted Gabriel had left. The following week Gabriel drafted his own statement to the press which he requested should either be published in full or not at all. All the music papers complied and printed it word for word.

I had a dream, eye's dream. Then I had another dream with the body and soul of a rock star. When it didn't feel good I packed it in. Looking back for the musical and non-musical reasons, this is what I came up with:

OUT, ANGELS OUT – an investigation.

The vehicle we had built as a co-op to serve our songwriting became our master and had cooped us up inside the success we had wanted. It affected the attitudes and the spirit of the whole band. The music had not dried up and I still respect the other musicians, but our roles had set in hard. To get an idea through "Genesis the Big" meant shifting a lot more concrete than before. For any band, transferring the heart from idealistic enthusiasm to professionalism is a difficult operation.

I believe the use of sound and visual images can be developed to do much more than we have done. But on a large scale it needs one clear and coherent direction, which our pseudo-democratic committee system could not provide.

As an artist, I need to absorb a wide variety of experiences. It is difficult to respond to intuition and impulse within the long-term planning that the band needed. I felt I should look at/learn about/develop myself, my creative bits and pieces and pick up on a lot of work going on outside music. Even the hidden delights of vegetable growing and community living are beginning to reveal their secrets. I could not expect the band to tie in their schedules with my bondage to cabbages. The increase in money and power, if I had stayed, would have anchored me to the spotlights. It was important to me to give space to my family, which I wanted to hold together, and to liberate the daddy in me.

Although I have seen and learnt a great deal in the last seven years, I found I had begun to look at things as the famous Gabriel, despite hiding my occupation whenever possible, hitching lifts, etc. I had begun to think in business terms; very useful for an often bitten once shy musician, but treating records and audiences as money was taking me away from them. When performing, there were less shivers up and down the spine.

I believe the world has soon to go through a difficult period of changes. I'm excited by some of the areas coming through to the surface which seem to have been hidden away in people's minds. I want to explore and be prepared to be open and flexible enough to respond, not tied in to the old hierarchy.

Much of my psyche's ambitions as "Gabriel archetypal rock star" have been fulfilled – a lot of the ego-gratification and the need to attract young ladies, perhaps the result of frequent rejection as "Gabriel acne-struck public school boy". However, I can still get off playing the star game once in a while.

My future within music, if it exists, will be in as many situations as possible. It's good to see a growing number of artists breaking down the pigeonholes. This is the difference between the profitable, compartmentalized, battery chicken and the free-range. Why did the chicken cross the road anyway?

There is no animosity between myself and the band or management. The decision had been made some time ago and we have talked about our new direction. The reason why my leaving was not announced earlier was because I had been asked to delay until they had found a replacement to plug up the hole. It is not impossible that some of them might work with me on other projects.

The following guesswork has little in common with truth: Gabriel left Genesis.
1) To work in theatre.
2) To make more money as a solo artist.
3) To do a "Bowie".
4) To do a "Ferry".
5) To do a "Furry Boa round my neck and hang myself with it".
6) To go see an institution.
7) To go senile in the sticks.

I do not express myself adequately in interviews and I felt I owed it to the people who have put a lot of love and energy supporting the band to give an accurate picture of my reasons.

The statement fudges the reasons why Gabriel did not announce his decision to leave earlier, for the sake of harmony with his ex-colleagues. In spite of its mystical introduction, the statement manages to convey Gabriel's feelings, and his doubts in 1975 about wishing to continue in the music business.

LOVE AND MARRIAGE

The Deputy High Commissioner in Singapore entertained the Rolling Stones in February 1965 despite their most recent outrage, being arrested for urinating against a service station wall. These were the days of headlines like, 'Would You Let Your Daughter Go Out With A Rolling Stone?'

The group were on a tour of the Far East and Australia and with their manager Andrew Oldham accepted the invitation to lunch with Mr Philip Moore. Mr Moore's two daughters, Sally, then fifteen, and Jill, thirteen, were proud their father was not stuffy like other diplomats, though the family's tolerance ended at Brian Jones asking Sally to go out with him.

The Moores were soon to come to the end of their seven-year stay in Singapore and return to West Byfleet, Surrey. "Singapore seems like my childhood and my home. Those years are very strong for me, I feel emotionally involved with them," remembered Jill.

"The most important thing to me was that we lived with Chinese, Malay and Indian people. The English – the local men were forces English – aren't an exciting memory. The memory is that those three nationalities, races, were incredibly different. As a child it stood out very much to me to have such extremes, and I think that has been the reason I have always been fascinated with people."

Jill, as the second daughter, was the dreamed of boy who would play rugby for England. Her father was an Oxford Blue in rugby and hockey, and had played rugby for England, and cricket for Oxfordshire.

Since rugby was naturally out of the question, Jill's chosen sport was swimming. She took it seriously from her arrival in Singapore aged six through to the age of eleven. "I was a sports fanatic. They were training me for the Olympics. Actually I wished to get sick and get out of it. When I saw the backstroke

67

record being threatened I couldn't face the idea of my dad running up and screaming at me. I managed to get a fascinating illness. They never discovered what it was." Her faked sickness and defeat marked the end of her swimming career.

Jill's parents kept their daughters with them, unlike many diplomatic families who sent their children to boarding school in England. "They were very anti the idea of us being spoilt kids and colonial kids. My parents were very unusual in that they were very close friends with all the servants. We would get into real trouble if we dared to be rude to the amah who looked after us."

Jill was self-conscious when their driver took them to school in the official limousine, and begged to be dropped before the school gates. This was during Singapore's transition from British colony to independent state and its breakaway from the Malaysian Federation. "We would drive in the riots. We had to come out of the gates of our driveway to drive to school, and stones were thrown. That was exciting, it was wonderful."

The family returned to Surrey in August 1965. Mr Moore became head of public relations at the Ministry of Defence. Instead of a residence with servants the girls were back living in a row of houses with their mother cooking for them.

While they were in Singapore, Jill had not been aware of her father's prestigious public position. But life in the stockbroker belt never got the chance to be too ordinary. Just over a year after their return Philip Moore, at forty-five was chosen as the Queen's assistant private secretary.

Jill had failed to get into the local grammar school and both Moore girls ended up at St Catherine's girls' public school, near Guildford, sister school to Charterhouse. "I hated that school because it was single sex and I felt very odd, terrible. I was really uncomfortable, the girls were crazy. They'd look out of the window for boys."

At the end of her first term, Jill was invited by friends to a Christmas party near Chobham. She was spotted by a Charterhouse boy dressed in a yellow satin shirt, a black velvet 'hippy' waistcoat speckled with gold, and black satin trousers. "I was standing in a group of girls and he came up and asked me to dance. He seemed incredibly full of himself. I didn't have any understanding of people. I thought, 'Well, he's good looking, so I'll dance with him, but I'm not sure I like this character.' I still say to this day that he actually smelled of beer, but he promises me he couldn't possibly because he never drank." Jill Moore had just turned fifteen and her new hippy-looking friend Peter Gabriel was sixteen.

"I must have given my telephone number because the next day he rang me up and we agreed to meet in a Wimpy Bar in Woking." Both were on Christmas holidays. "My mother was extremely worried about this, as she dropped me off. She was quite worried because I was a terrible flirt from the age of ten. Of course Peter does not eat meat, so it was a most extraordinary thing for him to arrange to meet in a Wimpy Bar. I couldn't understand it at all.

"There was something fascinating about him, although the main reason I went out with him from then on, for a long time, was that he was good looking.

"I remember going to a dance which he was singing at and it was flower power time, and it was wonderful to go along and be his girlfriend because he was the singer. And he started leading us around in a circle in this dance, we had to follow him."

Jill felt stupid following him around this circle. She realized that her first impression of him being aggressive was way off the mark. It was hard enough to get him to talk. "The fascination sank in for me, the life-long thing for me, which I enjoy most . . . people. He was the target for the rest of my life. I only know that in retrospect, but it was a matter of getting him to open up. I felt that we were both lost people. I loved the fact that he was different. And even then he had ambitions as a pop singer. To me that was wonderful. The analysis that I would marry a famous person, like my father, came a lot later."

Jill had experienced a traumatic transition from the near idyll of Singapore to the isolation and confusion of adolescence in an English girls' school. Her close and loving family was unaware of her sense of loss, and could have done little to alter it.

Philip Moore wanted his daughters to emulate his intellectual and physical prowess, giving Sally the mantle of brain and Jill the brawn. "I was this 'boy' sports player. It was uncomfortable to meet Peter when I'd just played in a hockey match, a lacrosse match, a netball match, and been captain. I'd change out of uniform when we met, I would pretend and do anything to avoid that image. So I was half trying to please my dad and half trying to please Peter. And I remember deliberately deciding to let go of the sports side. I would be a rebel, and pop music became stronger. I couldn't make it on the academic side, and so I hated those years." Jill got five 'O' Levels, like Peter, but this was regarded as a disaster.

Peter and Jill used to sneak out of school and meet at a lamppost in the middle of Guildford. They did not date enough for Jill's liking, but it was hard for Peter to escape. "He was a quiet rebel. The way he could exist in school was to be like that. I don't think he wanted to stir up trouble for himself. It was so painful he just wanted to withdraw. There was this excitement about meeting me, but he wasn't going to go too far and really blow it." Unfortunately for Peter he was spotted on one of his forays and was summoned by his housemaster, Mr Marriott. Peter had to drop his drawers so that the cane could be administered. "We had to shake hands afterwards, typical public school," he remembered.

Peter's picture of himself as a fat and spotty adolescent is a great exaggeration, according to Jill. "He said that by the time I met him he had fought that, but I don't think he was ever as bad as he imagined."

While Peter found his first taste of freedom when he went to London to cram for his 'A' Levels from autumn 1967 to summer 1968, Jill was stuck at home, and felt threatened by his independence when he later moved into Bramham Gardens, Earls Court, with friends David Thomas and Tony Banks.

"It was a very frustrating time for him, we were very close, we were like sister and brother, in a sense. But he wanted to be free . . . I think at that point he could already feel the grasping of me and knowing that he still wanted to be with me, but he didn't want me clinging, like a mother still there. When he was in the flat in London I would always write and he would even write letters back. I'm painting it as if he wanted to run away, but he wasn't, he just didn't want it to be so tight, and we were still so young. But I'd sort of blown my future, so my pressure was very heavy, 'How are we going to be together?' We were meeting at our parents' houses and I couldn't stand that." Jill was allowed to visit Peter in London for the day, but she was never allowed to stay the night.

In the winter of 1969 Genesis went into retreat in the isolated Macphail cottage near Dorking. During that period Jill left home for London to attend the Guildhall School of Music and Drama, moving into a flat in Swiss Cottage. Having failed to fulfil her father's dreams in sport, Jill tried to fulfil her mother's dreams – she had been an actress in rep in Oxford when she met her husband.

Jill gave up her 'A' Level studies and was admitted to Guildhall when she was seventeen, a year younger than the usual entrance age. Her intention was to eventually teach drama, though her mother hoped she would act.

Now it was Jill's turn to be free, fulfilling all her parents' fears. "I was completely the opposite to Peter, and still am, in that I am a chain smoker, I would try absolutely anything if I was given the chance. It was wonderful for me to be with Peter because he kept a rein on me in many ways in those years. Actually at college I tried smoking dope, which also Peter hadn't done, but he wouldn't approve. I had also heard of all these people and their acid trips, and I had in my head this image that they were all putting it on, making it up, it couldn't really be like these people were saying. I was always curious . . . terrible. And so I got this chap and said I wanted some. He gave me enough for seven people. I remember him saying, 'This is enough for seven people!' And me in my naïvety thought, rubbish! I don't believe this. So I took it. And I was actually going into a class at college.

"The next thing I knew was I found myself in this class – having missed out a whole section, I had no memory of it – and the panic came on. A friend there told the tutor and he said, 'Well, take her home.'

"I then found myself desperate to get to Peter. I had gone back to this girl's flat and I had to somehow find Peter, I was going mad. I saw creatures on the wall and everything. And I went on the tube. I said to this girl, I'll be fine! I'm going to get to Peter who was only just out of London for a concert at Brunel University in Uxbridge. So I caught the tube train with the doors slamming and shutting, I was absolutely determined to get there. When I got to this concert I thought, I'll be saved, I'm going to live! And when I told him he just went, 'I've got a concert, I'm too busy . . !' It was like, Oh, God, this nightmare isn't actually going to end! I'm never going to come out of it. It took three days really to come out of it. It was the first and last. I'm so glad that did happen because it stopped me from ever taking anything again."

Jill believes it was Peter's turn to feel threatened by her living in an independent environment. But she soon left the college, disillusioned and upset with the unwanted attention of a tutor. By that time her parents had moved from West Byfleet into the Old Barracks at Kensington Palace, a grace and favour home provided by the Queen. Jill moved in with them before deciding on her future.

The Moore girls kept their contact with the Royal Family to a minimum, in keeping with their rebellious hippy self-image. But they did have to go to Balmoral every summer. On one occasion Jill was able to take Peter with her. They both attended the Queen's Gillies' Ball for the gamekeepers and sportsmen. "Peter had to dance with Princess Anne and I danced with Prince Charles. I don't remember it at all except that I thought it was funny."

While she lived at Kensington Palace, Jill took a shorthand and typing course but got thrown out because her tutors could not read her shorthand, then she worked in a stationery shop. Jill and Peter wanted to live together, but their parents were set against it. Her mother persuaded her to join her sister Sally, who was taking her finals at Trinity College, Dublin. "It was a wonderful period. I worked as a waitress at nights. I really had deliberately gone away from Peter to think, 'What the hell are we going to do?' And just by going away I think it got him to think, 'Oh well, I'm not prepared to lose this.' And he actually came over and visited me."

Jill's sister shared her flat with fellow student Chris Davison, himself later to become a pop singer under the name Chris de Burgh. "I loved that time. It was somewhere where I could enjoy life. There was this side of me that thought this would be much better for me, this laughter, and total lack of intensity."

Jill stayed for six months and came back to find herself under the same pressure. "My parents were worried by Peter, although they have always been very fond of him. They were very concerned, my mother thought at one point he was schizophrenic." They were also worried about his pop career.

For Jill there was only one solution. "I remember very clearly we were walking in Hyde Park, and me saying to him, 'We get married or it's over.' And he said, this is our romantic proposal, 'Well, I haven't got much choice then, have I?' And when he actually told dad, my dad, who is a really good-natured character, completely freaked, and disappeared out of the house. I was absolutely astounded, and we went round Kensington Gardens in opposite directions, I was trying to find him. His fear was: 'How will you manage financially? Peter's getting £10 a week! What will you do?' He was very fond of Peter, and I think a genuine panic came over him. It was his first experience of a daughter saying she was going to marry. He calmed down very quickly and came round to the idea."

Jill had felt compelled to force the situation. "I couldn't think of another escape. We really should have lived together. My parents weren't incredibly strict, but you just didn't live together then. I just really think I wanted to spend all my time with him. My need for him was strong, excessively so." If Peter's need for Jill was not as strong, it was because his work was also a consuming passion.

Peter gave Jill an engagement ring on her nineteenth birthday. Jill's father could claim the privilege of seeing his daughter married in a royal chapel, and got his way despite Peter and Jill's opposition. "Peter and I were very unhappy about it. When I look back we were so naïve. He desperately didn't want to get married there, I didn't want to very much. Both Peter and I were anti-class and rebellious."

The wedding took place on 17 March, St Patrick's Day, 1971, at St James's Chapel and the reception at St James's Palace. "The wedding is a very vague memory. Just that it was incredibly flash and posh and there were these wonderful characters coming to the wedding from Charisma Records. My parents were wonderful in retrospect. My father was very tolerant. There was Tony Stratton Smith with his hair down to here, and all of them with their hair down to here, and these extraordinary clothes. And then my parents' generation in their top hats and tails. I'm very fond of my parents for that. It never seemed difficult for them."

Their honeymoon in Tunisia, a wedding gift from Jill's parents, was disastrous. "Peter got violent food poisoning and had to be injected. And it rained all the time." It did not fulfil the promise of their wedding night. Peter had booked a room with a four-poster bed in an historic hotel before their flight from Gatwick. "Driving out to that is my strongest memory because we got away from all these people," said Jill.

Back from their honeymoon they were faced with their marital home, a dingy basement in the then unsalubrious fading Victorian hinterland of the London Borough of Wandsworth. The first six months' rent of just over £7 a week was paid by Peter's parents as their wedding gift, clearly useful on Peter's £10 weekly wage from Charisma.

Jill had a frustrating choice: to travel around with the group and suffer the discomfort of the backs of vans, the boredom and the indignity of being an appendage, or to try and get a job with the likelihood she would not see much of Peter because of clashing hours. Her efforts to join the band on their first trip to America in December 1972 were thwarted through lack of cash, though she did go with them on tours of England.

A year after moving into Wandsworth Jill and Peter found

a new flat in Campden Hill Road, Notting Hill Gate. The combination of a new, cosmopolitan, lively area and a lighter flat prompted Jill into action. "Everything seemed to take off from there. Peter was trucking up and down to the North in vans, there was the feeling he was beginning to go somewhere."

She thought she would try going with him as much as possible. "I began to turn into something that wasn't me," she told Frankie Mcgowan in a 1978 interview with *Over 21* magazine. "I spent a great deal of time trying to look nice, which isn't how I normally behave, and constantly fighting something inside me which said, 'God, this is pathetic.' But it's what most wives do on tour. They start off trying to look good for every concert, which becomes impossible and exhausting after a while."

She took a job with a Notting Hill florist delivering roses in a van, which she enjoyed. Then, despite her lack of qualifications, she got a job at the Barbara Speake Stage School in East Acton teaching eleven-year-olds. It was the same school that Phil Collins had been to as a child actor.

"I loved that teaching. I got £16 a week and felt so rich and excited about earning money. It was very frustrating because although I really enjoyed it I was hardly seeing him. We would pass in the night. I would be getting up conscientiously to be at the school at eight o'clock, and he would be coming home from the north at five." Jill negated self-fulfilment at work for the sake of her husband's career. "I made my constrictions for myself. Peter would have loved it had I developed."

Being a relative failure at school, college and work was easier than matching the exacting standards set by her parents. But there was one role where she was sure she could win parental approval. "I remember distinctly my father saying to me, 'But you'll be a good mother and housewife.' That seemed to me the next thing to bash on with. It didn't occur to me that I could be anything else.

"I said to Peter, 'We should have our own kids.' And he didn't want that, either. He was quite right, again. But I was determined if I couldn't teach at school I would want my own kids. I was finding a role for myself."

Jill was pregnant before her twenty-second birthday in 1973. She had been touring with Genesis in Britain and joined them on their first tour of America where they were promoting their latest album *Selling England By The Pound*.

"That tour was good. I was healthily pregnant, and it was

really great to be there with him. It's just that it was a very difficult tour. He had very little time for me. It was a terrific strain because he couldn't be feeding me and my insecurities and doing his work. He tried his best but there were a lot of demands."

Jill found the emotional pressure of being in the background intense. Before she ever toured she remembers someone from the group management warn, "Never take wives on tour because the one thing they will do is go off with someone."

"But I went because Peter wanted me to, and eventually I did have an affair," she told Frankie Mcgowan. Instead of bringing Peter and Jill closer together her pregnancy only highlighted the emotional gap that had grown between them. It must have been extreme for her to have the affair with road manager Regis Boff at such a sensitive period.

"I desperately wanted to be famous, too. I used to dream about it right from when I was at school. But neither Sally, my sister, or I ever seemed to be able to succeed at anything. And we tried so hard.

"And there was Peter up on stage, glamorous, fêted, fawned over and not particularly liking it either. I was so jealous of him. So envious. The affair was my pathetic little bid for attention."

Jill was lonely sitting around hotels while Peter had interviews or talks with the management. Once she was picked up by the police while walking around the wrong area of Chicago and escorted back to the hotel. "Things that cheered me up were someone exciting coming out to join us or a good reception. But often Peter would be tired and he hated receptions anyway. Occasionally I went, not often, without him, but he didn't like it very much. Mostly I felt it was my duty to stay with him so I didn't go in the end either.

"I found it very hard to cope with him being the star. Most wives pretend to be very supportive but if they were really honest they would say that most of the time they were really jealous. Jealous of the person who is chauffeured everywhere, fêted, clamoured over by women, and you? You're just an appendage who gets things done for you because you happen to be with the star, never for yourself.

"I got very twisted about it all," she continued in her interview with Frankie Mcgowan. "Very bitter and then I had an affair. It was at the beginning of my first pregnancy, I was feeling really down like you do at the beginning. Every night I would go to the concert and there were always these beautiful girls hanging around.

"It was such an intense tour and Peter couldn't give me what I needed at the time, constant reassurance. It's not as though he went off with anyone else, it's just that I needed to know I was needed.

"My affair caused all sorts of problems. He was a good friend of Peter's and it caused a rift, obviously, between them. I think in Peter's heart he knew what was going on; that's why he was so patient. No one solved it except for me and Peter. It was terrible while it lasted.

"We both knew it had been caused by the pressure of a hard tour and the fact that I couldn't come to terms with this extraordinary fantasy that it should be me who was the star, the actress, the singer, whatever, up there.

"Watching Peter night after night, resenting the fact that he wasn't very struck with it, and then me dreaming all night that I could get up there too. Ridiculous. In a childish way I suppose I was trying to pay him back."

The affair and it's conclusion proved one of the most trying times for Peter and Jill. It brought to a head conflicts that had been present in their relationship almost since the beginning. He could never devote enough time to Genesis and Jill for both sides to be happy. She needed someone who would listen and give her attention. Jill carried on touring until May 1974, when she was seven months pregnant, and was then faced with living on her own at the Gabriels' new home in the countryside outside Bath.

Early in the summer of 1974 Peter felt torn by his commitments to Jill and the group. Leaving briefly in the hope of writing a screenplay with William Friedkin was an act of desperation and frustration. Matters did not improve after he rejoined the band to write *The Lamb Lies Down On Broadway* at Headley Grange in Hampshire and record it in Wales.

The day before Anna was due Peter and Jill went for a walk up Glastonbury Tor. "Peter wanted Leo children, and he's got two, only just. We walked up Glastonbury for the sunrise on the day it was coming into Leo. Two things happened. One was that we walked up to the very top and I was standing on my own, and there was this terrible screeching, sounding like hounds, and just as they stopped the sun came round. At that point I had this terrible fear that something was awfully wrong.

"We hadn't thought of a name, and he said, 'I shall ask the first person that walks by.' And I was saying, 'Oh, you can't do that, please don't, how embarrassing!' But he did, and it happened to be these nuns, a teaching nun and a student nun. The student nun said Bartholomew and the older nun said, 'If it's a girl, Anna-Marie'."

Anna was three months old when Peter insisted on taking her to Miami with Genesis on *The Lamb Lies Down On Broadway* tour. He felt it was better for her to see him under trying circumstances than not at all. Jill's anxiety over her baby combined with Peter's embarrassment at having to stop cars for nappy changes and feeds created a lot of friction. "I know touring definitely affected Anna. For a long while after a tour she wouldn't go near any men because quite often she would wake up, if I took her backstage at a concert, and find all these strange faces looming over her."

Nine months after Anna was born Jill decided she needed time on her own for the first time in her life, and left Anna with Peter, who had just played his last show with Genesis and was now free of the group. "The affair couldn't be, and yet it wasn't working with us. I went off for two weeks to Corfu, and I actually called myself different names. For me it was really like a breakdown point, not really knowing where the hell I was going."

Jill longed for independence, and the couple planned to separate. But Jill realized she could not be happy without Peter and Anna. "I came back and we had a pillow fight on the cottage roof. That was the only way Peter could let out his anger. Somehow that seems very relevant to me. I made a strong decision that I would make it work."

Jill chose a bizarre method of expressing her need for independence. "I went into the bathroom and shaved my hair off," she told Frankie Mcgowan. "When I came out thank God Peter just laughed. My mother cried and cried. I'd played this game of dressing up and being so cool for so long that I couldn't remember who I was. I was simply playing a role. I had waist-length hair that I used to hide behind, not confident enough ever to be without it.

"I thought, 'If I want to start again the hair has got to go too.' So it did. Peter in the end shaved his to keep me company. No one seemed to notice, which illustrates what I mean about wives. The best thing they can do is to fade away, pretend they don't exist."

Now she views it slightly differently. "I think it was very much an exorcism. In retrospect it was probably self-punishment, but at the time I wasn't aware of that."

Peter's sabbatical marked a period of peace for the couple and by Christmas 1975 Jill was pregnant again. Melanie was born on 23 August 1976, in St Mary's Hospital, Paddington, like her sister, though this time in the private wing. Jill and Peter were pleased they had another Leo daughter, though they were born at either end of the sign. "We had really committed ourselves to making it work again and so everything worked very well for Mel," said Jill. "Despite the problems we had when Anna was induced the doctor insisted on Mel being induced too." Peter was writing material for his first solo album and planning its recording at the time of Melanie's birth. He was able to avoid work pressures and devote time to his expanding family.

WAITING FOR THE BIG ONE

Larry Fast, who was to have a long musical association with Gabriel, first met him in 1973 when he was a law student. Fast also worked at his college radio station in Pennsylvania, and got the chance to sit in on an interview with Genesis.

Three years later Gabriel and Fast met for the second time. They had brunch together in New York to talk about working on Gabriel's forthcoming solo album. Gabriel was interested in Fast's skills at the synthesizer.

In those intervening years Fast had postponed a planned career in law to pursue music. He had played with rock band Nektar, and in May 1975, aged twenty-three, released his first solo album as Synergy, with the weighty title *Electronic Realization for Rock Orchestra*.

The Synergy album was released on small independent label Jem, parent company of Passport Records, then American importers of Genesis records. Fast knew Tony Smith through their mutual connections with the company. And through them word got back to Gabriel about Fast's skills.

"We found we had a lot in common, and a few months later when Peter was about to record the album I got a call saying can you be there with your equipment." Fast, Robert Fripp, and pianist Josef Chirowski, chosen after Bruce Springsteen's keyboards man Roy Bittan was prevented from participating by his management, were the only musicians selected for the album by Gabriel. He left the rest to producer Bob Ezrin.

Gabriel said, "I think I was very lucky. I had a lot of doubts about quite what to go for, and I made a decision to separate the style from anything I had been associated with before in Genesis, so I went to try and get a different rhythm feel using more American players, who were partly chosen by me and partly chosen by Bob Ezrin. And that was, in fact, when I met

79

Tony Levin who I have been working with ever since. There were some really fine musicians there."

The debut Peter Gabriel solo album was mainly recorded at Nimbus Studios in Toronto in autumn 1976. Ezrin's mighty ego, his 24-carat gold necklace dollar sign, and, worst of all, his whistle very early on started to annoy some of the band.

"It reminded me of going back to school when you know you haven't done your homework," says Fast. "Ezrin had a postman's whistle. He would walk up to anyone who was doing something he didn't like and blow the whistle at them. You lived in terror of him. Peter was terrified of exposing himself to all these hotshot musicians who had never heard of Genesis.

"It was very intense and tense at the same time. We broke into two distinct camps. Ezrin's boys went off to dinner and had 200-dollar bottles of wine, which Peter would be paying for. Peter, Robert and I would go to a vegetarian restaurant for our little intellectual discussions and talk about how the album was going. Peter was going for a very different sort of album from what he had worked on before and this was part of the price for breaking the mould. I didn't hear him complain about it, but Peter doesn't like anyone else to waste money so I am sure he resented it.

"I was very flattered to work with Peter. I didn't realize it was going to be anything as long-term as it was going to be." Fast was a member of Peter's band for nine years up to the beginnings of work on *So*.

Before Gabriel, Bob Ezrin had produced every Alice Cooper album, Lou Reed's *Berlin* and *Destroyer* by Kiss. He had no time for Genesis-style agonizing, though he did appreciate meekness in others.

"If there's anything that made me want to work with Peter Gabriel in the first place it was his natural sense of humility. Humility in the Christian sense of the word in that he is a humble guy. I was impressed that a person that brilliant could also hold himself on such a realistic level of esteem. Then I knew it would be a most fruitful match," Ezrin effused to *Sounds* writer Barbara Charone.

"He's so damned inventive! He's not a linear thinker. Because of that his inventiveness goes off in a thousand different directions. Consequently he needs someone to hold him down to the very best of his good ideas. All I do is edit him, cut out the bits that aren't necessary and reduce the thing down to the bare essentials. That way it's all great stuff.

"People criticize me for my attitude and say it's sterile cause I say I'm in it for the bucks. But this is a job, a profession."

Ezrin's stance could hardly have been more opposed to Gabriel's. Yet Gabriel found the no-nonsense Ezrin refreshing and stimulating after the posturings within Genesis. He also needed Ezrin because he lacked the confidence to direct such seasoned musicians. Never before or since has Peter Gabriel surrendered so much artistic control. Ezrin gave the album a live feel lacking in Gabriel's piecemeal and what Fast called "pointillistic" later method of working.

"Bob's a very smart man with good instincts. At the time of the first album I was nervous recording without the structure of a band, and was quite happy to let Bob take a strong role. I think it worked very well on most tracks. We wanted an acoustic, home-made quality to the music. However, 'Here Comes The Flood' was over-produced and the version I prefer is the German version or the one on Robert Fripp's *Exposure*, both of which are much closer in spirit to my original demo of the song."

Soon after recording began Gabriel began to prove his worth to the wary musicians. "Compliments have never meant so much as they have these last few days," he told Barbara Charone. "I love it cause these guys are musicians. In some ways I've never been respected by musicians before and this is a gas." He found the abuse hurled at everyone in the studio a refreshing contrast to the muted atmosphere of Genesis recordings.

Charone had seen him before he left London, and noted that his initial insecurities and self-doubt seemed to have since disappeared. "While clearly-enunciated sentences articulately replaced garbled half-phrases, several character traits remained. Slightly awkward, he still constantly changed position on the couch, shifted his legs often, and restlessly put his hands behind his head throughout the interview."

Gabriel was amused at the nickname bestowed on him by Ezrin. "He calls me the Overkill Kid because I have an endless stream of ideas but left to my own devices I tend to overcomplicate things. We were beginning to realize this as a band towards the end of my period with Genesis." The songs were more personal than the Genesis material. "More dependent on feel and emotion than sound," Gabriel said.

"I particularly wanted to get away from my past. It would have been very easy for me to come up with another European keyboard-orientated rock band. But that wouldn't have been right for me, that wouldn't have broken any new ground.

"I now want to qualify my success. Success no longer holds the key to happiness for me. I wanted it badly once but it's an experience I had. Now I can get on with being a human being among other things. I won't throw myself into it quite the same way I did before," he said during recording.

"I've got complete control now. The rock biz is a strange hybrid of hypocrisy. You get to the point where you're not really being yourself. You're selling something. You get the feeling that the rock star is really some sort of teenage creation realized for the most part by people who are no longer teenagers.

"All that tends to devalue things. It makes people eat out their souls because they begin separating what they are from what they're selling, yet still trying to sell themselves as an entity.

"I could see myself becoming that. I just didn't want to go on being a member of a rock group, growing old like the rest of them. Although there was a lot in Genesis that I'm proud of, there was always some sort of time clause on it for me for freshness and vitality."

The album took three weeks to record in September and October 1976, with extra sessions in London and New York, and was released in February 1977. "I am not sure he was making the album he was truly shooting for," said Fast. That, he believes, did not come until the third album. But for Richard Macphail, this album was crucial. He saw Gabriel maturing into artistic adulthood through it, and believes that tracks like 'Solsbury Hill, 'Moribund the Burgermeister' and 'Humdrum' are among his best. "I think people were a little surprised when they heard the songs. But pleasantly so." Some of the ideas for songs had germinated during the end of Peter's time with Genesis, though by the time they were put on the record they had gone through the extensive Gabriel filter.

Genesis had never been a singles band. The only hit while Gabriel was in the group was 'I Know What I Like (In Your Wardrobe)' from the *Selling England By The Pound* album which got to Number 21 in April 1974. His first solo single, 'Solsbury Hill', was released in March 1977, one month after the album, and got to Number 13.

"I was surprised with 'Solsbury Hill', because it's in 7/4 for a start, which is a bit unlikely for a hit. But I was very pleased when it was a hit. I think it was important that it did happen but it wasn't designed to be, 'This track's the single, let's radio it up a bit.'" Gabriel lived near Solsbury Hill, one of the ancient mounds that dot the West Country, and used it as a beacon of hope for his new life away from Genesis.

> *So I went from day to day*
> *Tho' my life was in a rut*
> *'Till I thought of what I'd say*
> *Which connection I should cut*
> *I was feeling part of the scenery*
> *I walked right out of the machinery*

'Solsbury Hill'; Gabriel, 1976

"It's about being prepared to lose what you have for what you might get, or what you are for what you might be. It's about letting go."

Apocalyptic imagery is scattered throughout the album, usually as a metaphor for personal change, as in 'Here Comes The Flood':

> *Lord, here comes the flood*
> *We'll say goodbye to flesh and blood*
> *If again the seas are silent*
> *In any still alive*
> *It'll be those who gave their island to survive*
> *Drink up, dreamers, you're running dry.*

'Here Comes The Flood'; Gabriel, 1976

"When I wrote this song I had an obsession with short-wave radio and I was always amazed at the way in which the radio signals would become stronger as daylight faded. I felt as if psychic energy levels would also increase in the night. I had had an apocalyptic dream in which the psychic barriers which normally prevent us from seeing into each other's thoughts had been completely eroded, producing a mental flood. Those that had been used to having their innermost thoughts exposed would handle this torrent and those inclined to concealment would drown in it.

"I also remember the night on which it was written. It was a warm summer evening and I was on the hillside above my cottage. With my eyes closed I used to run for a hundred paces and see where I found myself, and look for plants and animals of significance (I'd been reading books on American Indians and the Carlos Casteneda adventures). I felt as if I had found an

83

energy point on the hillside and after a burst of meditation stormed down the hill to write. In the case of 'Flood' it felt as if the song was writing me rather than me writing it."

He did not think it inconceivable that such a psychological breakthrough, or evolutionary leap, would one day be possible. "I had this vision of telepathic advance in the sense that people do have the ability to pick up what other people are thinking and feeling, much more than is acknowledged. If it is developed at one point within the species, which is how I pictured it, then those people who are used to being straightforward and expressing what they were thinking and feeling would be much better able to handle it than those people used to secrecy.

"This might sound too far-fetched, but I've seen it as Armageddon images. And this seemed to me to be something that might happen, whether it be the result of radiation or whatever."

Gabriel anticipated considerable emotional and social up-heavals for the rest of the seventies and beyond. "I am interested in changes of consciousness and the forces that bring about these changes," he told Allan Jones of the *Melody Maker* just before the release of the album in 1977. "There are a lot of things happening in religion, in the fringe sciences – new ideas, new concepts, that are beginning to change the way we live.

"You have to face the fact that there's a lot that's savage and terrible in the world, and you have to confront it and reflect it. It's obviously important to project something positive some-times, but you can't delude yourself. You risk becoming bland and shutting yourself off from reality. I'm concerned to achieve some kind of balance . . . I don't want to present something that's irredeemably bleak. There has to be some kind of humour or irony to make it tolerable."

That was most evident in the dry, tongue-in-cheek jazz and blues of 'Waiting For The Big One', a tribute to the style and wit of Randy Newman.

> *The wine's all drunk and so am I*
> *Here with the hoi-poloi, don't ask me why . . .*
>
> *Once I was a credit to my credit card*
> *Spent what I hadn't got, it wasn't hard . . .*
>
> *Waiting for the big one*

'Waiting For The Big One'; Gabriel, 1976

84

Despite his efforts, he was not entirely successful in shrugging off Genesis-like imagery and melodies. The opening track 'Moribund the Burgermeister', about St Vitus' Dance, has a typically Genesis fantastical title and grandiose melodic passages. 'Solsbury Hill' and 'Here Comes The Flood' in its over-arranged form could also have comfortably fitted onto a Genesis album.

Peter Gabriel's first eponymous solo album was released exactly a year after *A Trick of the Tail*, the first Genesis album without him. By now Genesis' success had confounded the commentators who had said the group were doomed without Gabriel. "The popular misconception when I was with the band was that I wrote everything, did everything. Then when I left and the band produced apparently just the same things without me, the popular misconception then was that I did nothing. And the reality lies somewhere in between." *A Trick of the Tail* was not a creative advance for Genesis, rather a statement of competence, proving the creative musicianship of the group did not rest solely with Peter Gabriel.

A twenty-date North American tour, Gabriel's first as a solo artist, was set up to promote the album for March 1977.

Bass player, Tony Levin, who had worked with Paul Simon, asked Gabriel if he could tour with him a few days after the sessions and is the only musician from the first album still with him. The rest of the session group from the album joined him, but, except for Larry Fast, they were replaced after the first tour.

Gabriel played New York's Palladium at the end of the month stripped of all the theatricality seen on his previous visits with Genesis. He was more restrained, projecting himself more as a musician, and surprising everybody by playing the piano. The elaborate costumes and masks of Genesis had given way to a simple grey track suit.

"Peter stands on the brink of massive success in America, if the reaction to his New York debut is any guide," wrote Chris Welch in the *Melody Maker*. "Songs like 'Solsbury Hill' are reaching a new audience in the vast American market who perhaps have barely heard of him before." 'Moribund the Burgermeister' was a throwback to Genesis, Marvin Gaye's 'Ain't That Peculiar' hinted at a greater soul influence yet to come, and for the encore he kept faith with sections of the audience by playing 'Back In New York City' from *The Lamb Lies Down On Broadway*, dressed in Rael's leather jacket.

Supporting him in New York were critically acclaimed New

Wavers, Television, who were booed by old wave elements in the audience. The music scene in Britain, and to a lesser extent America, was convulsing from the onslaught of punk. Genesis were members of the rock aristocracy that punk set out to depose. Gabriel largely managed to escape the stigma of being over twenty-five and an ex-member of Genesis. His album, and the single 'Solsbury Hill' were both hits in the UK, it looked like he had cracked it. But the records did not do so well in the USA despite well attended concerts.

Gabriel embraced punk more readily than his peers. He went to see the Sex Pistols in London before their infamy. "I didn't go for the music much, but I enjoyed Rotten. I was interested at that point because other people who I was with hated them with a venom I hadn't seen for a long time. I thought anyone who can produce that reaction must be interesting." And he enjoyed the music of the Jam and XTC.

In the autumn he played his first solo UK tour following a few initial dates in the spring. Looking forward to those concerts, stripped of costumes, masks and make-up, Gabriel said, "I'll live or die naked and exposed." According to Allan Jones of *Melody Maker*, he appeared uncertain of himself and was reluctant to confront the audience directly. "There was a detachment that frustrated the spectator and Gabriel's apparent informality seemed too choreographed to be genuine," he wrote.

But by September, at the start of the tour in Glasgow, all that had changed, according to Jones. ". . . such criticisms as I've directed at the London concert can now be declared redundant . . . His obvious relish at being faced with such an appreciative and demonstrably affectionate audience liberated him completely from his previously distanced stage persona . . . It's really rather curious this ability Gabriel has to communicate occasionally complex (and sometimes rather confused) emotions and ideas: he is essentially an awkward and clumsy performer – his attempts at dancing extend no further than a cumbersome goose-step and he has little of, say, Bowie's omnipotent presence. Neither has he the sexual drive of Jagger nor the camp flash of a Rod Stewart. Yet he had a convincing charm and a sincerity that demands the attentive concentration of his audience."

Gabriel's charm and sincerity was not immediately obvious to the vigilant Swiss police during the last leg of the European tour in October 1977. They pointed loaded guns at him and the rest of the group who they suspected of being terrorists in the Red Army Faction believed to be based in the Swiss-German-French border region around Basle.

They were halted while travelling in two dirty Mercedes on their way to Besançon in France for that evening's gig. They stopped off in St Gallen, Switzerland, at a phone box close to a bank because Gabriel wanted to phone his office in London. Gabriel looked suspicious with his face half-covered by his black scarf to keep his throat warm for singing. Some locals who saw him, bald-headed Tony Levin, and the two Mercedes with their engines running thought they were bank robbers and called the police. When the police nabbed them they dismissed the bank robbery idea, and thought instead they might be the terrorists responsible for the killing of the West German industrialist Dr Hanns-Martin Schleyer the day before.

"When we said, we are musicians, they said, where are your instruments," said Richard Macphail, then Peter's tour manager. The instruments had been transported separately. Police suspicions were not abated when they found Macphail's briefcase full of money in four currencies.

They were detained for three hours while the police checked their story. In a further attempt to prove they were musicians Gabriel and the rest of the group sang the apt a capella song 'Excuse Me' to the police. "There was a slight quaver in the voices," said Gabriel. "But otherwise the performance was intact."

"A week or two before we had played in Berne and I still had a copy in my briefcase of the local permit which the promoter had to organize," said Macphail. "It was a very official-looking document with the names of the musicians on it." They were finally released after three hours' detention when their Swiss promoter verified their story, and they managed to reach that night's gig within minutes of its starting time.

After the first hit album and single, and a successful audience response on the tour – despite a phenomenal financial loss of $200,000 – Peter Gabriel looked set to fulfil expectations that he would soon be a major rock figure to rank alongside David Bowie and Bryan Ferry. But though he enjoyed his commercial success, Gabriel was not happy with all of Ezrin's work.

Robert Fripp's minimalist approach was the opposite of Ezrin's, as was his attitude to the music business; being commercial was his last concern. Gabriel had admired Fripp's work since the King Crimson album *In The Court of the Crimson*

King, which the fledgling Genesis listened to incessantly stuck in their cottage near Dorking.

Fripp reluctantly played on Gabriel's first album out of friendship. Ezrin was not enamoured with him, and kept trying to make him play rock guitar, a style Fripp could not stomach.

"I liked a lot of the material on that album, but I have severe reservations about the way it was recorded and the kind of pressures Peter worked under. Basically, it was the producer's album, with Peter as an excuse for the producer to make his solo album. That was how I read it. Peter maintains that choosing Bob was the right decision, that it was what he needed at the time. Bob gave him a lot of confidence, push, and support. But I have other considerations. I wasn't really allowed to be myself on that album and, if I'd had the courage of my convictions, I would have left on the second day. In fact, when I agreed to do the album, I said I reserved the right to leave if it didn't work out. But, in fact, when you turn up, and you're booked there for two or three weeks, and you're doing a friend's album, you don't actually turn around and leave.

"I originally agreed to play on the album pseudonymously – and that was a number in itself. I had a lot of pressure put on me to have my name on the album – which I was unhappy about, because I didn't feel that Robert Fripp played on the album." Fripp also toured with Gabriel under the alias Dusty Road. He insisted on playing to the side of the stage, hidden by the speakers, because he did not want to be associated with the guitar parts.

Despite this, Fripp agreed, albeit with serious reservations, to produce Gabriel's second album in Holland and New York in late spring 1978. He wanted to capture the essence of Gabriel, but found giving Peter Gabriel all the freedom he needed also had its drawbacks. "I would describe Peter as being a person who knows exactly what he wants but is unable to make up his mind. If you think that sounds paradoxical, you're right. He writes beautiful songs but he's not spontaneous; he is more compositional. He has a conception of how a piece should sound and he's not happy until he hears on tape what is in his head. I wouldn't call that being a perfectionist, either; I would call it being a fiddler or pussyfooter. Recently I wrote this little blurb for Charisma Records as a publicity thing, explaining what it was like to produce Peter; the title was 'Peter Gabriel: Pussyfooter or Creative Giant?' I concluded that Peter is a pussyfooter," said Fripp, soon after the album's release. He

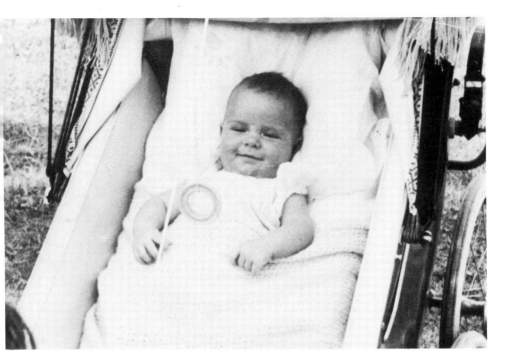

The utterly contented angel
Gabriel, aged nine months

His mother calls this his 'dirty
grin'. On holiday in Bognor
Regis at the age of two

Peter and Anne aged five and four discussing naval strategy by the paddling pool in the garden of Deep Pool

His early enthusiasm for dressing up was rewarded with first prize for this matador outfit at the age of eight on holiday in Wengen, Austria

Peter aged fourteen with his first modest drum kit getting help from a
schoolmaster at Charterhouse

Peter and an attentive Phil Collins at Genesis's first foreign gig in Belgium,
1972

A fetching flared glitter suit worn at Dury Lane Theatre, London in January 1974 during the *Selling England By The Pound* tour was one of his more sober costumes. Note the shaved forehead, here reaching the end of its two year life span

Tony Banks is troubled with more than Gabriel's self-defiling haircut during the writing and rehearsing for *The Lamb Lies Down On Broadway* at Headley Grange, Hampshire in June 1974

With his hair newly shortened, Gabriel applies make-up for his Rael incarnation on *The Lamb Lies Down On Broadway* tour in March 1975. (*Robert Ellis*)

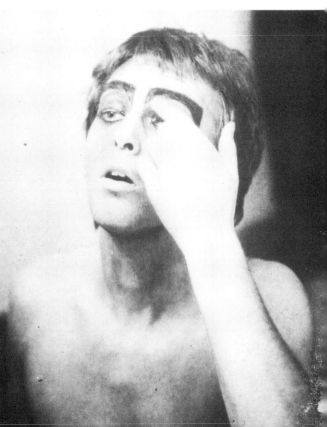

The parental line-up. *Left to right:* Ralph and Irene Gabriel, Peter and Jill, Lord Philip and Lady Joanna Moore

The long haired contingent at Jill and Peter's wedding outside St James's Palace on 17 March, 1971. *Left to right:* John Anthony, first Genesis producer; Tony Stratton Smith; Richard Macphail; Steve Hackett; Gail Colson.

The young father with Anna, left, and Melanie wearing his Genesis masks at home near Bath in 1977

Kate Bush and Gabriel during her vocal sessions for 'Games Without Frontiers' and 'No Self Control' in October, 1979 at the Townhouse Studios, London. (*Larry Fast*)

David Rhodes and Gabriel recording the third album outside Ashcombe House, near Bath in early autumn 1979. They developed a close friendship and Rhodes became Gabriel's fifth and final permanent guitarist. (*Larry Fast*)

felt Gabriel was trying to become too sophisticated which would remove all his gaucheness, a quality he felt endeared him to audiences.

Gabriel saw himself and Fripp as 'passive aggressives', a tag given to them by a friend. "I can see something in that because I can float along quite happily, but when I get moved to do something then I can get quite . . . obstinate."

Gabriel finally got Bruce Springsteen's keyboard player, Roy Bittan, to play on the album, overcoming the managerial problems encountered before the first album. "He plays exactly what I would play if I could play the piano as well as he could," Gabriel said. Tony Levin and Larry Fast were still there. By now drummer Jerry Marotta had joined the band, which also included guitarist Sid McGinnis, who had played with Leonard Cohen and Barry Manilow, and saxophone player Timmy Cappello, later to find fame pumping iron and playing in Tina Turner's band.

Most songs contain a variety of frequently complex themes. 'Animal Magic' with its 'Join the Professionals' chorus is, according to Gabriel, about virility and the politics of the battlefield and bedroom.

The album marked the first recorded songwriting collaboration between Peter and Jill, on 'Mother of Violence'. They had worked on a song to be used as a kids' Christmas carol in their village church. Peter liked the melody so much he adapted it and used it on the album. Instead of the innocence of a carol he twisted the meaning on itself, leaving it with a sense of foreboding; 'Fear is the mother of violence.'

'D.I.Y' was a plea both for personal independence and for people not to be intimidated by society.

> *Don't tell me what I will do, 'cos I won't*
> *Don't tell me to believe in you, 'cos I don't*
>
> 'D.I.Y'; Gabriel, 1978

"Rather than just change your attitude, change what you do. In other words, one has responsibility for a lot more than most people are prepared to accept. I believe in small groups of people having a lot more control over themselves than they do at the present," he said.

Gabriel was unhappy with the production on various tracks, like 'DIY', where he felt the vocals were not as light as he intended. "Robert was very keen to get everything fresh. We kept a lot of early takes and kept the production very dry. The second album is more spontaneous. There are some rough edges and some mistakes but leaving them in makes it more alive."

Despite his reservations he said he thought it was a better album than the first, not a view taken by Atlantic Records in the United States. Their fears that Fripp would produce a less commercial record were confirmed. They were after another album filled with 'Solsbury Hills' and 'Modern Loves'. They were assuaged by an idea of Gabriel's for a singles project. "It's not a concession to the record company. I do what I want on albums, but I'll see if I can give them something they can go out and sell to all those people they are sure won't buy my album."

The second album bore no title, something else that rankled with the marketing men, though it was informally known as *Scratch*. "Other acts on each album very much try and present a brand new face, a bit like marketing soap powders; new added ingredients, WM7 and sparkling blue bits and all the rest. So I thought much more interesting for me would be just to keep exactly the same title, the same typeface, the same position, so the only way of telling the difference from the outside was by the difference in the picture, so it looks a bit like a songwriter's magazine that comes out once a year."

The cover picture was as stark as the mood of the album with Gabriel's clawed hands ripping giant white scratch-marks out of the black cover. On the reverse side a bleak figure scurries along a slushy desolate New York street. And on the inner sleeve an unidentifiable Gabriel is hunched and looks like he is under secret surveillance.

A hit album would have been very useful. His bank balance was still reliant on royalties from Genesis. "If I consider my current financial situation realistically, I would say that I'd be able to survive in this cottage with my wife and two children living fairly decently for five years. No more than that, and that's being generous, and therefore I am concerned about compromising, that's all . . ." he told Nick Kent of the *NME* in June 1978. He wanted to be a commerical success.

On the melancholy track 'Indigo' he was inspired by Paul Robson's song 'Old Man River' which was played on tour while people were leaving the auditorium.

I was good at the art of survival
I've always tried
To keep my troubles deep inside
Where I can hide them
Now I'm wide open . . .

I got nothing to fear from the showdown
I'll go down quiet.

'Indigo'; Gabriel, 1978

In writing the song he had in mind the father of a small family who as he approached death had a change of attitude, "a new rush of sentimental and romantic feelings". Gabriel stressed that his songs have a universal application, there is a danger of reading too much into them. Even so, the lyrics to 'Indigo' were prophetic of Gabriel's later voyages of self-discovery.

THE RHYTHM TAKES CONTROL

Shaving his head never made Peter Gabriel look very pretty. Not that it was done for aesthetic reasons. "People react to a shaved head differently to how they do to a soft hairy one," he said. "There were experiments in stations in London to test people's reactions to the same subject with different outfits and hairstyles, and there is no question that you are seen as more aggressive with a shaved head, whether you are or not."

In the summer of 1978, he aired the style in public for the first time. It was "not to get attention" but for what he termed spiritual and practical self-improvement.

The second album had just been released, and proved only a moderate success; his solo career was not taking off. This was all thrown into sharp relief by his erstwhile colleagues who were getting their first taste of megastardom.

By September 1978 when Gabriel gave two open-air concert appearances he looked like a skinhead 'Number One' crop. Gabriel shared the billing both times with a big furry punk panda toy, with a chain around its neck, accompanying him on the humorous 'Me And My Teddy Bear', a song from his childhood, for which he adapted the words.

First he supported Frank Zappa and the Tubes at Knebworth where earlier that summer the increasingly successful Genesis headlined a triumphant concert before 100,000 people. He was then special guest star with the Stranglers at Battersea Park. This appearance left the *Melody Maker* reviewer, presumably a punk fan, confused. "Peter Gabriel (motto: 'A festival a week keeps the blues away') was the first of the day to get the audience off its collective ass, but his recent surge to credibility is perplexing: to me, he is as anonymous today as he ever was with Genesis. But the rest of the audience enthusiastically endorsed Gabriel's oddly-arranged music and went quite wild over his punk parody of 'Whiter Shade of Pale', which I found both unfunny and unspectacular."

After Genesis' concert at Knebworth in June, Gail Colson, managing director of Charisma Records, quit her job. She had rowed with Strat over his A&R policy. When she left after working with him for ten years he forced her to sign a piece of paper stating she would not poach any of his artists for rival record deals.

"I had no idea what I was going to do," said Gail. She had considered leaving for some time, and had hinted as much to Peter before he re-signed his recording contract with Charisma Records. "I was trying to tell him that I would not be there forever."

Tony Smith had carried on managing Peter after his departure from Genesis. The group were getting increasingly unhappy with Smith dividing his time between them and Peter. They wanted his full attention, but Smith resisted their pressure and pledged his loyalty to Peter. However, the workload for Genesis and Peter Gabriel was increasing and Tony was forced to delegate the handling of Peter's affairs to his office staff.

After a holiday following her departure from Charisma, Gail returned to London for a meeting with Tony Smith who offered her the job of managing director of Hit and Run Music, the management company for Genesis and Peter Gabriel. "Genesis were a different band without Peter. Within two months of working there I realized that was not what I wanted to do and that Peter needed separate management."

Peter was aware he needed personal attention and asked Gail to manage him. She came to an agreement with Tony Smith and together they set up Gailforce Management. Gail and her assistant Norma Bishop still share the same Knightsbridge offices with Genesis. Tony Smith still retains his share in Peter Gabriel's management through Gailforce.

In the autumn of 1978 Peter Gabriel went on a tour of America and Europe under Gail's guidance for the first time. His next London appearance was in the week before Christmas, playing seven dates at Hammersmith Odeon. Promoter Harvey Goldsmith had inadvertently double-booked Christmas Eve for Peter Gabriel and Tom Robinson. A gentleman's compromise was suggested by Goldsmith: Gabriel and Robinson should do a joint show for charity.

On the last song of the last show on the last date of his tour, the day before the charity show at Hammersmith, Gabriel got more excited than usual and inadvertently drew blood from Tony Levin's shaved head.

"I turned my back on Peter as I did a lot, I used to face Jerry.

93

I thought a rock hit me from the audience, a very heavy rock," said Levin. "I started to bleed and left the stage before the song had ended. Every night during that show Peter used to pick up his mike stand and smash it into the footlights. On the last night he was holding a swivel mike stand by mistake which swung round and hit me." Levin did not turn his back on Gabriel for more than ten years, and still has the Fender Precision bass with the blood stains.

Tom Robinson's first public encounter with Gabriel was through the pages of the *NME*. In the spring of 1977 he was guest singles reviewer, and the releases for that week included 'Solsbury Hill'. This was six months before Robinson had his first hit with '2-4-6-8 Motorway'. He remembered, "The first sentence of the review read, 'I never listened to Gabriel's Genesis, because I didn't like them,' like the Guinness ads that said, 'I never tried it because I don't like it.' I'm pleased to say that I gave it a rave review."

Gabriel and Robinson agreed to meet to see if there was any common ground for a joint concert. Robinson took the train to Bath. "This very shy individual met me at the station in his car and drove me through the streets of Bath, off to the little cottage where he lived at the time. I was very struck by a children's swing which was in the garden, which was stuck together by gaffa tape. Gaffa is used by roadies to stick everything together on stage, it was nice to see it extended to the children's swing as well."

Their friendship soon developed once they found they were the same age, and shared common schoolboy influences like the Spencer Davis Group and Manfred Mann. Any fears about musical incompatibility were soon overcome, and they decided to turn the show, still two months away, into a party. It was billed as 'Rob and Gab Xmas 78'. Each chose a worthwhile charity to donate the proceeds to and approved the other's choice. Gabriel's was One Parent Families and Robinson's the Northern Ireland Gay Rights Association.

They collaborated on two new songs for the show. 'Merrily Up On High', on Robinson's next album *North By Northwest* had Robinson's lyrics with Gabriel adding the music. 'Bully For You', the next Tom Robinson Band single, had Gabriel's music inspiring Robinson's lyrics.

Instead of separate sets they decided to appear together, playing each other's numbers interspersed with rock and roll standards. The illustrious backing band included Elton John on piano, Andy MacKay from Roxy Music on saxophone, Phil Collins on drums and Paul Jones, their old Manfred Mann hero, on harmonica.

The show was memorable more as an occasion than for the quality of music. "I massacred 'Solsbury Hill', for my sins, and he sang 'Hold Out'," remembered Robinson. He recalled one reviewer complaining, "One sings, the other doesn't."

Chris Welch in the *Melody Maker* was kinder. "It was an unlikely, unexpected pairing, and yet it seemed to work. Tom, the brotherly fifth-form prefect, took Peter, the Owl of the Remove, under his wing, and between them they presented a bold front to the school bullies in the audience." The rowdy crowd did not take kindly to magician Simon Drake's opening act, and used the paper hats, balloons and whistles to disrupt the evening, quietening only on the arrival of Rob and Gab.

Welch continued, "Take the piano player, for example, an oik from the senior school called Elton John who gave his keyboard a severe thrashing, his percussive power adding to an already impressive rhythm team under the tutelage of the old master, Phil Collins. The whole evening was just full of surprises . . .

"The music was not just aimless jamming. They had rehearsed well, and on rock standards they sounded like hard-bitten pub rockers. On a more artistic level, it was intriguing to hear Rob and Gab (as they were billed) swop songs, although Tom had a struggle singing Peter's tricky 'Solsbury Hill'. They were at their best singing together on the co-written 'Merrily Up On High'.

"Their slightly neurotic voices twinned surprisingly well, but the best vocal performance of the night came from Peter with the moving 'Here Comes The Flood', the maestro accompanying himself on piano with saxophone prompting from Andy MacKay."

In the new year Gabriel started to look for musicians he could rehearse and form a band with for his third album. He mentioned he was on the lookout to a friend, artist Graham Dean, who still admits to little knowledge of the rock world. But Dean did recommend rock band Random Hold, who he had seen play in Oxford where the group members were at college. David Rhodes was the group's singer, songwriter and aspiring guitarist. "Technically I could barely play, but I used to make some nice noises," said Rhodes.

Gabriel, Gail Colson and Tony Stratton Smith went to see Random Hold at the Rock Garden in Covent Garden. Gabriel was impressed and wanted Gail to manage them and Strat to sign them to Charisma. In the end they did neither, though Peter Hammill later produced the Random Hold album *The View From Here* after they signed to Polydor. The album failed commercially but the group still hung together.

Gabriel asked Random Hold to go to Bath to rehearse with him. "It was pouring with rain when we got to the house and we couldn't find him anywhere. Then we heard some people making noises around the side of the barn, and there were three people covered with mud. The barn had been flooded and Peter had been helping with a few of the road crew to dig a channel to divert the water. He was wearing a pullover and wellingtons and an old school cap," said Rhodes. They eventually got down to work by the fireside in the barn on the reeking damp carpet.

It became clear that Gabriel was mainly interested in Rhodes who later went down on his own for three weeks of rehearsals. Though Rhodes did play on the forthcoming album, he was still committed to Random Hold who toured with Gabriel the following year, though the group fell apart soon after that.

Gabriel had leased Ashcombe House, down the hill from the Mill Cottage where he then lived, for £12,500 in 1978. He needed somewhere he could write, play and record without the restrictions of time and money imposed by commercial studios. The rambling farm house had a croquet lawn and a long low barn at the bottom of the garden that Peter first converted into a primitive studio using egg boxes. By the time Rhodes came down to join rehearsals it was still a fairly basic eight-track studio. They rehearsed new songs including 'Biko', 'Not One Of Us' and 'Milgram's 37', a song that had to wait six more years before it got on vinyl.

Gabriel considered using guitarist Anthony More, from the quirky Slap Happy, to produce the next album. He was impressed with their albums. More and Gabriel rehearsed several times at Ashcombe. "He is a colourful person, a bon viveur. He was positive and gave me confidence with some of my new approaches," said Gabriel.

Gabriel's writing was changing, developing rhythms first instead of chords and melodies. It was a crucial change that helped shape his future success, and was spurred on by a breakthrough in technology. Larry Fast got him the first programmable drum machine, a little rhythm box called a PAIA, made by friends of his in Oklahoma City. There had been drum machines before, but they were the home organ variety that could give you a tango or bossanova beat from preset buttons.

The PAIA dispensed with that giving the user the ability to tap in his own rhythms and store them for later recall, a facility now common to many home electronic keyboards.

"On the first two albums Peter wasn't working to get a rhythm, he was writing more in a traditional 'sit down at the keyboard and play your chord pattern' mode of songwriting. When he got this box it was working the music through the rhythms. It became the fundamental part inspiring what was going to happen," said Fast.

"I felt I wanted to write music for the eighties and that the place to begin was with a rhythm track. Rhythm being the spine of music, if you change the spine, the shape of the body changes as a matter of course," said Gabriel.

The first song written with the help of the rhythm machine was 'I Don't Remember'. "I wrote much more simply on top of that. Whereas if the rhythm isn't there I'll normally try and keep my own interest alive by making things a bit more complicated in terms of chords and melody."

He needed a producer willing to experiment in a similar way. Gabriel was impressed by the feel of Siouxsie and the Banshees' records. They were produced by 24-year-old Steve Lillywhite whose hit productions included 'The Sound of the Suburbs' for the Members, 'Hong Kong Garden' for Siouxsie and 'Making Plans For Nigel' by XTC.

When Lillywhite got a call from Gail Colson to arrange a meeting with Gabriel he thought it was one of his mates phoning up as a joke, although working with Gabriel was not totally unacceptable to a post-punk producer. Unlike Genesis, Gabriel had leapt over the credibility gap on the arrival of punk.

"He had heard my XTC work, but my feeling was, 'Peter, you could use anyone, you know, why do you want to use this kid who came from a completely different school?'" said Lillywhite. His engineer on the XTC albums was Hugh Padgham, just three weeks Lillywhite's senior. "I remember we were doing a project one day and Steve said, 'You'll never guess what! Peter Gabriel's rung up. I can't believe it. I'll go down and have an interview.' But we were still fresh-faced in those days and we didn't think we'd have a chance of doing something like Peter Gabriel. He was a big act," remembered Padgham. His bigness at that time was more reputation than sales. When Lillywhite was offered "the gig" he asked Padgham to join him.

The one rule they established when they got together was that if something sounded normal, it should not be used. "That was the basic thing we reminded ourselves of all through the LP, which really helped open me up," said Lillywhite. "It was great for me because I was experimenting with a lot of different dimensions of sound."

During their first meetings Lillywhite asked Gabriel to play him some songs. What he got instead were musical ideas without lyrics. "Lyrics are the most difficult things for him to put together, and without any lyrics you don't really have a song, so you were always slightly in the dark. It wasn't as if he would say, OK this is the song and this is how we are going to present it. It was always, well, I've got this riff and I'll do this, and it sort of evolved."

Since the split with Genesis, Gabriel had maintained sporadic contact with the group, mainly through sharing the same offices. He was friendliest with Phil Collins, whose first marriage broke up in 1979. Collins, always a workaholic, had even more time to play on other people's sessions. "Pete wanted to rehearse some songs for his new album, and I heard from Gail that he didn't have a band because he could not afford to keep them on a constant pay cheque," said Collins. "I said, 'Look, if he wants a drummer I will be there any time he wants.' He rang up and said, 'That would be great, come down to Bath.'" Gabriel was booked to play at Reading Festival on August bank holiday and at the old Genesis haunt Friars of Aylesbury. Collins played at both, playing Gabriel's new material and duetting on *The Lamb Lies Down On Broadway*.

Recording for the album started in summer 1979 using a mobile at Ashcombe House. And then mixing and overdubbing was done at Virgin Records' Townhouse studios in Shepherds Bush where Padgham was a house engineer. Studio Two, where Gabriel was to record, has stone walls that made the sound "splashy". The studio exaggerated the resonance of the cymbals. Padgham and Lillywhite had countered this before by distancing the microphones away from the drums, a technique Gabriel also used in his own studio.

Collins was booked to record with Gabriel for the first time since *The Lamb Lies Down On Broadway* more than five years earlier. The components were now in place to create what was to become one of the most distinctive and influential sounds of the eighties.

"Peter suddenly announced that he didn't like cymbals and hi-hat because they were too normal. We said this is great news because now we can get a really big ambient sound by putting the mikes further away," said Padgham.

Phil Collins became very disorientated. His cymbals and hi-hats were taken away leaving him to thrash out where instinct told him they should be into thin air. "It was so strange for him that he couldn't stop himself from going up as if to smash the cymbals. So we hung two or three drums off big mike stands where a cymbal should be and that cured the problem. He'd do a roll where normally a drummer would hit a cymbal, and he hit a big drum." Collins was fooling around on his kit trying to develop a drum pattern for 'Marguerita', a song that has not yet made it onto vinyl. As Collins was playing away he became aware of the effect he was creating via a cheap microphone relaying the sound back through his headphones. The sound he heard went through a gate compressor unit, the first of its kind fitted to the studio's new Solid State Logic desk. The gate compressor unit both shut off the sound and squashed it. Lillywhite and Padgham were experimenting with these devices.

"For some reason I had this thing in and Phil was playing," said Padgham. "It was suddenly boom-boom tshh . . . and then the noise would suddenly close up before the next boom-boom started. I was just playing around with things, and then he started playing to the sound, in other words the way the noise kept shutting off. Pete was in the control room and he suddenly heard it and he said, 'Fucking hell, listen to that!' And we said, 'Yes, that's amazing!' and Phil said, 'Yes, that's amazing.' It was something we had never heard before, nor had anybody else. It was an enormous sound because we were compressing the death out of this microphone, and it wasn't what it was supposed to be used for.

"So Pete said to Phil, 'Play along for five minutes,' so Phil just sat there and played boom-boom tshh . . . boom-boom tshh . . . for five or ten minutes. And Pete said, 'Thank you very much. I'll go home and write a song to that.'" Gabriel decided to use the drum sound not for 'Marguerita', but instead for another track. That drum sound opens Gabriel's third album on 'Intruder'.

The technique became known as the 'gated reverb'. The 'reverb' came from the reverberation in the studio, a sound that can be imitated electronically, and the 'gate' from the cut-off device on the control desk. Phil Collins was inspired by the sound he helped develop on 'Intruder', and used the gated reverb extensively on his own album *Face Value*, recorded in the same studio with Hugh Padgham as co-producer and engineer. It featured on the song 'In The Air Tonight', his first major solo hit. Collins ultimately got more recognition for creating that sound than Gabriel. "It's silly really. At the time I was pissed off because Phil's album was an enormous seller, and then people would say to me, 'Oh, you are copying the Phil Collins sound,'" said Gabriel.

Collins saw all this slightly differently. "That was one of the best examples of Pete's bloodymindedness. He didn't want any metal on the album, so I said, 'Why? Some sounds would sound great like that, but others would be great with metal.' He said, 'No. I don't want any metal.' So I said, 'What do you want me to do?' And he said, 'Instead of hitting a cymbal you hit the drum.'

"I started playing this drum sound and Pete straight away put his hand on the intercom and said, 'Listen, that sounds great. Play that for ten minutes.' At the end of it I said to Pete, 'If you are not going to use that I would like that,' because as far as I was concerned I had written this drum part and I said I would like to use it. So I took a tape away with me that night. I took it to mean, 'OK, you can use it if I don't.'

"Now that opens up a whole can of worms. When I used it was I ripping Pete off by using my sound? To me I was using my sound and I would defend that to my dying day. It was my brain, it was me that played the part with the sound that Hugh created. I am not saying that I created the sound at all, but I didn't think it was particularly Pete's thing. You can see how tricky it was.

"I heard he had this song called 'Intruder' and he rearranged it to fit with what he had on the drums. When I heard about this I said to Gail, 'Can you ask Pete if he could give me credit on the album for writing the part,' because I felt it was very me. So he wrote: '"Intruder" – written by Peter Gabriel, drum part by Phil Collins' – which was fine by me.

"Of course when my album *Face Value* came out everyone said it was very Gabrielesque and I didn't think any of it was apart from the drum sound which I had used on Pete's album. If you listen to 'Intruder' and 'In The Air Tonight' and all the other drum parts I have done they are all very different."

"Phil was not nicking that idea," said Padgham, who as well as co-producing *Face Value* also went on to produce Genesis. "He was just impressed with an engineer's ability to create new sounds, his enthusiasm and everything else. Phil had never heard his drums sound like that before."

"I really think the third album was the first where a Gabriel style crystallized," said Gabriel. "We have pioneered a few things. I felt bold enough to say to the drummers 'No cymbals!' and made a few rules like that which I think gave it character.

"I stopped the session we were working on and said, 'This sound is going to revolutionize drum sounds.' I didn't create it, but I saw some of the possibilities and used it. Hugh and Steve had done something with XTC using the gated reverb, so it was not the first record it was on. But it was the first record where it was really allowed to happen in the sense that it was the dominating sound.

"I remember talking to Nile Rodgers afterwards and he said as soon as he heard that he said, 'I've got to have this!' and spent a bit of time creating it for himself. When you get those moments and there are few in the studio, and you think 'here's something we've come across and struck gold' which is a really exciting feeling, something that is really going to excite musicians all round the place and you feel their sense of discovery, it's a great moment."

"I think a lot of people have quoted Peter's third album as being a new departure in sound. It's been used so much now I've gone off it a little bit," said Steve Lillywhite.

He had a unique perspective on Collins and Gabriel working together. "They are complete opposites. Phil will say, 'Right, let's do it.' Whereas Peter will say, 'Right, let's do it. What are we going to do?' Or, 'How do I do it?' Or 'How can I do it differently?' For Phil there's no questions, for Peter it's a hundred questions leading to another hundred questions."

After the initial sessions at the Townhouse the Gabriel party moved down to Ashcombe House with the Manor mobile studio parked outside. Larry Fast took charge of the electronic production as well as keyboards, with the now regular team of Tony Levin, Jerry Marotta taking over on drums, and David Rhodes, plus visiting musicians.

"I see Peter as a really important artist," said Lillywhite. "He's extremely talented, but he has to push himself. He has to work hard. It doesn't come easy, unlike Phil. Things probably come easier to Phil than to anyone I've ever met. And things come more difficult to Peter than to anyone I've ever met. He will put off making a decision until the last possible moment, but that's only because he doesn't con himself into thinking he knows what he's doing."

The new rhythmic approach prompted Gabriel to explore an idea that had been with him since September 1977. That was when he heard the news of black South African political activist Steve Biko's death on the radio over breakfast. It prompted Gabriel to acquaint himself more with the situation in South Africa, though the lyrics were the last part of the song to be written. Biko's death generated what was to later become Gabriel's commitment to the cause of human rights throughout the world.

The music for 'Biko' was inspired by music heard on the radio at breakfast on another occasion. Gabriel had been fiddling around with his short-wave dial and picked up a Dutch station playing tribal rhythms from the soundtrack to *Dingaka*, a South African film that starred Stanley Baker. That sound formed the rhythmic core of the song. " 'Biko' and 'Normal Life' are probably the farthest away from my old style of writing. 'Biko' is much simpler musically than anything I had written previously, it only has three chords. This is an approach I would not have used before if I hadn't begun with the rhythm first," Gabriel said. 'Normal Life' was a variation on a Bo Diddley melody.

While 'Biko' was being recorded Gabriel came across the soundtrack of a news documentary on Biko's funeral. Some of the singing from this tape was used at the beginning and end of the track. "The remarkable thing to European ears is that the music is really hopeful – happy is perhaps the wrong word – and positive. Western funeral music is always very down and sombre and serious," said Gabriel.

As well as the 'gated reverb' on 'Intruder', and the African rhythms of 'Biko', Gabriel also pioneered the use in rock music of the marimbas, an African and South American instrument similar to the xylophone, on 'No Self Control'. Avant-garde 'systems' composer Steve Reich's album *Music for 18 Musicians* was the inspiration for the marimbas, played by percussionist Morris Pert. 'No Self Control' also saw the first collaboration between Gabriel and Kate Bush.

But Gabriel also broke new technological ground as the first person to use the Fairlight CMI (Computerized Musical Instrument) synthesizer in a British recording studio.

Sid McGinnis, who had been with Gabriel on his second American tour, was playing on a session with Carly Simon at the Power Station in New York when Peter Vogel, the Australian co-inventor of the Fairlight, came by to show his wares. The Fairlight was named after a hydrofoil that crossed Sydney harbour.

McGinnis knew this new gizmo would interest Gabriel and Larry Fast and telephoned them both. "Larry wasn't that convinced by the instrument," remembered Gabriel. "He comes from a different background where part of his craft is synthesizing sounds, which he is brilliant at. Whereas the sampler seems like a cheating device to him in some ways because it is taking wonderful textures that exist already and manipulating them. So it is collage rather than creation. For me that was a dream come true because I had pictured in my head something that would just allow you to go round with a microphone and grab anything and start manipulating it and being able to use it in your palette."

Fast's memory varies from Gabriel's. "I thought it was amazing and I said to Vogel, I am going to be working with Peter Gabriel, this is where I will be, when I get to England phone me, I am sure you can be picked up. Peter is always pushing the boundaries, from high-tech with the Fairlight and very low-tech, using cheap horrible amps and abusing equipment, but using it always creatively. That's where Peter's mind is brilliant, he can use either way."

Vogel did contact Gabriel when he got to England with the Fairlight a few weeks after meeting Fast and took it to Ashcombe House where he stayed for a week. Gabriel put the Fairlight to immediate use smashing milk bottles and banging bricks, and then playing melodies using the sampled sound. Though it did not change the album drastically it did give it additional colour. It can be heard in the fade out to 'I Don't Remember', a pulsating drone drowning out the incomprehensible whisper of the amnesiac's memory.

Also invited to the studio when Vogel arrived was Gabriel's cousin Stephen Paine, then trying to mark out a career as a synthesizer session player. Paine was well versed in synthesizers through selling them at the London Synthesizer Centre.

Paine shares his cousin's fascination with technology and was inspired to get in on the act and propose to Vogel that he represent him in this country and start importing the Fairlight.

That was the impetus to set up Gabriel's company Syco Systems, in 1980, which had the exclusive rights to import Fairlights and Synclaviers. The initial European distribution of these Rolls Royces of keyboards was conducted from the ramshackle and rat infested Ashcombe House.

"Although the commercial opportunity was fairly easy to see, it was not the main stimulus," said Paine. "Syco deals with high end, state-of-the-art technology. Peter's interest was in establishing a company that was involved in music production

103

technology so that it could allow him quick access to the latest and the best technology as it became available." Paine uses terms like techno-artist and techno-flow. He believes Gabriel is one of the former and in the latter.

"Now we take that technology for granted. What the Fairlight was doing was incredibly basic. It was able to record a sound and play it back on the keyboard at any pitch, polyphonically and as chords. Up to then something similar only existed on the Mellotron. On that each note on a keyboard has a continually rotating tape loop. When you press a key it places a replay tape on the head. It is incredibly laborious and expensive."

Steve Lillywhite and Hugh Padgham were not the only representatives of the New Wave on the third album. Paul Weller of the Jam was recording in another studio at the Townhouse when they returned there to complete the record. He accepted an invitation to play guitar on 'And Through The Wire'. "There was one track which we couldn't get the right guitar feel on at the time and Paul was able to go straight to it," said Gabriel. "We were looking for a certain rhythm that Paul was very good for. The way he plays that rhythm stuff is amazing; he's got this sort of liquid energy in him and in the way he plays."

"Peter was always interested in punk, and was always fascinated with what kids are doing at any point. You have to have the right attitude working with Peter rather than technical ability," said Lillywhite.

All this breaking of artistic sound barriers was the last thing Gabriel's American record company Atlantic wanted if it meant being uncommercial. During the recording the musicians had to put up with the visits of Atlantic's head of A&R, bearded Californian John Kolodner. After the Townhouse sessions the bulk of the album was recorded at Ashcombe House using the Manor mobile studio. It was the first recording Gabriel had made on home territory. Kolodner went to hear what was going on.

"His big thing in music is 'fuck art'. The best record in the world is the one that sells the most. End of story. And he used to come over occasionally during the album and hum and ha," said Lillywhite.

"We were very childish in a way. And when we knew Kolodner was coming over we'd make sure the control room in the studio was really cold because we knew he liked it warm. And we used to have table tennis tournaments during the recording of the album.

"We would think we had something really good going, and he

would come in and put a damper on it. Everyone was nice to him, there was never any animosity."

Kolodner's most memorable remark came while he was listening to 'And Through The Wire'. "I was in the studio when Kolodner said, if you do this, this, and this it will sound like the Doobie Brothers. I had enough, I walked out of the studio," remembered Gail Colson. Paul Weller's guitar was used as a suitable antidote.

When the album was finally completed in February 1980 Gail went to New York with the tapes. "I made the mistake of making them sit down and listen to it," said Gail. In the room were Kolodner, managing director Jerry Greenberg and the president and founder of Atlantic Records, Ahmet Ertegun. Gail attempted to explain every song as they went along, but was met with hostility. "Ertegun said there was no point in writing a song about Biko because no one in America was aware what was happening in South Africa. He thought 'Family Snapshot' was too controversial (the song is based on the thoughts of an assassin stalking his prey). And when he heard 'Lead A Normal Life' (about conformity) he asked if Peter had any mental problems.

"The meeting went downhill," remembered Gail. "I think they had decided they were going to drop him. Kolodner didn't want Lillywhite, he had wanted an American whizz kid."

They broke up for lunch, and Gail met them again in the afternoon. "They said, we have an idea," said Gail. "When Peter comes to his senses we will have the next album. And I said that's not on, you either have him or you don't, so they passed."

Kolodner concluded the album would be "commercial suicide", believing it would not sell above their minimum requirement of 100,000. Atlantic was forced to pay Charisma Records £75,000 for passing on the option. The album would have been Gabriel's last for Atlantic anyway as his contract was due for renewal.

Gabriel called Atlantic's decision "an example of the short-sighted, bigoted attitude commonly found in the hierarchy of the American record industry. It will be ironic if this album turns out to be more successful." It was, and Gabriel derived great satisfaction when 'Games Without Frontiers' became his first UK Top 10 single, reaching Number 4 in April 1980 and boosting sales of the album. But Gabriel could not take credit for the release of 'Games Without Frontiers' as a single; he and Lillywhite disputed Colson's belief that it should be the first single from the album.

Gabriel enjoyed the idea of being out of contract in America for the first time, believing he now had a free hand to find a company sympathetic to his work. What he did not realize was that Tony Stratton Smith still held the option for his American releases, and Strat placed the album with Polygram's American label, Mercury Records.

Gabriel and Colson had their doubts about Mercury, an arm of the giant Polygram group who were strong in Europe but lacked marketing muscle in the United States. It was known as 'The Graveyard of the Record Industry' and someone referred to the company as 'Mercury Poisoning'. Their fears were unfounded; the third album sold a healthy 250,000 copies in the United States, outselling the second album by 100,000 copies. Sales were helped by extensive play of 'Games Without Frontiers' on US Top 40 radio, though the song was not a hit in the States. Atlantic Records apart, the third album is regarded as the one that established Peter Gabriel as an important artist, and paved the way for future success. Within two years of dropping Gabriel, Atlantic were offering to buy him back for an advance of $750,000.

In the UK the album, again just known as *Peter Gabriel*, went straight to Number 3 after its release on 31 May 1980. The following week it became Gabriel's first Number 1 record.

The album's themes are frequently disturbing, even if the music is more accessible than his previous work. On 'Intruder' the menacing whistling and scratching guitar echoes the lyric; 'The sense of isolation inspires.'

"I liked the idea of the intruder and intrusion of different sorts. Implied within that there's obviously the cat burglar, just the house-breaker, but there's also the implication of sexual intrusion as well which I tried to leave fairly open and I think I was trying with some of it to exaggerate the moment of fear.

"I think there are various physical states that we get in when our adrenalin is pumping hard which leave much bigger mental imprints than information which goes in under normal circumstances. So it was trying to cultivate a sense of urgency.

"I have a belief that in some ways a victim is guilty as well as the assailant," explained Gabriel to Bruce Elder of *Melody Maker*. "We are excellent casting directors and writers of our own psychological dramas, and we choose to surround ourselves with people who will perhaps produce a certain set of reactions that something within us needs." That message reflects EST and Zen teachings.

But it is a belief Gabriel takes to its extreme, agreeing with an American study that in certain cases people might psychologically invite a mugging and other crimes.

"I think that rape being such an explosive subject it's very hard for anyone to logically accept that a victim has any responsibility, but where it maybe is easier for a rational mind to see some sort of pattern is in wife-beating, where some wives will go from one man to another man to perhaps a third, all of whom would be violent men. And in a sado-masochistic tie-up that sort of pattern and relationship is present, and in a lot of other things that consciously or logically we can't accept, nor could our legal system."

The terror is continued on 'Family Snapshot', this time it is the assassin and his victim. The song is based on *An Assassin's Diary*, the notes and scribbles of Arthur Bremmer, who shot and crippled Governor George Wallace of Alabama in 1972. When Gabriel introduces the song live he relates how the discarded diary was found under a bridge in Washington DC by a passer-by before finally reaching the hands of a publisher. "It was a really nasty book, but you do get a sense of the person who is writing it," said Gabriel. "Bremmer was obsessed with the idea of fame. He was aware of the news broadcasts all over the world and was trying to time the assassination to hit the early evening news in the States and late night in Europe to get maximum coverage." Bremmer originally went after Nixon, which explains the references to the presidential cavalcade in the song. Gabriel has dropped his stage references to Kennedy's assassination having been convinced a solitary assassin was not responsible for that murder.

> *I don't really hate you*
> *– I don't care what you do*
> *We were made for each other*
> *Me and you*
> *I want to be somebody*
> *You were like that too*
> *If you don't get given you learn to take*
> *And I will take you*

'Family Snapshot'; Gabriel, 1980

The song is viewed from inside the assassin's head. Gabriel believes that criminals are not the alien beasts caricatured in the popular press, but merely act out what is for the rest of us an imaginary part of our existence. The assassin and victim both had an impending sense of their fate. "As though they're each preparing, getting dressed up for this occasion," Gabriel said.

When it is over the killer flashes back to his unloved boyhood. "Some cliches are true – patterns of behaviour begun in childhood do carry through. I see that in my own life."

There is not much more cheer throughout the rest of the album. 'Games Without Frontiers' suggests war is as simple as child's play, while satirizing the slapstick and frequently inane TV contest *Jeux Sans Frontieres*. 'Not One Of Us' and 'And Through The Wire' deal with alienation and isolation, while 'Lead A Normal Life' proffers the banality of what is on offer to those of us who conform. Gabriel agreed that anguish is a common theme on the album, but it was not by design. One track that never made the record because the lyrics were unfinished was the frivolous 'I Go Swimming', later to appear on his live album.

"I see some parallels between this new album and blues music in a way, although not obvious at all. People ask me why is it always so depressing and dark, this new music, and I think that blues music can be very depressing and dark and quite often self-pitying, but at the same time it does provide people, when they listen to it, with an opportunity to release those feelings within themselves and perhaps come out of it more optimistic, more positive, but only by having been through or experienced that sort of negativity and pessimism," he told Bruce Elder of Melody Maker.

Again the album had no title and the cover was stark, this time one half of Gabriel's face was distorted, a process achieved by rubbing the emulsion on a Polaroid picture before it was dry. It is literal self-effacement. He was still holding to his belief that all the albums should look like magazines.

The critics were mixed in their views, he was anything from a genius to a middle of the roader. Dave Marsh got carried away down an intellectual black hole in *Rolling Stone* in September 1980. "Lucid and driven, Peter Gabriel's third solo album sticks in the mind like the haunted heroes of the best *films noir*. With the obsessiveness of *The Big Sleep* (or, more aptly, Jean-Luc Godard's *Breathless*, since Gabriel is nothing if not self-conscious about his sources), the new LP's exhilaration derives from paranoia, yet its theme isn't fear so much as overwhelming guilt. If rock and roll is capable of comprehending original sin, then Peter Gabriel might be the man for the job.

"Gabriel's methods are similar to those of Graham Greene, Raymond Chandler and Eric Ambler. The singer establishes an 'innocent' character of society from a distance until he finds himself being pulled inexorably towards the centre of events. Finally, he's uncertain where observation ends and complicity begins. This is the essence of modern-day moral geometry – even the passive man must act – but that doesn't make it any less scary . . ." And so he continued for a few hundred more words, concluding, "Peter Gabriel has seen a hellish future, and there's no exit."

Nick Kent in the *NME* wrote: "Although I've only possessed the record for some three days, the sheer ferocious power of conceit, vision and performance that blazes out of virtually every bar of music on this, Peter Gabriel's third solo album, is so obvious and so courageously implemented that this reviewer is currently in a state of virtual awe at the achievement."

Kent concluded, "It is destined, I'm already convinced, to become one of the eighties' seminal works. On the one hand it is the sound of a man breaking stride and grasping for his moment, on the other it is the sound of an artist fully coming to terms with himself and his sense of values. The result is a courageous tour-de-force that anyone who even cares slightly about the current state of rock should take heed of."

The following week, Kent's *NME* colleague Paul Morley was less charitable, calling Gabriel "the thinking person's David Essex". He went on: "A suitable package of puzzlement, pessimism, abstraction and paranoia, acted out professionally and containing enough philosophical and political flavour to soothe the rumbling guilt of the passive rock consumer . . ." Morley called Gabriel's "honesty admirable; the art shallow".

Gabriel was stung by Morley's gratuitous insults, and has gradually grown to distrust the music press, rarely granting them interviews. "I think for any artist to pretend that he isn't hurt by bad reviews would be dishonest. They hurt and they're discouraging," he said of reviews for another record, though the same holds true for all his work.

The *NME*, apart from Nick Kent, were particularly scurrilous in their attacks, provoking intolerance in return from Gabriel, who instructed that no concert tickets, press information and records should be sent to the *NME*. In 1987 hostilities abated and the paper, under a new regime, made attempts to repair the fractured relationship.

109

TRANSFORMATION

Gabriel did not relish baring his soul to a room full of strangers. He found it hard enough to open up on an individual basis. So he was not over-keen when Richard Macphail urged him and Jill to take part in an Erhard Seminar Training session in 1978.

He shelved responsibility and said he would abide by Jill's decision, feeling sure she would say no. "I thought I was quite safe there, because she's sceptical about all these things. But she said, 'OK, I'll do it.' So I was thrown." Actually, it was not that Jill was seeking enlightenment so much as jumping at the chance of getting away from the kids for two weekends.

Richard Macphail was so enthused by EST he encouraged all his friends to follow suit; most did not want to hear about it.

Together with Macphail and his girlfriend, Peter and Jill did the EST training at a London hotel in July 1978, one month after the release of the second solo album. They paid around £170 each for two intensive weekend sessions.

EST was portrayed by the media as cranky and a rip-off. This was not surprising considering founder Werner Erhard's background. Originally a car salesman named Jack Rosenberg from Philadelphia, he left his family to seek a new life. His new name was inspired by West German Chancellor Dr Ludwig Erhard, who transformed post-war Germany's economy, and the rocket scientist Dr Wernher von Braun.

Werner Erhard went to California where he became a successful businessman selling educational aids for an organization called Parents. He became involved in the burgeoning 'human potential movement' of the late fifties and sixties, and devised the training from his own experiences at the Esalen Institute in Big Sur, California, the centre of the growth movement in the sixties, as well as involvement with Zen Buddhism and Silva Mind Control. He was later reunited with his family.

The EST training aimed to force participants into confronting their deepest emotions, motives and relationships, in the hope this would unlock their hidden potential. Part of that process of self-confrontation included the discomfort of sitting for hours and hours on end, baring your soul if you chose, or listening to others bare theirs. People frequently screamed in anger and burst into tears. All this public heartrending was a revelation to Gabriel and Macphail, who were brought up to not show their emotions.

"My parents never rowed openly, it just wasn't done, so I just learned never to express anger," said Macphail. "Anger was unacceptable. It's something I've relearned to do to overcome that sort of conditioning. And I think Peter's done the same. I think it's a great mark of our relationship that we allow ourselves to be angry with each other."

Gabriel also never heard his parents row, and their voices were hardly ever raised against him. As a child he expressed his frustration obliquely. "I remember quite often when I was angry with my parents slamming the door and going down to the piano and playing particularly discordant things which I knew would bug the hell out of them, particularly my mum. Totally senseless," said Gabriel.

"Expressing anger is something I had to try and come to terms with and I'm still working on it. It's difficult because it is a sort of wild impulsive thing that I've been taught to buckle up. And it's absurd, really, because people know when you are angry, it's just that you can't make it honest. And if you can't get angry with other people then they can't get angry with you and all this hidden resentment builds up, so it's really unhealthy."

Gabriel had already read about EST in Californian underground magazines. "It was a real sort of threatening experience, in a way, which I think is partly why I didn't do it up until the time Richard decided to go for it.

"It's a hotch-potch of ideas culled from all sorts of places. I view it now mainly as a vehicle, something you can use to get from point A to point B. People were very critical about Erhard and about money and the philosophy. When I buy a car I don't ask for psychological backgrounds of the people that built it. If it's going to get me from one place to another then I'm happy to use it," said Gabriel.

"I think for some people it's a useful training, so I have recommended it to a few people, one of whom actually committed suicide, I don't think as a consequence of that, but he got very involved with EST. He was unstable, I think, before then. But it's strong stuff, and the most important single idea, I

111

think, is that it says, 'You are responsible for what happens to you. You are not a victim.' And that, I think, has enabled me to do a lot of things that perhaps I wouldn't have done before.

"It was part of a process of a much more honest communication between Jill and I, and between other people, key friends and relationships. For instance, one of those jobs that you don't want to do, like firing someone, maybe in the old days I would have asked someone else to do it. Now I would do that myself. I have a lot of difficulty doing it, but I feel better for having done it."

"It was a very dramatic event. Trainers were purposely very, very straight with people in a way that is quite unusual. I sat bolt upright in my chair and it terrified me and fascinated me at the same time. It was such an enormous relief for me," said Macphail.

"There is something about it being in a large group that stops people being damaged. It's hard to explain it any more than that. In terms of emotions I experienced everything there was to experience during that course. You agree not to hit anyone else or intrude on anyone else's experience. You are in the chair for those hours and hours and hours. People are sharing and interacting with the trainer, and it just sparks off stuff because you begin to empathize and realize you've felt like that, you go through that, so you don't have to get up and say anything, just by being there it rubs off on you.

"It had an enormous impact on all of us, and immediately afterwards we went and spent a whole week down at their cottage together, just the four of us, and continued the process. In a sense it started a process that has never changed. It drove our relationship down, much deeper, we just opened up to each other in a way that is quite extraordinary, unprecedented, because that is what it is about. It is the basis of a very close bond between us. It shifts your attitude to things in a way that, if you choose, will never leave you.

"It had a very powerful effect on Peter and I would say that I can still see the effect. For instance, the whole character of his lyrics changed after the training. He may not put it down to this but instead of being all this wishy-washy gnomes and goblins stuff that characterized Genesis, you know, pretty unspecific and heavily symbolic, it became much more straightforward and he just started to write what he was feeling in a way that wasn't tricky to understand. So he discovered a sort of directness of approach. It was a very important turning point in my life and in

112

my relationship with Peter, and I would say his life too," said Macphail.

"Peter did change dramatically, he was able to talk openly to people in a very different fashion. So there was much more of an extreme change in him than me," said Jill. "Richard would like to be stronger about the EST influence than I think Peter or I would, partly because he was so involved. I don't think EST changed my life, though it did have a positive influence. I think it did change Peter's lyrics, but I still have the feeling Peter would have got there anyhow, it was just accelerated growth."

Macphail reviewed the training in 1981, he supervised courses and organized weekends, though despite earlier aspirations decided not to become a trainer. The original EST training has now been softened and moderated. EST, according to Macphail, had a lot to do with helping Peter and Jill through later crises in their marriage.

EST was an effective tool helping Gabriel confront his own conditioning. Though it was capable of having deep psychological effects there was nothing mystical or necessarily spiritual about the experience. When he wanted to probe further into his psyche he preferred esoteric teachings to formalized religion. He shunned the short-cut to Nirvana chosen by so many of his contempories through drugs, notably LSD. But he was willing to experiment with technological devices that appeared to have similar effects to meditation.

"Acid was the only drug I was interested in, but I was too frightened ever to do it. I used to have a pretty powerful dream life and I think I was afraid of losing control. Maybe I'm less afraid of losing control now, but I'm not so interested in it any more. Sometimes I have been pretty scared when my head gets going into overdrive, and I didn't want to unleash it."

Part of his resistance to trying drugs was his loathing of peer pressure from schooldays, whether it was being one of the sports set, in the art group or smoking cigarettes and drinking. "I was pretty much of a dud growing up, so I thought, don't go into competition you might not do well in."

He had two experiences with hashish. The first time he giggled a lot and then threw up. The second was more scientific; he ate some hash cakes provided by a roadie at Ashcombe House and sat down at his desk with a notebook and tape recorder. Nothing happened, so he ate a lot more. He then leaned over the desk and felt "these two bolts of metal shoot up the back of my neck, like mercury in a thermometer. They came crashing round the front of my head, and I thought, 'Uh-oh.' And panic began to set in deep."

Convinced he was going to die he headed for home. "I decided I would try and get home in time to say my last words to my wife and kids. It was about half a mile across fields to where I was living, and I was still talking to the tape recorder, so there's this very funny tape of me thinking that I was going to die. I was getting revelations, as I approached my death, about the meaning of life. I was certain that life was actually organized into five videotapes, which were all running slightly out of sync. And very soon after I came upon this profound piece of wisdom, you hear me collapse into a ditch."

Eventually he found his way home, where he had milk with sugar and went to bed. "Jill thought I looked very pale and thought I must have been in a traffic accident. I looked shocked, was her assessment, but my kids didn't notice any difference."

A failure as a drug user, Gabriel prefers the intellectual and psychic to the chemical search for enlightenment. He was to try what appear cranky methods to help induce dream-like states. "I feel I have had experiences that are a little out of the ordinary. Just being at some remote place and getting a very quiet meditation. Maybe there's a clear sky and a full moon and my mind starts zapping. I think we keep our other lives incredibly contained.

"Dreams are important. We spend a third of our lives asleep, and probably a third of that time dreaming. And I think it's part of the process through which the brain organizes what has been going on in the conscious and the unconscious, and not to take notice of it is, I think, foolish. I do jot them down when it's strong, but it's not a daily event, maybe once a month. It is all influential stuff going on in our head and it is not often acknowledged. I think it is quite a powerful and a motivating force."

He has extensively read the works of Carl Jung, and like him jotted down dream experiences. Jung wrote in his autobiography, *Memories, Dreams, Reflections*: "I wrote down the fantasies as well as I could, and made an earnest effort to analyse the psychic conditions under which they had arisen . . .

"In order to grasp the fantasies which were stirring in me 'underground', I knew that I had to let myself plummet down into them, as it were. I felt not only violent resistance to this, but a distinct fear. For I was afraid of losing command of myself and becoming a prey to the fantasies . . ."

114

Jung continued: "It was clear to me from the start that I could find contact with the outer world and with people only if I succeeded in showing – and this would demand the most intensive effort – that the contents of psychic experience are real, and real not only as my own personal experiences, but as collective experiences which others also have."

Dreams have served a dual purpose for Gabriel, as well as helping him delve into his psyche they were an inspiration for songs. He paid homage to Jung in 'Rhythm of the Heat' on the fourth album. It was originally titled 'Jung In Africa', but he abandoned that because it sounded pretentious.

> Smash the radio
> No outside voices here
> Smash the watch
> Cannot tear the day to shreds
> Smash the camera
> Cannot steal away the spirits
> The rhythm is around me
> The rhythm has control
> The rhythm is inside me
> The rhythm has my soul.

'Rhythm of the Heat'; Gabriel, 1982

This final verse is similar to a description of Jung's while in Africa in 1925: "Thousands of miles lay between me and Europe, mother of all demons. The demons would not reach me here – there were no telegrams, no telephone calls, no letters, no visitors. My liberated psychic forces poured blissfully back to the primeval expanses . . ."

'Rhythm of the Heat' has a pulsating, primeval drum sound that builds into an all-encompassing crescendo. It is one of Gabriel's most direct expressions of rhythmic power.

Gabriel described 'Rhythm of the Heat' as "the adventures of Carl Jung in the Sudan – Great White Thinker – inventor of the concept of the shadow, frightened by his own shadow emerging as a result of rhythm".

The song refers to an incident when Jung, trekking across Africa, became terrified of the very thing he was searching for, the continent's mystical power. Though no humour is apparent in the song, Gabriel was amused at Jung's comical attempts to shut off the magic. A tribal dance was put on for the visiting psychologist, but he was alarmed to see the participants possessed like a wild horde as the rhythm of the dance and drumming intensifed. Cracking his rhinoceros whip, swearing at them in Swiss German and passing around cigarettes Jung managed to scatter them into the night.

The promise of more dream-like states encouraged Gabriel, in early 1981, to buy a Samadhi flotation tank. Not quite the fiendish sensory deprivation tank depicted in Ken Russell's film *Altered States*, the tank is a calm, immensely relaxing environment. The Samadhi, resembling a fat wedged coffin, has about eight inches of water and Epsom salts, kept at skin temperature to give the sensation of gravity loss.

Gabriel has not cited any musical inspiration that has come to him in his tank. "I've daydreamed a lot. You know, in that state in which ideas do come." It would be a useful escape over the traumatic next few years. The songs on *Peter Gabriel* four, recorded in the year after he got the tank, do show more of a mystical leaning – 'Rhythm of the Heat', 'Lay Your Hands On Me' and 'San Jacinto' – but the songs are also the result of many other influences dating back several years.

He was inspired to get the tank after reading *Centre of the Cyclone* by American psychoanalyst John Lilly who designed and experimented with tanks to attain "psychological free fall". His findings were the opposite of those of CIA researchers who first developed tanks in the fifties to explore sensory deprivation which they believed could induce madness.

Lilly's book is full of flowery out-of-the-body experiences which became even weirder when he started experimenting with LSD. It was these experiences which inspired Paddy Chayefsky to write the fictional *Altered States* on which Russell based his film.

"I moved into universes containing beings much larger than myself, so that I was a mote in their sunbeam, a small ant in their universe, a single thought in a huge mind, or a small programme in a cosmic computer . . . Waves of the equivalent of light, of sound, of motion, waves of intense emotion, were carried in dimensions beyond my understanding." Lilly concluded: "All and everything that one can imagine exists."

The isolation tank highlights one of the paradoxes of Gabriel's character. He never indulges in drugs because he fears losing control. The isolation tank promised altered states. He was willing to gamble on losing control in the tank, although in the end there was little risk.

Whatever mystical possibilities first enticed Gabriel to buy a tank, he has used it to help enhance creative thinking. The scientific explanation for this is the tank's stimulation of the brain's theta waves. Beta waves are generated when we are awake, alpha when we are relaxed and calm, delta when we are deeply asleep. But theta waves occur in fleeting instants when we drift in and out of sleep.

According to Michael Hutchison in *The Book of Floating*: "The theta state is accompanied by unexpected, unpredictable, dreamlike, but very vivid mental images, accompanied by intense memories, particularly childhood memories – theta offers access to unconscious control, reverie, free association, sudden insight, creative inspiration. It is a mysterious, elusive state, potentially highly productive and enlightening."

Gabriel lent his copy of *The Centre of the Cyclone* to Richard Macphail. "He wrote in the front, 'Peter Gabriel's – feel guilty if not returned.' I actually gave it back to him about five years later, and stopped feeling guilty," said Macphail.

Present day advocates of floating point to more practical benefits more suited to the age of the Yuppie, like weight loss, reductions in smoking and drinking, and counteracting drug withdrawal symptoms. Floating is said to stimulate the brain to secrete endorphins, the pain-killing euphoria-creating substances described as the body's natural opiates.

Gabriel's interest in machines that could induce mood changes or detect them dated back to his days in Genesis when he first investigated bio-feedback machines. He saw in them a potential for increased self-awareness. Bio-feedback machines with electrodes attached to the body monitor involuntary bodily movement like brain waves and heartbeat. Seeing the level of these normally unconscious movements on a dial or oscilloscope can supposedly help the individual gain conscious control of them.

In the early seventies Gabriel visited companies in the United States that made the devices. He planned to attach the machines to the group on stage to alter the light and sound according to the moods the machines monitored, for *The Lamb Lies Down On Broadway*. The band were doubtful it was technically or financially feasible and the plan was eventually abandoned.

During his sabbatical period in 1975 Gabriel learnt a yoga technique called Breath of Fire, which induces a form of hyperventilation. Gabriel demonstrated with some fast breathing, then took a deep breath and held it. "You can mess yourself up if you don't do it right. But you sort of flush the system. It's quite strong medicine. That, too, gets my head floating."

In 1982 during the recording of the fourth album he was introduced to gravity boots by Jerry Marotta. The boots were strapped to the legs and had large metal hooks protruding from them which could support someone hanging upside down from a gravity bar. Gabriel then had prolonged struggles with a children's climbing rope to find a satisfactory way of hanging upside down. The theory is that the spine and back benefit greatly from stretches and exercises performed the wrong way up, more blood is pumped to the brain and the endocrine system is stimulated.

By now Gabriel had got rid of the aversion to most sports he developed at school, and became a keen jogger. During various sessions at Ashcombe House, particularly with David Rhodes, he would go for a run up to Solsbury Hill, and still jogs sporadically.

Physical exercise and the expansion of the psyche were part of his continuous quest for self-improvement. Despite being open to many esoteric influences, he had a natural aversion to organized religion. "I'm not a practising religious person, in the sense of belonging to a faith or a church. I've been very interested in Zen Buddhism and Taoism, those two I think fit my way of looking at the world better than anything else, and yet in moments of crisis I still pray hard because that is instinctively built in from childhood. So I think there is a mixture there, but I think religion is one of those things that once you have created the hole in the psyche for religion, it always has to be filled with something, even if it is anti-religion."

Jill retains stronger church links through her father Lord Moore, ennobled on his retirement as Private Secretary to the Queen in 1986, who is vice-president of the Society for Promoting Christian Knowledge. Jill has been an active member of her village Anglican congregation, once putting on a play which sent roller skating children through the church to the consternation of some older members. "Peter believes in God, and he believes in Christ, but I don't think he believes in the church, and I can see that, and I have great battles myself."

Anna and Melanie were both confirmed and christened at the Self-Realization Fellowship in Los Angeles. "It was lovely, actually, a mill in the middle of this wonderful lake, and they were christened in six different religions," said Jill.

Much of Gabriel's inner search is, of course, way out of vogue in the eighties. But he makes no apologies for it. "My formative years were in the sixties. I was born in 1950, so I was seventeen years old in 1967 and I think seventeen is a critical age for a lot of people because they are just getting a sense of how they fit into the world. You are trying to think things through an awful lot during that period. There was an openness then that made a big impact on me. My father has always had this inquiring mind, there were always books around. And it seems to me that a lot of those ideas which went underground in the seventies are beginning to resurface again in the eighties, except that they are a lot less naïve, partly because a lot of the people who are still working with them are now in their thirties, rather than in their teens or their twenties, so that's exciting me." He sees these attitudes seeping into our lives, from healthier food and exercise through to the global awareness generated by Band Aid.

Gabriel is a long-time fan of the *Whole Earth Catalogue*, which has promoted alternative technology and campaigned on environmental issues since its inception in the sixties. Through an introduction to one of the people closely involved with the Californian community around which the catalogue is based, Gabriel was offered the chance of the most extraordinary journey he, or anyone else, was ever likely to make.

Gabriel had been corresponding with Tom Mandell, a fan who worked as a futurist at Stanford Research Institute in Palo Alto, just south of San Francisco. Mandell, an engaging letter writer, informed Gabriel that Peter Schwarz, his boss at the institute, was visiting London, and suggested a meeting. Schwarz was familiar with Gabriel's music and was sure he was the musician he needed for the first documentary feature made in space.

Peter Schwarz, a brilliant thinker with a child-like enthusiasm for the ideas that captivated him, was a good friend of Stewart Brand, founder of the *Whole Earth Catalogue*. Brand, a former army photographer, campaigned to get the first picture of the earth from space published, naming the catalogue after it. "The picture was significant because it showed the unity of the whole planet," said Schwarz. The catalogue is one of the few successful surviving remnants of hippy idealism.

Schwarz, a self-confessed old Californian hippy, wanted Gabriel to join his mission to make a film on the Space Shuttle after their meeting in 1978.

" 'Why me?' he said. Peter is a modest man. He thought, 'It

couldn't possibly be me.' On the other hand he loved the idea, and he was tickled and fascinated by it," said Schwarz. "Like anybody in his situation you are approached with lots of hair-brained schemes. And this, in fact, was one of the hair-brainier he had encountered. He took it seriously because I presented it seriously and I came from a relatively serious organization. I had come recommended by someone he knew, so he didn't think I was a nutcase."

Schwarz wanted Gabriel to compose the film soundtrack inspired by what he would experience in space. The project would also include writer Peter Mathiessen, a traveller and "spiritual explorer" who would write the narration; Schwarz would go as producer, with a yet-to-be-chosen cameraman shooting in 70mm. Schwarz had also interested Tom Wolfe, then working on *The Right Stuff*, in writing about the project.

It is easy to see how Gabriel became captivated with Schwarz's scheme. Schwarz has an incisive mind and talks with conviction. Both Schwarz and Gabriel, who have become close friends, share similar 'spiritual' ideals. That idealism inevitably makes them appear naïve and cranky, but that is the risk any innovator takes. It has not stopped Schwartz's high-powered career which has involved working on identifying 'future critical problem areas' for the White House, and his current role steering a large team as acting head of strategic planning at the London Stock Exchange.

Schwarz had been fascinated with space travel since boyhood, and nurtured dreams of becoming an astronaut into his adult life. In 1968, as a student of aeronautical engineering, he spent his vacation working as a junior engineer on the Apollo mission for the National Aeronautics and Space Administration in Philadelphia. Then, in 1974, at the Stanford Research Institute he worked for NASA again, in mission planning for the Space Shuttle Programme.

Schwarz was convinced Gabriel was perfect to write the space film soundtrack. "Firstly, I liked the aesthetics of his music. It is just very good entertaining music. Secondly, it was clear that he was prepared to push the frontiers of music, and this was going to be an innovative enterprise. And third he has brought together – and this is, I think, remarkable – a kind of broad cultural diversity, global in character, and a depth of spirit, which is quite unique. And that is what I wanted the movie to represent, all of those together. And no one represented that better in music than Peter.

"There are not many people who can integrate across the kind of profound gulfs you find between the arts and sciences. There are people who are comfortable in the world of science and people who are comfortable in the world of arts. But there are very few who can meaningfully bridge across that.

"Peter has the discipline to master the tools, and it takes a lot of discipline. It's really quite remarkable to watch him work in the studio. Getting something down right will take him not hours, but days, weeks, sometimes months."

Schwarz was dismayed that the American pioneering spirit had all but disappeared from the Space Shuttle programme. "Somehow or other we had to communicate the real sense of adventure, the profound phenomenon of man going off into the universe." The men from NASA were unsure how to respond when they received Schwarz's request in 1978. Their idea of commercial spin-offs from the space programme was creating new products like Teflon.

One of the film project's advisers was Rusty Schweickart, an astronaut on the 1969 Apollo 9 mission. Schweickart had undergone what amounted to a mystical conversion during a forty-minute space walk. He later formed the Association of Space Explorers dedicated to the peaceful, non-nuclear use of space, which he co-chairs with Alexei Leonov, the first Russian to walk in space. Schweickart still keeps in touch with Gabriel.

Gabriel was told that if the space film did go ahead he would have to undertake the same rigorous training all aspiring astronauts undergo. All the participants would have to go into wilderness areas to see how well they functioned as a team and train on gravity machines.

The loss of Schwarz's financial backers combined with NASA's procrastination and delays in the Shuttle programme forced Schwarz to abandon his dream at the end of 1978. "The whole thing caught my imagination for a while. It looked like it might happen," said Gabriel. Schwarz is still convinced he will one day travel in space.

At the time the space film was starting to look shaky, Schwarz was approached by two Hollywood scriptwriters who wanted to model a film called *The Genius* on him as a child. Schwarz does not blanche from confirming he was a child genius.

Schwarz recommended a more interesting plot, partially based on his own experiences as a youth when he became one of the first computer hackers, breaking into two Department of Defense computers, one controlling the trajectory of missiles.

The film became *War Games*, which grossed $100 million at the box office.

On the basis that it takes one to know one, Schwarz is sure he can recognize the qualities of genius in others. "Peter is a great genius. Genius is not simply a function of the blinding insight. That happens from time to time, sure. It has to do in part with having very open eyes to be able to see clearly. And I think Peter forces himself to look hard at the world.

"He travels a great deal, he visits people, he doesn't really sit in his little studio in England and say, 'Well, I'll read some things and listen to the tapes people send me.' He's out there! 'What's happening there in the world? What do I feel when I take a trip to Senegal and Brazil, or Nicaragua?' I took him to the high technology places in California, and he, like a good trained observer, sees things that others don't see. So he has very open eyes, I think that is terribly important.

"I think another part of genius is the ability to bridge. That is, to make connections that others don't make. What is beautiful about Peter's connections is that they cut across so many curves; the cultural, i.e. he really is able to tap the rhythms of many cultures – they are still very much in his own idiom of rock and roll of the West, because he's intimate in that idiom. There is a kind of political-spiritual dimension; he wants to make the world a better place. It isn't simply 'I like to make nice sounds', it is 'I have a deeper purpose in life'. And that affects both him as a person and his thinking, it moves him, inspires him. I don't think he has an innate love of hardware technology; he loves the tools and what they can do for him. He has to discipline and really force himself to master it and not be satisfied until he has got it. I think very few artists have that."

THE MASTER PLAN

The conflict over the creative input and ownership of *The Lamb Lies Down On Broadway* lingered long after Gabriel left Genesis. More than any of his other group projects, Gabriel felt most possessive towards *The Lamb*.

Having got the group to originally agree to give him complete artistic freedom in devising the story and lyrics, Gabriel decided he deserved to own them as well, and without consulting the rest of Genesis, copyrighted it.

That action in itself, in a group that had prided itself on its democratic ownership of all material, caused a rift. But then Gabriel compounded the sin in 1979 by writing a screenplay and then asking his former colleagues to return to the studio to re-record the soundtrack. He had no choice but to ask them to help as the Genesis line-up of 1974 still jointly owned the music.

"The band were a little reluctant to re-work old material, and also old material in which I had figured so prominently. So there was a certain amount of resistance. It occurred to me that up until the time of my leaving Genesis everything had been co-owned. I should have, through writing melodies and lyrics and quite a few things, done quite well. But I had been possessive enough to copyright the story of *The Lamb*, which caused a certain amount of friction at the time. I thought that as it had been my story I should have the right to do other things with it as I wanted to, and was able to. The music, of course, is co-owned."

When it became clear the band weren't prepared to re-record, Gabriel thought about writing some new material for *The Lamb*. "I think I could have legally recorded my own version of *The Lamb*. But that would have been a somewhat dumb thing to do."

Gabriel felt deeply about Rael and *The Lamb* not only because he believed in its visual potential, but also because of the resemblance Rael bore to himself. Superficially Rael, the Puerto

123

Rican punk from the Bronx, created over a year before the real punks hit the music scene, was far removed from Gabriel, the polite product of middle-class Surrey. But as if to confirm how much of himself was in Rael, Gabriel planned to put himself in the lead role of the film.

In the early seventies Gabriel had been greatly impressed with the film *El Topo* directed by Alejandro Jodorowsky. "There are scenes in *El Topo* which will stay with me forever," Gabriel said. The film appears to defy description. Gabriel's attempts to locate Jodorowsky, the Chilean-born son of Russian Jewish parents, were thwarted several times, but he eventually tracked him down to his Paris home and met him in early 1979.

"I had an original story, it wasn't very long, about twelve pages or something. Alejandro then did his own version of that. I don't think my thing was very strong in the first place, I certainly didn't like it, where it had gone, so I sort of killed it off."

The Lamb Lies Down On Broadway was to be a twentieth-century *Pilgrim's Progress*. Rael, the young Puerto Rican convict from the Bronx, was carving out a career in New York City. But the street punk and graffiti artist was forced to make an unexpected detour into his own psyche. Rael was thrust into a fourth-dimensional world inhabited by mythical creatures and bizarre characters. It was a surreal tale of sex, violence and death. Gabriel, who had mounted a highly theatrical live show when performing with Genesis, planned to make extensive use of cinematic special effects.

"We spent about four to six weeks working together, developing a script. It was great, a very exciting time." After a break Gabriel and Jodorowsky continued their work during the summer of 1979 in Bath at Ashcombe House. "He's an incredible character, and has been a breath of fresh air in helping me re-evaluate my own career," Gabriel said at the time. "We've been talking about getting a producer, and it's very exciting for me because he's the master and I am the apprentice." They modified the story considerably. Jodorowsky persuaded Gabriel to abandon plans to play Rael and stay behind the scenes as co-author.

"At the time I only knew his songs, I had never seen him on stage," said Jodorowsky. "I said he should not play Rael, but now I would say yes because I know how he performs."

The proposed feature film was entrusted to Charisma Films who looked to raise a relatively modest £5 million. But when

Gabriel was dropped by Atlantic in 1980 there were immediate delays in getting the necessary American backers. Charisma were told financiers wanted to see Gabriel selling records in America first before they would commit themselves. Despite the third album's ultimate success, they were still not convinced.

After working with Jodorowsky, Gabriel hoped filming could begin in the summer of 1981. He hung on tenaciously to the idea for a few years after that. "It just died, it wasn't ever resolved with the band," he said. Conflict was avoided by default.

Gabriel was captivated by Jodorowsky's "cosmic enlightenment". Soon after working with Gabriel he made a children's film about elephants called *Tusk*. But his Russian and Latin temperament and surreal vision were too much for film financiers who doubted his commercial appeal. Jodorowsky survived by giving Tarot readings.

"I think Peter has a marvellous unconscience [sic]. In some ways he understands me, but in an enormous way I understand him. In order to understand Peter you need to close your ears and look at how he walks. There you can start to understand him," Jodorowsky attempted to explain.

Jodorowsky's career never took off, despite being the first to hold the film rights to Frank Herbert's science-fiction epic *Dune*. He wrote a script for the movie and put together the design and special effects team only to have the project taken off him and given to director David Lynch.

Film was not an infatuation for Gabriel in the way it becomes for most successful rock stars who believe they can carry their talents over to celluloid. He gave up the chance of a course at the London School of Film Technique at the age of nineteen to stay with Genesis in 1969. It was ironic that film, through William Friedkin's invitation in 1974 to write a screenplay, was instrumental in spurring his departure from the group.

Gabriel's visual sense had always been strong. Jill remembered a painting he did at school depicting the skeletons of dinosaurs all in a line in a cavern with a man walking over the bones into the cavern. The psychological explanation is open to debate.

When Gabriel was offered the chance to go to film school he wrote a screenplay based on his feelings having run over and killed a bird in a car.

"He was so intensely moved by that. That's why I loved him. I mean, that was partly what attracted me to him, he felt it really deeply, and he wrote the most amazing film script because of that, and was accepted," said Jill.

Little more than a year after Rael was conceived, Gabriel invented the "mercurial stranger" Mozo. "He was partly based on Moses, but he was a fictional character who came from nowhere, disrupting people's lives and causing changes and then disappearing," said Gabriel. Mozo was part of a "master plan" dreamed up during his sabbatical in 1975–6 which he alternately wanted staged or filmed.

Mozo was inspired by *Aurora Consurgens*, a medieval alchemical treatise based on The Song of Solomon. It was brought to light by Carl Jung who thought it the work of St Thomas Aquinas. The text is full of alchemical and religious symbolism and apocalyptic imagery.

Jung saw alchemy and psychology as having the common aim of self-transformation. Gabriel was captivated by Jung's alchemical writings. "I have always been interested in transformation of one sort of another," said Gabriel. "When Mozo came in he upset the status quo and the story is about the struggles after his appearance." Mozo was a catalyst for spiritual change. This was true alchemy of which changing base metal to gold was a mere analogy.

Mozo was at the core of what Gabriel tries to express in music. Perhaps he sees himself as that mercurial stranger able to transform and uplift people.

Gabriel wanted to scatter songs about Mozo over several albums, though they would make a complete story when put together. The songs were 'Here Comes The Flood' – an apocalyptic vision: 'Down The Dolce Vita' – a ship leaving harbour on an intrepid journey; 'On The Air' – Mozo and his fantasy world; 'Exposure' – the struggle for salvation; 'Red Rain' – denying one's in her feelings; and 'That Voice Again' – judgment.

"Mozo is set in this fishing village, which is very upmarket, not quite Mediterranean, but something of that ilk," explained Gabriel in 1987. "There is this volcanic sand which gives the sea a red colour. Everything is focused on the sea, which is very rough, and the great macho feat is to cross the water, which no one has done.

"Mozo is discovered in a tip, in a house built out of rubbish, on the edge of the city. And initially kids and passers-by are just very curious to look inside this little shed, and they see in it what they are most afraid of. They project their fears on to him because he is different.

"I remember in Horsell Common near Chobham, where my parents live, there was this beaten up old caravan, with newspapers in the windows. I used to think there was a witch inside there. And I think it probably fuelled this setting for Mozo.

"Eventually the people who have discovered Mozo in this hut on a tip get disturbed. They are getting upset by what they are seeing, by what they are projecting onto him and they try and kick him out. He escapes, and he proves later on that he has crossed the sea. So he goes from being the tramp underneath society to the hero on top of it.

"And then having been placed above other people he is challenged by the people who put him up there. They then have him as a target to push down to the bottom again."

'On The Air', on the second album, introduces Mozo, who lives in a fantasy world created by what he picks up and transmits on his short-wave. "Through short-wave radio he becomes whoever he wants, but in real life, on the street, he's totally ignored," explained Gabriel.

> *I got power, I'm proud to be loud; my signal goes out clear*
> *I want everybody to know that Mozo is here*
> *On the air . . .*

'On The Air'; Gabriel, 1978

'Down The Dolce Vita', from the first album, introduces characters setting out on the intrepid journey across the sea. Aeron and Gorham, like Mozo, have corrupted biblical names.

'Here Comes The Flood' was written at the height of Gabriel's fascination with short-wave radio. If radio signals got stronger at night, he reasoned, maybe psychic and telepathic awareness could be similarly increased and made to flood the mass consciousness. Those who were honest and straightforward could take on board their new insights, while those who hid their thoughts and feelings would be lost.

> *When the flood calls*
> *You have no home, you have no walls*
> *In the thunder crash*
> *You're a thousand minds, within a flash*
> *Don't be afraid to cry at what you see*
> *The actors gone, there's only you and me*
> *And if we break before the dawn, they'll use up what we used to be*

'Here Comes The Flood'; Gabriel, 1976

127

'Exposure', from the second album, is stark and minimal. The music was co-written by Gabriel and Robert Fripp, who named his 1979 album after the track. The version sung by Gabriel on Fripp's album is introduced by a recording of English sage J. G. Bennett uttering, "It is impossible to achieve the aim without suffering."

The final Mozo-linked songs to appear on record were 'Red Rain' and 'That Voice Again' from the *So* album. 'Red Rain' is about repressed feelings and pain that become expressed by the elements.

'That Voice Again', Gabriel explained, was about "judgmental attitudes being a barrier between people. The voice is the voice of judgment. A haunting internal voice that instead of accepting experience is always analysing, moralizing and evaluating it." The song was originally called 'First Stone', but Gabriel abandoned the biblical allusions. He went through three sets of lyrics before David Rhodes came to the rescue and co-wrote them with him.

Gabriel first sought backing to perform Mozo in early 1976, soon after the Genesis album *A Trick of the Tail* became their biggest success to date. It was an unfortunate time to make an approach. Genesis' good fortune overshadowed Gabriel's. There was little enthusiasm from publishers and record companies for what promised to be an expensive exercise and Gabriel was forced to wait until he had commercial success as a solo artist.

He had discussed his ideas with Bob Ezrin, the producer of his first solo album. Ezrin told him about the Czech theatre Laaterna Magica and the pioneering Josef Svoboda. Gabriel visited him twice in Prague in the late seventies. He was interested in Svoboda's 'perforated screen' combining cinema with theatre. In it a film was complemented by live action using a device that made actors appear to go in and out of the screen.

Gabriel was later introduced to Czech animator Raduz Cincera who developed his 'Kineautomat'. Cincera was working on opera sets for the London Coliseum when he met Gabriel. "The Kineautomat has cinema seats with yes/no buttons," said Gabriel. "There were about a dozen decision points, the plot chosen by vote. So, for example, an actor would come out of the screen and say to the audience, 'Should I stay with my wife, or go with this woman?' And the cinema would become as lively as a football match."

Eventually the Mozo idea lost impetus, though in autumn 1985 Gabriel was still considering working on developing the story into an hour-long video. "Maybe I should look at it again some day, there's still stuff in it I like. It's always the thing, the new is more attractive than the old," Gabriel said in 1987.

Teaming up with Jodorowsky, Friedkin or Hall before him, was indicative of Gabriel's belief in cultural cross-pollination, developing ideas from those he admired in all the arts. Graham Dean, who he met in 1978, gave him several books including Leni Riefenstahl's photographic essays *The Last of the Nuba*, and *People of Kau*.

"The first time we met was at a private viewing theatre in Soho where he invited me to see a film by Jodorowsky opening in London. We went to shake hands and missed. People who know Peter would say, 'Yes, I understand.' Things are slightly off with him," said Dean.

"Peter and I have been battering ideas over the years. As you get to know him you see he is an ideas person, he goes off on many tangents. He is one of the most creative people I know. The trick is to discipline the creativity, he would admit that himself. Everyone can come up with ideas."

Dean has never been in favour with the art establishment or critics. 'Leo and Mona', his 1974 visual joke, showed the master and subject in bed together. The following year he exhibited Memories, originally titled 'Refugee From England'. It shows an exiled Queen Elizabeth looking through a scrapbook at her days of former glory. His earlier work in acrylics had a photographic clarity, now he is more emotional, painting giant smudged watercolours.

In 1981 Dean asked Gabriel to do the soundtrack for *Undercurrents*, a fifteen-minute film. The title was a pun on images of water blended with the sinister undercurrents of Dean's disturbing paintings of skin disorders.

They booked a recording studio for an afternoon to make the soundtrack, and went on for three days and three nights. Dean repaid Gabriel with a painting called 'Tropicans 7', an unsettling image of a young negro with a multi-coloured skin disease. A six-minute extract from *Undercurrents*, with its atmospheric music, was shown on the BBC2 arts magazine programme *Riverside*. It was a useful test bed for Gabriel's later feature film soundtracks.

Dean travelled around London with Gabriel, frequently using public transport. "He is the least likely looking pop star you will meet. I can't remember a single instance where he has been recognized because he doesn't act the pop star." But that was before the success of *So*, which has certainly robbed Gabriel of the luxury of virtual anonymity.

Gabriel now has a keener sartorial sense. But Dean remembers when it was otherwise. "On one occasion a few years ago I was having an exhibition in Paris at an international art fair. It was raining when we arrived in Paris. He had a dark grey roll-up plastic mac like the ones your parents used to make you wear. He suddenly unrolled one of these and put it on and we walked through the streets of Paris to the show at the Olympia.

"International art fairs are mega European style conventions, the rich of Europe parade themselves, and there was Gabriel walking around wearing his mac. I kept giving him hints, saying are you sure you aren't warm inside that. They looked at this funny person in this peculiar looking mac. Once I said Peter's name people recognized him. The funny thing is he is so visually oriented, yet the way he put himself together was the opposite."

Dean introduced Gabriel to sculptor Malcolm Poynter in early 1980, then working in a studio in Butler's Wharf, opposite the Tower of London. Gabriel was impressed by Poynter's sculptures: "white, bald, naked figures that stood around in little sets". Poynter talks about wanting to "gobsmack" people. "Throw the image straight into people's eyes, jarr them, shatter them. I like disturbance levels. All these things are perception raisers or lowerers. We are basically myopic in the way we see things, we are cotton wool surrounded, we never experience much nowadays, we are becoming visually blasé because there is so much visual imagery everywhere. I am just using ordinary images, but you can really disturb people by the context you use them in."

Gabriel and Poynter enjoy collaboration. It is not just a matter of using other artists as source material, but, for Gabriel, also having enough courage and belief in what one is doing to make it happen. "If you have people who inspire you with their work, very often, if you are determined enough, you can get to them, and it's like touching Jesus' cloak. It is possible if the willpower is there," said Gabriel.

"And when people send tapes to me, which they do all the time, I think it's very rarely the music that is going to make the difference with whether they make it or not, it's their psyche: a) whether they need it badly enough, and b) whether they have the willpower to go for it. I think, different to most people, that a lot of talent is acquired and not God-given or hereditary."

Gabriel found Malcolm Poynter, a bluff South Londoner,

refreshing. "I think Peter is very unused to being challenged personally because of his manner and who he is. I love people like that because I know underneath them they're really waiting to get out.

"Peter has the ability to draw people out, but because of his attitude most people give in to him. The only way to counteract or contradict him is actually not to take any notice of that but to confront him as the individual that he is and not to worry. I have felt like shaking the shit out of him sometimes."

Gabriel and Poynter discovered a mutual interest in the work of Professor Stanley Milgram. "It was a revelation that both of us knew and had an understanding about his work. It made it easier for us to become friends." Milgram's book *Obedience To Authority* is based on his psychological experiments at Yale University in the late fifties and his disturbing findings about the cruelty people are capable of inflicting when ordered to do so by a figure of authority, in this case a white-coated scientist in his imposing laboratory.

"Two people come to a psychology laboratory to take part in a study of memory and learning," wrote Milgram. "One of them is designated as a 'teacher' and the other a 'learner'. The experimenter explains that the study is concerned with the effects of punishment on learning. The learner is conducted into a room, seated in a chair, his arms strapped to prevent excessive movement, and an electrode attached to his wrist. He is told that he is to learn a list of word pairs; whenever he makes an error, he will receive electric shocks of increasing intensity."

But the real focus of the experiment is the teacher, the learner is merely an actor feigning pain. "At what point will the subject refuse to obey the experimenter?"

Gabriel grew up hemmed in by the authority of an English public school. He was obedient despite his alienation from the system, joining the Combined Cadet Force, and in his last few weeks at Charterhouse even becoming a monitor. Much of his adult life has been spent peeling away the protective layers culture and convention imposed on him through authority figures. He identified with Milgram's experiments, though they were prompted by a hell far removed from the playing fields of Charterhouse: the Nazi concentration camps.

"Facts of recent history and observation in daily life suggest that for many people obedience may be a deeply ingrained behaviour tendency, indeed, a prepotent impulse overriding training in ethics, sympathy, and moral conduct," wrote Milgram.

Gabriel first started performing his song 'Milgram's 37' in 1979. It referred to one experiment highlighting the easiest form of cruelty – getting someone else to do the dirty work, in this instance to administer the shock. "In this situation thirty-seven out of forty adults . . . continued to the highest shock level on the generator. Predictably, subjects excused their behaviour by saying that the responsibility belonged to the man who pulled the switch. This illustrates a dangerously typical situation in complex society: it is psychologically easy to ignore responsibility when one is only an intermediate link in a chain of evil action but is far from the final consequences of the action."

Gabriel first intended recording 'Milgram's 37' for the third solo album, released in 1982, but the track never made it. The live version of the song at the time had just one line: 'We do what we're told, told to do.'

It was repeated in a moronic virtual monotone, with a steady hypnotic beat. Almost unheard was the crackle of electricity. On this occasion when the audience sang the words it was not an expression of unity, more an uncomfortable reminder of how crowds encourage obedience and conformity.

By the time 'Milgram's 37' reached the *So* album seven years after it was first conceived the song had changed into 'We Do What We're Told' with the subtitle 'Milgram's 37'. The song gently builds up into an eerie chant against a pulsating rhythmic backdrop. After the repeat of the lyric 'we do what we're told' the song's chorus is:

> *One doubt*
> *One voice*
> *One war*
> *One truth*
> *One dream*

For Peter Hammill, it is Gabriel's least satisfying work. "I thought it was pretty half-baked. I just thought, it won't do. As a comment or a song about the Milgram experiments, I don't think that the lyric as it stands is acceptable. 'We do what we are told' is not the point of the Milgram experiment.

"For somebody who doesn't know anything about Milgram it just presents another Kafka-esque vision. The whole point is much deeper than that. It's the stuff of what we are inside. It is my belief that if you are going to do something about an area like Milgram's that it becomes a very complex thing, you want people who don't know anything about it to become interested to find out something about it, you want people who do know something about it to have their perceptions changed in some way, or at least to present them with an alternative view.

"I think if it was to be reduced simply down to one line, more accurate would be 'we aim to please'. In reality, in terms of writing something like this, I would obviously write a different song. But if I had been doing it in Peter's psyche, writing it in terms of various phrases like that, I would probably want to combine 'we aim to please', 'we do what we are told', 'we suffer the suffering'. Something like that so one would end up with a bit more of a spread of the psychic disturbances involved.

"The only reason I bring this up is I do think he gets elements of that into other quests. 'Biko', obviously, is an epic stand precisely because it flips from the mundane to the absolutely global, and that is what 'Milgram's 37' doesn't."

Gabriel spent a long time tracking down Professor Milgram on the telephone to ask his permission to use film excerpts of the experiment for possible use in videos or on stage.

"I was interested in the film because they seemed very ordinary American people, the type who would quite happily shop next to you in Safeways. Yet they were capable of performing horrific things on their fellow human beings. It was quite an eye opener. At the time it was quite controversial and Milgram got into a lot of trouble because it was seen as potentially harmful for the volunteers in the experiment." When Gabriel finally got through to Milgram on the telephone he found him cordial. He believed Milgram was well-disposed towards him after checking him out before their conversation and finding some of his students were fans. But Milgram's attitude changed on the second call.

"I think he was cautious of another spate of sensational publicity, as he saw it. His quote in the end to me was, 'Academic research and entertainment aren't happy bedfellows'. He came up with this quote after he talked to his colleagues, so I think it was peer group pressure." Milgram died in 1984, two years before 'We Do What We're Told (Milgram's 37)' was finally released on the *So* album.

Gabriel and Malcolm Poynter first teamed up in 1980, before they knew of each other's interest in Milgram, to make an experimental video at the offices of Syco Systems in Paddington. Poynter took along some of his sculpted heads, and film editor David Gardener borrowed a VHS camera. Poynter got Gabriel to crawl around the floor, while Gardener shot Gabriel's reflection in a giant flexible mirror with elongated shots of his head. Gabriel was mainly static, in different poses, looking as if he were just about to do something.

Gabriel wanted to experiment with reversing the conventional 'write a song and then make the video' process. He wanted to create a video scenario and then write a song that worked with it. "When you have a strong point in a video you make something happen to a drum beat or whatever. There is no reason why you cannot write music that works for that video image," explained Gardener, who had edited the video for 'Games Without Frontiers'.

Gabriel, Poynter and Gardener drew up a list of effects and ideas they wanted to use, though there was never any story line. Some of the ideas on that list, like using a newspaper-style image of a moving picture made up of black, white and grey dots, have since been used by other people.

Nothing came out of that evening at Syco until two years later when Gabriel was stuck for a cover design for his fourth album. He contacted Gardener and Poynter and they met up at a Soho editing suite to try and get some stills from the video.

They played around with a vision mixer adding special effects to the original video and swopping colours. They found a video camera in the next door studio and started making another film, using a piece of blue plastic tubing that was lying around which Gabriel put between his teeth. Poynter took slide shots of the images on screen, and Gabriel used them on the inside cover of his fourth album, released in 1982. Gabriel never realized his aim of writing a song around a video, though he hopes to create the technical facilities to make that possible at his new studio in Box, near Bath.

Gabriel was unsuccessful in his attempts to produce films of his own stories and lacked the time, facilities and budgets to fulfil his video ambitions. But his music did interest two major Hollywood directors, Martin Scorsese and Alan Parker.

Scorsese was the first to approach him in 1983 to see if he was interested in contributing to the soundtrack for *The Last Temptation of Christ*. Gabriel was delighted at the chance of working with Scorsese.

The film was to be based on the novel *The Last Temptation* by Nikos Kazantzakis, author of Zorba The Greek. The story depicts Christ as a man for thirty years until he accepts his destiny and returns to the cross. False rumours spread that the film depicted Christ as a homosexual. But Paramount started getting paranoid.

The film's commercial prospects looked bleak when the owner of America's largest cinema chain, Salah Hassanein, who had not read the script, felt he did not want to show it in his theatres. He had trouble with religious films.

Paramount Studios had agreed to put up $12 million; they then slashed the budget in half. Sets had been built in Morocco, costumes and wigs made in Italy, all the cast booked, and locations organized. Then Paramount pulled out altogether. Scorsese persisted in his attempts to get finance, including one scheme to get backing from the Greek Government, but without success. He met up with Gabriel and said he hoped one day to resurrect the idea. In 1987 the film, renamed *The Passion*, found new backers, and Gabriel once again agreed to Scorsese's invitation to do the soundtrack.

Alan Parker's request for Gabriel to write the soundtrack for the film *Birdy* was more straightforward. Chastened by his first experiences with the world of rock and roll working with Roger Waters and Pink Floyd on *The Wall*, Parker was hesitant about approaching another rock musician. But as a fan of Peter Gabriel's music he suspected he might be dealing with a different temperament. "Peter's not of that world. He's a very exceptional person. He doesn't have any of the hang-ups or the unpleasantness of that particular business. We got on so well, he's such a sweet man, it was such a refreshing change from working with megalomaniacs like Roger Waters."

Parker, director of *Midnight Express, Bugsy Malone, Fame,* and *Shoot the Moon*, had been given a list of suggested musicians to write the soundtrack for his latest venture, *Birdy*. The production company were A&M Records who, for business reasons, listed only their own artists, with one exception: Peter Gabriel. His name was included because he had a fan in their A&R department.

In September 1984 contact was made and Gabriel met Parker and his producer Alan Marshall at Pinewood Studios. Gabriel was shown the two thirds of the film that had been shot. Already behind preparing his next album, Gabriel agreed to halt that project to work on the *Birdy* soundtrack; he enjoyed the discipline.

Parker had made a tape of excerpts from Gabriel's music that he liked, including 'Rhythm of the Heat' from the fourth album to give Gabriel an idea of what he wanted. Parker had already put some segments from Gabriel's fourth album onto a rough mix of the film soundtrack.

Gabriel needed some assistance in the studio and approached Daniel Lanois on the recommendation of David Rhodes, impressed with his production of composer Harold Budd's album *The Pearl*, which features the multiple sounds of pianos. A Canadian, from Hamilton, Ontario, Lanois had also produced more mainstream acts Martha and the Muffins, and co-produced the U2 album *Unforgettable Fire* with Brian Eno. Gabriel contacted his old friend and occasional collaborator Eno who assured him Lanois could handle the project. Lanois was able to join Gabriel and Alan Parker at short notice.

"We went back to the original 24-track masters to a great deal of the things that I love, I couldn't believe the richness of them – things that weren't even on the album," said Parker.

"Peter's record company were very difficult to begin with, and so I phoned them to ask if they'd mind if Peter took off a little time to do this, and they said as long as it didn't take more than a couple of months because Peter was already a year late, or something."

For once Gabriel found the strict deadline invigorating. During October he worked a 14- to 16-hour day trying to meet the Christmas deadline. The film opened in New York in December 1984, without Gabriel's soundtrack, to make that year's Oscar nominations. It was premiered in London in February 1985 with the soundtrack. He may have had to speed up, but Gabriel still made sure he had the final say in what he did. "He had strong views and I would never be able to persuade him to do something he didn't feel comfortable with, but we didn't have any confrontation as such," said Parker.

Gabriel's music had inspired Parker, but he was also attracted by similarities between Gabriel's nature and the two main characters in the film. Birdy himself is naïve, unworldly and obsessive, but with an inner strength. He is not affected by the scorn of his peers, pursuing his passion, paying little attention to the condemnation of others. In contrast his friend Al is worldly and good with the girls. Al and Birdy are conscripted to Vietnam where they are both injured. In hospital Birdy withdraws into a catatonic state, sucking strength from Al, who disintegrates so that his friend can come back to life.

"It is a film with a number of layers. It is a bit dodgy just zooming in on one thing," said Parker. "The reason I wanted to make the film was that it was about friendship, but it was also about the way in which war in general takes away young lives. And also it's about the dreams that we have to explain the world that we are in. We all take flight one way or the other, through music or film or whatever."

Gabriel was sparse in his use of music to aid the narrative. "When you have wall to wall music in the classic Hollywood movie scores the music ceases to have any effect because there is no light and shade. It's the same as an album mix, really. If you just have head on stuff right the way through it ceases to be powerful. It is the quieter moments that make the louder stuff work," said Parker.

"The rhythmic percussion on the flying scenes was the most original use of his music in the film. It was not the normal way to do that kind of scene. It was a much harsher sound than goes with the fluidity of flight. Normally it would be very lyrical, but it's not, which makes it very powerful."

Concerned that his fans might feel ripped off by the repetition of music that had been released elsewhere Gabriel put the equivalent of a Government health warning on the album cover.

When I was asked to do this soundtrack, the intention was to build it out of elements of existing tracks. Some of these Alan Parker had already chosen.

We worked for a couple of weeks with unorthodox explorations of some of the sounds, rhythms and themes of existing tracks. This provided many moods, but I felt some new material was needed as well. So, what you have here is a combination of both.

For those people who know my records, I have included (in brackets) the titles which have been obviously raided. I do not wish anyone to be deceived by the sleeve. However, I am not revealing all my sources. I leave that for your detection.

Three of these tracks did not make it to the last round – the film. But the music on this record was chosen to make a compatible collection of moods . . .

Birdy sold far fewer copies than Gabriel's previous albums, just 25,000 copies in the United States, though worldwide it reached 150,000, a respectable number for a soundtrack.

Gabriel enjoyed the idea of making diehard fans work out his musical sources. His own sources are drawn from a wide range of stimuli, not least a prodigious reading list. He has occasionally acceded to requests from fans wanting to know his influences. In autumn 1982 he gave a list of his favourite things: '*The White Hotel* by D. M. Thomas – book of the month; *Sergeant Bilko* – TV programme of the month; Spike Milligan – favourite comic; Talking Heads – favourite group; Nusrat Fateh Ali Khan – singer of the month; *M* by Fritz Lang – favourite film; *Sunday Times* – favourite newspaper; Ian Pollock – favourite illustrator; Crest – favourite toothpaste; Redcurrant and Peach – favourite yogurt flavour; New York – favourite city; Italian – favourite language; 'Old Man River' [no category, presumably favourite song] – Paul Robeson; Nicol Williamson – favourite actor.'

He repeated the exercise in similar fashion in spring 1984: 'Books: *The Dream and the Underworld* by James Hillman; *The Complete Poems of Anne Sexton; The Life and Death of Yukio Mishima* by Henry Scott-Stokes; *An Anthology of Modern Day Japanese Haiku* by Makoto Ueda; *Hotel* – various authors and photographers; *My Last Sigh*, autobiography of Louis Buñuel; *The Tree* by John Fowles and Frank Horvat. Magazines: *New Scientist; Coevolution Quarterly; Zoom*. Favourite illustrators: Ian Pollock, Matt Mahurin, Janet Long, Russell Mills, Grizelda Holderness, Glenn Baxter, Peter Till, Duncan Robert-Wilson, George Hardie.'

During 1985, there was one other vital influence without which the *So* album would apparently not have been made – Sainsbury's wholewheat shortbread biscuits.

Before working on *Birdy* in autumn 1984, Gabriel had already tasted involvement in Hollywood. He contributed a track to *Gremlins*, the furry fantasy from the Steven Spielberg factory, directed by Jo Dante. Because of Spielberg's insistence on strict secrecy Gabriel was only given a copy of the scene he was to write for. He came up with 'Out Out', featured in a bar where the mischievous gremlins create havoc.

The music was an indication of the funkier direction Gabriel's next album was to take. 'Out Out' was recorded with Nile Rodgers, the producer who funked up David Bowie at New York's Power Station. But Gabriel was also attracted to Rodgers' less known more playful sound, heard on Carly Simon's song 'Why'.

Gabriel took up the offer to work with Rodgers some time after receiving a telex from him when he became successful asking if they could work together. "I thought maybe this is a good chance to try it out," said Gabriel. "The trouble is I am used to working at such a slow pace and experimenting, and I hadn't actually got the song ready when I went over there. So it cost a fortune in American studio bills and really wasn't a very good song. There were sections in it I liked, but it didn't work a hundred per cent." He was not too impressed with the way the song was put over in the film. "It's a bit of a disappointment when you think, 'This is it! Films! Hollywood!' And then you get smothered by some gremlin throwing up!"

Gabriel could not resist delivering the finished track personally to get a peep at Warner Bros' studio in Hollywood. He received "medium VIP" treatment on the set and met director Jo Dante, though Spielberg was nowhere to be seen.

Also in 1984 Gabriel recorded and produced the song 'Walk Through the Fire' for use in the romantic adventure *Against All Odds*. The film was directed by Taylor Hackford, who made *An Officer and a Gentleman*, and starred Rachel Ward and Jeff Bridges. Gabriel's optimistic rhythmic conga-tinged music was used as background in a tense bar-room scene where Bridges seeks information that will help save his life. 'Walk Through the Fire' was released as a single in May 1984 but only got to Number 69 in the charts. "It could have been a good song. The ingredients are there but it's not quite right," Gabriel said. The song had originally been intended for the third album before getting reworked for *Against All Odds*.

He was invited to contribute to the soundtrack by Tony Smith, the film's music producer. He naturally asked the members of Genesis to write songs, and Mike Rutherford and Phil Collins obliged. Just over a month before Gabriel's single was released Collins' got to Number 2 with his title track 'Against All Odds (Take A Look At Me Now)'.

Gabriel used *Gremlins* and *Against All Odds* to gain experience in the film world, as well as earning some pocket money during lulls in his own recording. In 1985 he was reluctantly drawn into another film, *Lorca and the Outlaws*, again through Tony Smith, who became executive music producer. Smith, who also had Tony Banks writing for the film, pressed Gabriel to take part as a favour. Gabriel was filmed at Shepperton Studios performing 'San Jacinto' from his fourth album and can be seen performing the song as a supposed holographic image brought up on a twenty-first century jukebox. The film, a weak science-fiction thriller, was only released on video in the UK.

Gabriel has not ruled out acting, though his enthusiasm appears to have waned. "As a rock musician and writer you get to act out the characters you created, so theoretically the job should be less hard. An actor is really hollowing himself out and fusing someone else's character with the residue. It is a very skilled profession and it's very presumptuous for musicians to think they can do it, or for actors to assume they will make good musicians."

WOMAD

First it was going to be called Music From The Edges of the World, but that implied that Britain was at its centre. Then it was going to be Rhythm '82, but that was abandoned because it sounded too much like a BBC jazz programme. The only way to encapsulate everything memorably was to find an acronym.

At that point, in early spring 1982, a choice had to be made. A World of Music, Arts and Dance certainly summed it up. But some wag suggested WOMAD might be mistaken for a drug to combat menstrual pain. Even now there are inquiries for more information on this supposed women's festival. WOMAD's suffix seems apposite given the débâcle that followed.

WOMAD developed from an idea Peter Gabriel had in late 1980. "I was getting very excited by some of the things I was coming across. So I thought, if they are so exciting to me, I'm sure they will be interesting to a lot of other people too. So I was sitting on a train one evening and I thought, wouldn't it be great to have an event which could bring in a large audience with a few rock and roll groups, and have that audience exposed to a lot of this stuff."

He had started gathering tapes of music from around the world, including Africa, Bali and from Australian aborigines. "I feel that an important influence on music over the next few years will be ethnic in origin and I can hear it being combined with electronics and more expressive, emotive use of the synthesizer," he said at the time. "Also I have been listening to and enjoying some of the recent material by Talking Heads who seem to be in that area and the tape made by David Byrne and Brian Eno. What I am actually trying to do with some of this stuff is to sift out rhythms which have a clarity and a simpleness to them. I think that much of the Afro-rock and Afro-influenced music of the past had tended to use the more complex rhythms which I find less interesting."

Producer David Lord, who owns Crescent Studios in Bath, introduced Gabriel to Thomas Brooman, known as Thos. Thos was one of a group of Oxford graduates living on the dole in Bristol who had developed the *Bristol Recorder Talking Book*, a combined magazine and LP. The mix of community arts and politics in the *Recorder* appealed to Gabriel, and he agreed to an interview as an almost local musician. Gabriel also donated three tracks from his 'live cassette box': 'Not One Of Us', 'Humdrum' and 'Ain't That Peculiar'.

The *Recorder* people, Thos Brooman, Martin Elbourne, Stephe Pritchard, and Jonathan Arthur, with their eclectic tastes, seemed ideally suited to help organize his planned concert since no commercial promoter was likely to take it on.

"We felt quite flattered to have been asked. We'd just been listening to Gamelan music (from Java and Bali in Indonesia) and a bit of Pakistani music, and were getting fairly bored with local pop groups," said Thos. "Peter said he had been listening to some sounds and he just thought it would be a good idea."

"We had meetings in Ashcombe House and started getting up plans, it was a very exciting time," said Gabriel. He was also encouraged by a positive response from Talking Heads, and Bath neighbour Steve Winwood.

The event was originally planned for spring or summer 1981. "We started talking to people and the whole process of finding the music was like a detective trail. It was a very potent idea and the further we went into it the more it became clear that if we were going to go to the trouble of assembling people from elsewhere it would be a good idea to do it with more than just African groups. And that in terms of logistics and costs it would have to be more than an indoor venue because it became quickly clear that finance and backing was not readily available."

In April 1981 Thos went to the eighth Rennes Rhythm '81, part of the French Festival of International Arts. In particular he wanted to see the Sabri Brothers from Pakistan, masters of Qawwali, the musical and ceremonial expression of Sufism, the mystical branch of Islam. He also came across the Master Drummers of Burundi, peasant farmers from the hills of this tiny impoverished nation, and was spellbound. Thos wanted both acts to come to what was to become WOMAD.

The Burundis were already known in the west through a somewhat obscure sixties album of their music. Since then there had been some borrowing, notably by Joni Mitchell on *The Hissing of Summer Lawns* in 1975, and later by Adam Ant and Bow Wow Wow, offshoots of the Malcolm McLaren image factory.

"The Burundis were very angry about all this because it was done with a lack of understanding of what it was being borrowed from. They were called warrior drummers, which they are not, never have been and never will be," said Thos.

On his return it became clear that the summer 1981 deadline would be impossible to meet and WOMAD was put back a year. "Looking back it was completely naïve, because this decision to delay it by a year did not imply we knew what we were doing."

It grew from a single concert to a planned six-day festival that was to include everything from traditional music from a wide range of cultures to hi-tech Western music.

The WOMAD workers set about trying to raise finance from the Arts Council, public bodies and private sponsors, including Coca Cola, but without success. Gabriel used his influence to contact people in the music business on both sides of the Atlantic. Apparent salvation came from Charles Levison, then chairman of WEA Records UK, who agreed to a $150,000 advance on a double album to be released prior to the festival. Pete Townsend, David Byrne, Gabriel, Peter Hammill, the Beat, the Burundi Drummers and several of the Third World acts contributed tracks.

Another apparent breakthrough came when the BBC agreed to film the festival for their prestigious *Arena* arts documentary slot.

The date was finally set for the weekend of 16 to 18 July 1982 at the Royal Bath and West showground near Shepton Mallet, Somerset: six days had become three. As well as the promised extensive TV coverage of the 300 performers from 21 countries there were cultural exhibitions, lectures, films, workshops, and arts, crafts and food from around the world. There were four stages with concerts running concurrently.

The idealism that shaped the festival was also to contribute to its downfall, best exemplified by the festival poster. All musicians, regardless of fame or prestige, were given equal and alphabetical billing. The alternative, which was rejected, would have put the British like Gabriel, Echo and the Bunnymen and Simple Minds above artists like Tian Jin from China, Les Musiciens du Nil from Egypt and Sasono Mulyo from Indonesia. But if the big names could draw in the crowds and turn them on to the different traditions, then perhaps it would have served a purpose.

142

"It was just not a commercial poster, it reflects a mistaken sense of idealism," said Thos. "A fundamental principle of what we have always done, which was directly as a result of Peter's influence, was that all the artists were to be respected as artists and that their billing is part of the respect that the festival has for them. His sense of principle and his ideas completely shaped what we did."

They had to rely on financial dribs and drabs and a tolerant bank manager. The *Bristol Recorder* staff put in the few thousand pounds' profit they had made, and Martin Elbourne from the *Recorder* cashed £4,000-worth of shares, Gabriel gave £3,000 and fundraising events amassed a few thousand more. It was hopelessly underfinanced, but benefited from a lot of gifts and goodwill – for example, the colour programme's only real cost was the paper.

Any real chance of making back the investment was scuppered by the showground authorities insisting that rock acts like Gabriel and the Bunnymen performed inside the Showering Pavilion, restricted to an audience of 4,000. They were the biggest crowd-pullers so the authorities perversely limited how many people could see them, fearful of a repetition of the crowd problems at the heavily over-attended Bath rock festival of 1969.

"We were over-ambitious and inexperienced, but a cardinal error we made was to be dictated to by the site. They demanded we put all the pop acts indoors and we very foolishly agreed," said Thos. Tickets for Gabriel and the Bunnymen were sold out three weeks in advance.

Projected costs were approaching £250,000. This included £90,000 in air fares for the fourteen Burundis and two Government officials, plus a further twelve musicians from around the globe.

The deal with the BBC was a co-production. That involved the BBC bringing their services and filming, but the "above the line" costs were to be paid by WOMAD, who had found American backers. That allowed WOMAD to have the rights to sell all the material to TV companies around the world. "That was the cornerstone of our finance. We were being asked to come up with £50,000 in front of the project. But our co-producers in the States in the end would not come up with the money because they did not trust that it was all above board," said Thos.

The BBC unexpectedly announced they were pulling out two weeks before the event. The news was received just as the Burundi Drummers were in the air. "To say it was a bodyblow would be an understatement. It started to feel like we were building a hotel on quicksand. We had got to the point where we had spent around £40,000 in a gamble that might recuperate £200,000. The question then is, do you say goodbye to £40,000 or carry on to the end of the road to risk getting all that £40,000 back or lose still more? In any promotion, big or small, there is always a deciding point like that. We passed that point fifteen days before."

The WOMAD double album, which included many of the acts appearing at the festival, should have provided much-needed publicity as well as vital revenue. But the album, planned the previous summer, was delayed. It finally took eleven months to complete and was not released until two weeks before the festival. The final instalment on the advance from WEA Records was forwarded to WOMAD. "When the advance finally came through it completely cleared the overdraft and we carried on spending, which sounds in retrospect like it was almost calculatingly foolhardy. But it was simply what had to happen because the machinery was in process then, it was running and it couldn't stop."

The financial débâcle obscured what was a mammoth cultural achievement for Gabriel and the WOMAD team. They provided a British audience with a glimpse of a wide range of different musical styles whose influence on Western music is still being felt.

Gabriel was keen to stress the input of children at WOMAD. With 7,000 schoolchildren attending the first day's event he could justifiably regard that as a success. But it was also obvious on that first day that the adult audience was badly lacking.

"It wasn't until the Friday had actually been that it was quite clear that the audience was not coming on the day," said Thos.

By now Gail Colson, who had advised Gabriel the idea was a folly from its inception and refused to have anything to do with it, could no longer bear to see it go so badly wrong. She brought an accountant from Hit and Run to Bath to try and sort out the mess.

"By Saturday morning the accountant had been working all night, finding out the liabilities, and we realized we were potentially anything up to a quarter of a million quid adrift.

"Then the decision was, 'What do we do now?' And on the advice of people much more experienced than ourselves we decided to go through the weekend on the analogy, say, of a Laker aeroplane that has already taken off from Heathrow to go to New York. What do you do? Turn round and take it back to Heathrow or carry on to New York and then say the company's bust? So we just carried on, feeling like the end of the world had come."

The question of the glaring gap between revenue and costs was raised with Gabriel by *NME* writer Vivien Goldman a few days before the festival. "Yes, that discrepancy might lead us to interesting places . . . like the bankruptcy court," he said.

Goldman also asked him where cultural exchange stops and ripping-off begins. "Gabriel seems to love debate and dialogue; a warm smile shows he's thought the subject through many times. 'I'm not sure of the value of that argument. All art steals from other art. The important thing is deciding what to steal and doing it with respect. If through WOMAD, rock people acknowledge their sources, the sources are also much more likely to sell.'"

Goldman bumped into Gabriel towards the end of the third day. "As far as I can see, Peter Gabriel deserves a slap on the back and some red roses. But the man did not look happy, despite his brightly-coloured festival waistcoat that probably doubled as a pair of hiking boots." This was a reference to the festival's popular consumer buy, clothes that changed into other clothes, hats into bags, trousers into shirts.

"I knew instantly. Artistically, the Festival had been an unqualified success, a three-day musical orgasm, in fact. It could only be the bucks that brought a frown.

" 'Have you had enough people here to cover costs?'

" 'In a word . . . no,' said Peter, bravely trying to force a smile. I recalled his crack the week before about there being interesting places like the bankruptcy court."

Throughout the eighteen months while the festival was being planned, Gabriel had been writing and recording his fourth album. He finished it less than a fortnight after WOMAD, and first performed some of the songs from the album at the festival. His band were dressed in black track suits, but presumably they were not in mourning. They played 'I Have the Touch', and 'Rhythm of the Heat' with Ekome. It was filmed by London Weekend Television for a *South Bank Show* documentary. Gabriel gave an impassioned performance of 'Rhythm of the Heat', falling to his knees, his body vibrating and swivelling, looking like he was making love and performing the limbo at the same time.

He also premiered 'Across The River', which later appeared

on a compact disc single with 'Big Time' in 1987, with L. Shanker on the violin and Stewart Copeland of the Police on drums. The song is one of Gabriel's most haunting. The surrounding trauma no doubt helped add authenticity to the venting of his tortured soul.

"Peter was panicked. I think all of us were," said Thos. "There was still this complete conflict of things. On the one hand, well, it's a great event. And on the other, God, haven't we fucked up. Just an absolute turmoil of contradictory things."

"We started to realize things were collapsing during the event," remembered Gabriel. "There were concerns before then, but we were confident we were going to get a much bigger audience than we had. We had the rail strike against us, and we had appalling publicity, which was a pity because I thought it was ideal colour supplement material.

"Because I wasn't working on it full time I didn't want to tell the WOMAD people how to do it. Some of the pros in the business were very sceptical and cynical about the whole thing, Gail particularly, saying, 'This isn't going to work and blah blah blah.' We were saying, 'Oh yes it is. People will like this idea.' We were very confident and naïve. But I didn't want to come in the big rock star; 'You've got to do it this way. This is the way things are done.' I think I was a bit stupid in that way. I should have been more aggressive. I had no idea I was going to be seen as the only one worth chasing as things went down."

Gail and the accountant salvaged what they could. "She worked almost the whole weekend at the festival itself, helping where she could and advising with a very limited amount of cash on who should get paid the cash on the weekend," remembered Thos. "And as a result of her advice all the visiting artists were paid cash first. I think there was a sense of really active involvement by then, and almost a sense of energy generated by it. There were several creditors who came personally for us, they felt so angry. Afterwards nobody could understand how the festival had happened with the minimal investment that it had received.

"But it was limited and we were protected by the law. At the same time I think the pressure on Peter was so much worse because the companies we owed money to realized that he was the only one of us who might have any, and so he was under real personal pressure."

The final debt was £189,000. Gabriel was the main target, and had irate debtors at the door. "I was the only fat cat. Jill actually got a death threat aimed at me, an anonymous caller saying, 'I'm going to kill you afterwards,' and all that stuff, very nasty. Not the sort of thing I want to live through again."

Help came from an unexpected quarter. Tony Smith, who still owns 50 per cent of Gabriel's management company, discussed the débâcle with Genesis. "We said, 'Listen, this is ridiculous, why don't we help him out?' said Phil Collins. "We can't have Pete go bankrupt, though it didn't turn out to be that serious. We offered to give him some money towards it or play a benefit, or lend him the money until he could pay us back."

The offer of money never got as far as Gabriel's ears because everyone knew he was bound to refuse. "We decided maybe the money was not such a good idea, so why not do a concert," said Collins. That autumn Genesis were on a tour of the UK, so it was not difficult to slot in an extra date for a WOMAD benefit.

"Peter has a tendency to get involved in this sort of thing, which is great as it's part of his personality," said Tony Banks. "Originally it was not going to be with Peter, although doing it with Peter seemed like a good idea. In rock music it is very easy to raise a large sum of money. And this particular thing was to help a friend, so it seemed to be a damned good thing to do. And it also got rid of this terrible thing of everyone wanting a reunion, so we killed two birds with one stone."

"At that point I was so freaked out I would have done anything," said Gabriel. "I was very touched that they were prepared to do it, to bail me out. Because although I didn't feel personally liable, I had been part of a team that was naïve. A lot of the decisions which were partly responsible for the problems I didn't feel I had created. Except that I had instigated a thing and left it to the WOMADers. I felt responsible in neglecting to take a heavy-handed financial role. I think I would have made some attempts afterwards to pay off what could have been paid. But I wouldn't have been able to get that sort of audience."

He agreed to the suggested reunion immediately, despite artistic reservations. "I had been trying for years to get out of these associations, and here I was jumping back into it."

Five weeks after the WOMAD festival the Genesis reunion was announced in the London *Evening Standard*, which called the event the year's major rock event after the Rolling Stones. It was set for the open-air Milton Keynes Bowl early in October with everyone gambling on the clemency of the autumn weather.

Rehearsals took place at the Hammersmith Odeon just before the shows. Gabriel listened to new tapes and studied lyric sheets to refresh his memory. "We felt a bit strange. We had to decide what songs to do, and obviously the idea was if we were going to do a reunion we should do the classics like 'The Musical Box' and 'The Knife'," said Phil Collins. "Pete has always had difficulty remembering words. It was understandable then, he had not sung them for years and his head was full of other things.

"I thought some of the songs I had been singing for years didn't sound that much better with Pete singing them, take that as you like. But when we sat in Milton Keynes and did it, it was the overall thing."

On Saturday 2 October it rained all day, turning the Milton Keynes Bowl into a mud lake. Despite that 47,000 people came, some flying in from Japan and the USA, and many bravely watching the support acts throughout the afternoon.

"Genesis drifted onto a blue-lit stage. The lights broadened and four pallbearers brought on a white coffin which opened up to reveal Gabriel in make-up. It was his old Rael disguise, and it became obvious that Gabriel was prepared not just to sing old Genesis numbers, but to perform them with his old costumes (brown cloak and mask/the sunflower etc) brought out of the mothballs," wrote Paul Strange in *Melody Maker*. "Rael's anthem 'Back In New York City' opened up the historic set, the sound initially dodgy and variable, with Gabriel valiantly coping with a naff mike."

This was not viewed so charitably from the stage. "What was extraordinary was having seen Peter quite a few times since he left the band, I noted how his mike technique had improved so much and his pitching was great. They were all the things he had trouble with in the group," said Tony Banks. "But then at the reunion he was right back to where he was before. It just shows, because he was singing other people's melodies, the complexity of them made it much more difficult for him to do. Whereas with his own stuff he had no problem because he could sing exactly as he wanted."

"His mike technique was as bad as it used to be. Which must be why he wears one of those radio mikes, he can't muck that up," said Collins. "There were some wild moments, but we carried it off because people were so pleased to see us together again."

The group included the newer Genesis recruits Chester Thompson on drums and Daryl Stuermer on bass. The set included some post-Gabriel material, including 'Turn It On Again' where Gabriel and Collins embraced each other while passing on stage as Collins went to the front to sing while Gabriel took over the drums. The fans were then surprised by the appearance of Steve Hackett for 'I Know What I Like (In Your Wardrobe)', finishing off with 'The Knife'. "A reunion that is unlikely to ever happen again. The rock event of the year," the *Melody Maker* concluded.

"It was just like returning to some sort of family reunion," said Gabriel. "It felt really warm, though it was terrible weather. Musically it wasn't very good, but emotionally it was very strong. I was given at Strat's funeral his notebook in which he wrote some notes around that concert, and he was obviously touched."

NEW DEAL

The bids to win Peter Gabriel's recording contract for the United States peaked at one million dollars in 1980. The major American record companies, including his former label Atlantic Records, were after him, following the success of the third album.

The year was to be taken up with touring, so Gabriel had time to carefully consider the offers since he had no plans to start on his next album until the following year.

One of the companies most interested in Gabriel was Geffen Records. It had only just been set up that year by David Geffen, respected for his work with Asylum Records which he ran in the sixties with acts like Joni Mitchell, Neil Young and Jackson Browne. Geffen was known for his persuasive powers. His latest achievement had been to tempt John Lennon back into the recording studio.

Both Peter Gabriel's and Phil Collins' contracts for America were available in 1980. Geffen Records considered both artists. At the time, before *Face Value* helped make Collins the most successful British artist in America in the eighties, Gabriel looked a safer proposition. After all, his last single, 'Games Without Frontiers', was his first to get airplay on US Top 40 radio. It is a moot point whether Collins would have signed to Geffen if they had made an offer, considering his close relationship with Ahmet Ertegun at Atlantic Records.

David Geffen and company president Ed Rosenblatt did not see Gabriel in concert while he was touring North America in June and July 1980. But they had clearly made a decision to get him if they could by the time they flew to Portugal to see him perform and discuss a deal. Geffen and Rosenblatt arrived in Lisbon in October 1980 and went to the coastal resort of Cascais to meet up with Gail Colson and Gabriel.

"Peter Gabriel is someone we were both familiar with from his Genesis days," said Rosenblatt. "We knew his first couple of albums and then all of a sudden the third album was out on Mercury and we were unaware why." They soon found out when John Kolodner, ironically, joined their company from Atlantic as A&R director.

Geffen and Rosenblatt met Gabriel and Gail Colson in the lobby of their hotel in Cascais. They all drove up the coast for an early dinner before Gabriel's concert that night. Gail and Peter were wary, they were not happy about Kolodner joining Geffen. They were also meeting opposition back home from Tony Stratton Smith, who wanted a new deal allowing Charisma to license them in America. Rosenblatt believed a rival company was spreading rumours that he and Geffen knew nothing about Gabriel's music.

"I'll never forget this," said Rosenblatt. "After saying, 'Hello, hello, how was your trip' and things like that David immediately went into the John Kolodner situation and answered the remarks that this person from another company had told Gail. I believe David completely disarmed Gail and Peter.

"These are things you normally get in the pursuit of an artist: 'I'm the greatest, you're the greatest, we're the greatest!' And you leave any kind of negativity under the rug some place. But the reality of life was that a 3000-pound rhinoceros was sitting with us on the dinner table while everybody was looking around pretending it's not there. We got that out of the way within the first five minutes of the dinner.

"Peter was quite hurt over this Kolodner situation. But John feels very badly about it to this day. He didn't feel at that time that Peter was being as commercial as he could have been. He certainly knew that Peter was a great artist. I don't think he ever believed Ahmet Ertegun would ever allow Peter to leave the label. He was just giving his opinion as an A&R person. It's not John Kolodner who should be blamed, but Ahmet Ertegun."

Geffen's offer was not only below the biggest advance of one million dollars from a company Gail Colson refuses to name, but also below Atlantic's $750,000. Gabriel's prime consideration was not to get a huge advance, deductable anyway from royalties. He needed complete creative independence from an artistically sympathetic company with a sharp business sense. He took David Geffen at his word and agreed to the deal.

After their dinner in Cascais, Rosenblatt and Geffen stayed an extra day, travelling on the tour coach to Oporto in the north of Portugal. The tour was nearing its end having started back in February 1980 in Britain.

Perversely, Gabriel had called it The Tour of China 1984. It was his little dig at groups getting competitive about being the first to play Russia or China and then producing expensive merchandise to commemorate the event. Since Gabriel was twisting the truth he made it the 1984 tour for its Orwellian overtones. He thought he would take a short-cut and not bother to go east, while still issuing the merchandise.

Gabriel explained, "I thought it would be a lot more interesting than The 1980 Tour of England." The tour programme was a little red book made up of cut-out graphics from Chinese newspaper advertisments, political posters, comic books and the odd exotic girlie shot dug up by Gabriel on a visit to Soho's Chinatown. His head, usually with a contorted expression, was stuck on other people's shoulders, including a muscle man's, and used as part of a political propaganda poster.

Gabriel wanted someone with studio experience to be sound engineer on the 1980 tour and asked David Lord, who ran the local Crescent Studios in Bath, if he wanted the job. For Lord, a softly spoken classically trained composer, it was an enticing idea, though he could not predict how much of a culture shock life on the road would be.

Gabriel had met Lord in 1977 and the following year asked for his help in transcribing some of the music from the second album for the band to perform live. Crescent Studios was growing in popularity thanks to a healthy local punk music scene.

Lord found life on the road somewhat disconcerting. In Las Vegas, in empathy with Tony Levin, Gabriel decided to once again shave his head. "He likes upsetting plans very much," said Lord. "If a tour has been carefully worked out by the tour manager he likes looking for the unusual. It is very difficult organizing a tour, but at the last minute he'll want to change it.

"He loves cutting things fine, he doesn't like being in good time for things. He is always a madman catching planes and things. I think there have been many times when they have had to virtually reopen the doors.

"I remember us getting onto a train very early. The tour manager had given us the wrong time to make sure we would be there early, and we sat on this train for twenty minutes and everyone was relieved because Peter was there, it was the last train, and about two minutes before we were due to go he said, 'I'm just going to get a paper,' and dashed off to the paper stall a few platforms away and the panic started. It was like that all the time."

The Bath tribal look for a photo session in February 1981. (*Retna Pictures*)

A powerful performance at the first WOMAD Festival in July 1982 was given added tension by the looming financial crisis. (*Robert Draper*)

Newly shorn in Central Park, New York City in July 1980

Gail Colson, Peter Gabriel's manager since 1978, in a break during touring in summer 1987

Bon viveur and raconteur Tony Stratton Smith holds forth. (*Barrie Wentzell*)

Gabriel and Rhodes jump to it at the Tourhout Festival in Belgium on 1 July 1983 during the Playtime '88 tour. Picture taken by Larry Fast from his synthesizer position during 'I Have The Touch.' (*Larry Fast*)

The 'monkey' mask make-up was the most elaborate facial adornment of his solo career used on the 1982/3 tour as here in Los Angeles, August 1983. (*Retna Pictures Ltd*)

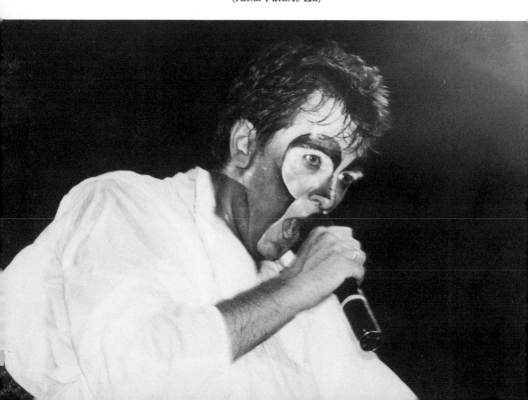

The multi-award winning Sledgehammer took 100 hours to shoot over eight days in Bristol, April 1986. (*Armando Gallo/Retna Pictures Ltd*)

At Ashcombe House with the Fairlight CMI Synthesizer in 1986. Gabriel predicted the synthesizer would become the most important instrument of the eighties. (*Rex Features Ltd*)

The clenched symbol of solidarity during the song 'Biko' was acknowledged as one of the most powerful moments at the Amnesty Conspiracy of Hope Tour of the USA in June 1986. (*Larry Busacca/Retna Ltd*)

Gesture plays an important part in Gabriel's carefully choreographed stage movements. During the first leg of the This Way Up tour on December 16, 1986 at the Los Angeles Forum. (*Margaret Maxwell*)

The song 'Lay Your Hands On Me' is the cue for the most dramatic moment of Gabriel's stage show as he plunges into the audience. It frequently results in a loss of clothes and shoes as here at the L.A. Forum also on December 16, 1986. (*Margaret Maxwell*)

Jill and Peter at the Ivor Novello Awards in London in April 1987.
(*Syndication International*)

Peter Gabriel and President Daniel Ortega of Nicaragua, his ministers and
officials during their hour and half meeting in May 1987. (*Matt Mahurin*)

In June 1980 Gabriel and the band spent a week rehearsing for their American tour at a Los Angeles warehouse belonging to Supertramp. They wanted to play a warm-up gig and found a small club in Santa Anna, Los Angeles. "We were playing some quite big venues, so we were attracted to the idea of playing a 200-seater club," David Lord remembered. "The word got around that he was going to play there. People hitchhiked down from Canada and tickets were being sold for vast sums. We started the show and it was absolutely packed until the doors were bursting."

The fire marshalls who had been monitoring the club for possible offences decided to stop the show. Police helicopters were called in with spotlights shining down. "The police raided the place, they drove all their cars up against the doors so nobody could get out. They came in and photographed everybody so they had proof the fire regulations were being broken. It was touch and go as to whether the audience would riot because they were so annoyed at the show being stopped.

"Peter was trying to persuade the police to let us carry on, saying it would be less dangerous, but they wouldn't listen to him." The club owner, who had broken the hire agreement by advertising the show, was prosecuted for the fire offences.

The American leg, which ended in New York three and a half weeks later, was buoyed by the success of the third album. It moved into the US Top 40 while the tour was on, proving to be Gabriel's best seller yet. It gave Gabriel the satisfaction he wanted in proving Atlantic Records wrong in dropping him.

Later that summer David Lord worked on his first major recording project with Gabriel, mixing the German album which had translated lyrics at Crescent Studios before setting off on the final European leg of the 1980 tour finishing in October 1980.

The following year Lord engineered Gabriel's first attempt to produce another artist since the Charlie Drake episode. This time it was someone equally unexpected; Jimmy Pursey, leader of the then defunct Sham '69, the yobbo punk group whose success proved too much for its eccentric leader, sending him into premature retirement.

"I think Peter took pity on him," was Lord's assessment. "They started off writing songs together. It was pretty hard going, he was a bit over the top, but Peter was very clever with him." In March 1981 Lord engineered the single 'Animals Have More Fun' at Crescent Studios, matching Pursey's lyrics to Gabriel's music. The B-side, 'Sus', was also co-written.

Gabriel, who was impressed with Pursey's energy, had first met him in 1978, when he invited Sham '69 to open for him at a concert in Belgium. Three years later it was Pursey who contacted Gabriel when he was looking for a producer for a single. "I was despondent about me as a producer," said Pursey. "The only person I could think of who could do the job was Peter Gabriel. I gave him a buzz, he liked the idea of the song, and about two days later he came to see me on my farm in Guildford.

"We talked about all the ideas I had. We walked around the farm and chatted. He thought I had some great ideas, he wanted to carry them a bit further. I told him about this line I had, about 'Animals Have More Fun'; he said that's a great starting point."

About a week later Pursey went to Bath to rehearse at Ashcombe House. "I spent one night out in the garden. I refused to sleep in his barn because it was full up with his heads and masks. It was very, very eerie to say the least. There were ethnic masks and also ones he'd used on stage, surrounding the whole room, just piled on top of each other. It all looked like something out of a Ken Russell movie. My imagination was running too far ahead of itself. I wasn't even on marijuana, I was straight as a die.

"In the kitchen I saw a rat run across the floor. I didn't think I was going to get any peace and quiet that night. I pulled one of the settees out, stuck it in the middle of the garden and sat in the garden all the time contemplating the next day and trying to forget about these masks and heads that had been staring at me in the next room.

"The day after that we continued to work. He was very amused by the story. He made me breakfast and we chatted about what had gone on. In the studio he would be in control of the music side of what was going on, while I was coming up with the lyrics to the song."

'Animals Have More Fun' was released in June 1981, three months after it was recorded. Pursey disputed the press comment that his pairing with Gabriel was a strange one. He believed they were compatible as musicians and people. Pursey's lyrics went:

> Piggy banks, Russian tanks,
> Animals have more fun.
> The human race, are we lost in space,
> Animals have more fun . . .

Pursey explained: "As we sit around and think of certain things, there are other things that don't think, they are just living. Whereas we spend most of our time analysing and making judgments, and these are the judgments and analysations [sic] that are not necessary in life." The B-side, 'Sus', originally titled 'The Shining', was about extra-sensory perception and telepathy, a subject that certainly has interested Gabriel. "He was very, very patient with me. I can be an arrogant and self-opinionated sod. Peter Gabriel was the perfect producer," Pursey said.

The single was greeted by Radio 1 DJ Simon Bates as a future Number 1. That, in Pursey's opinion, ruined its chances because it was a record that was meant to grow on people. The record received unfavourable criticism in the music press. "Co-written with fellow self-styled tortured artist Peter Gabriel, this shows Jim the Baptist trying to drop us in the same hole that he's in. The puerile lyrical theme is off set by a grinding 'n' grandiose backing track," commented *Record Mirror*'s reviewer. 'Animals Have More Fun' failed to make the Top 75.

Early in 1981 David Lord helped Gabriel upgrade the equipment at the Ashcombe House studio, helping redesign the control room. Lord rented Gabriel a console, but there were various technical problems which ended up delaying the recording of the next album, Gabriel's fourth.

Six years after leaving Genesis, Gabriel was still lacking in confidence. "I think we are both very similar characters in the way that we are never quite sure that we are right. It was the first big production that I had done, I was probably too much in awe. If I had a strong idea I should probably have stuck with it much more. He could probably have done with someone a bit sterner, his manager always hoped there would be somebody who'd make him bring in a record on time, an eternal desire that never happened," Lord said.

Gabriel already had a clear idea of the direction he wanted to go in, even if the material had not yet been conceived. He told Ray Coleman of *Melody Maker* in February 1981, "I can hear in my head now a sort of music which involves a lot of percussion, very little of the regular drum kit, and a lot of electronics. In other words pulling out and virtually removing the emphasis which has always been there from guitar, organ and piano and leaving it more naked.

"This is my ultimate direction. I don't expect to have much on the next album that will sound like that, but that's the direction that's consuming me at the moment and that I'm involved in getting down."

In spring 1981 London Weekend Television started filming a documentary on Gabriel for the *South Bank Show*, narrated by Melvyn Bragg. They wanted to chart the progress of an album from start to finish. They expected to stop filming that autumn, but were hopelessly optimistic, having to wait until October 1982 when the fourth album was released and they could transmit their show.

Gabriel showed them a case-full of cassettes with recordings of different rhythms from around the world taken from the radio, *The World About Us* TV programme, and records. He was being helped in his research into different musical cultures by the people at the *Bristol Recorder*, then starting to plan what became the WOMAD Festival in July 1982.

"I'm certain the Third World can have an increasing influence on our culture and in music a very vigorous hybrid will be produced which is based on this non-European influence and the new technology which is going to get very cheap and this facility will open up a new age of electronic skiffle," he told the *South Bank Show*.

"Initially when you first walk into the studio it's like walking into another world of masses of knobs and buttons which are totally foreign. Then, as you spend more and more time in the studio, you learn what they all do and how to manipulate things . . . At this point in the process much the most important tool for me is the drum machine and the rhythm box. This allows me with the sound of real drums to store in computer memory any drum pattern I can conceive of or steal and use this as the basis for my songwriting. When I have the rhythm set up I can start adding patterns in there. When I've got my rhythms locked into the drum machine I can begin improvising and finding which synth sound then forms around the rhythm.

"In the process where you start to develop these rhythms there's probably over one hundred starting points. I then begin developing the best of these ideas." Gabriel already had his demos of 'Jung In Africa', later to become 'Rhythm of the Heat'. Lord described it as having "just a raw voice and backing, there's no words". The embryonic song showed that Gabriel was continuing with his technique, started on the third album, of building songs around rhythms rather than chords and melodies. On 'Rhythm of the Heat' most of the music had already been composed, for other songs they would have to work on musical ideas in the studio.

"At this point I've only got outlines for lyrics, so I use odd sounds. I'm trying to enlarge what I do with my voice not through technique but by the sound. We all make noises, particularly when we get emotional about something. The tones of those noises change, they are all representative. There are gutteral noises that are built into the rhythms and into the atmosphere as a whole, the tension and the excitement of it.

"In opera you have this very abstracted form of singing – a brilliant technique, but to me it doesn't have the emotional impact that I get when I listen to great soul or blues rhythms. I think in rock as a whole there's been many great songs which have had really appalling lyrics and others which have had great lyrics and appalling music. You might as well make the music as appropriate as you can and try and communicate something."

Having amassed a selection of rhythmic ideas and rough recordings, Gabriel was ready for the musicians booked for the new album to start recording with him. Drummer Jerry Marotta was the first to arrive to work on the rhythms. Marotta resisted Gabriel's increasing reliance on the drum box. "A machine is a machine and you can't programme emotion at all into a machine," Marotta told the TV interviewers. "In this case it's important for me to feel this emotion. It's basically what music is all about, the emotion inside you. The machine and I split the work fifty-fifty, it's very hard."

The other musicians arrived to put down the backing tracks, laying down each instrument individually so that Gabriel could later manipulate the sound as much as he liked. "I like to leave my options open and always think tomorrow I'll find a way in which it will work perfectly," said Gabriel. The nucleus of musicians on the album was still the same as for the third album, with Tony Levin on bass, Larry Fast on keyboards and synthesizers, and David Rhodes now installed on guitar.

Having left Random Hold the previous year, David Rhodes was signing on the dole and had sunk into a depression. In his misery he too shaved his head. "I stayed in my bedroom for six months and wrote some not very good songs," said Rhodes, who sent Gabriel copies of his songs. Gabriel wanted to use him. Gail Colson was instructed to send a keyboard to Rhodes with demos for the forthcoming album. "I would get called in to do bits. I was given a nickname while we were working on 'Wallflower', they called me 'Dial-a-weirdie'," said Rhodes.

157

"There were loads of people better than me technically. It's the rhythmic feel, the grooves that Peter liked. No fancy finger work."

David Lord was still finding his confidence as a producer, and with hindsight felt he was not stern enough with Gabriel. "I hope very much to interpret his ideas because I don't think he needs very many of mine," Lord said at the time. "People tend to think they need producers, but I think it's more a liaison between what he wants to get and overcoming technical problems."

After several weeks' work at Ashcombe House, Gabriel was left with twenty-seven 16-minute tapes, over seven hours of material comprising eighteen possible songs, seven of which were running over ten minutes. For the next three months Gabriel, Lord and Fast used the latest technology to develop the material. According to Melvyn Bragg's TV narration they "began a search for an entirely new sound".

"We try treating sounds to put them in perspective in this picture we're building up. For instance, you could have a keyboard sound which you think is occupying too much space and has too much weight. Then I may stick it through something to make it thin and wavy so its personality changes. Everything will at some time go through the electronics and be blended in with newer sonic textures.

"It worries me sometimes that I'm taking so long over these things, then at the end I think it doesn't really matter anyway if the end product works. There are mountains of reels, of try-outs and overdubs. Very often, when you get down to the final mix, very little of it is used. But that's a sort of compositional process, really. Some people would go through it before they go into the studio, most of Peter's work in that aspect is done in the studio," said Lord.

Both Fast and Marotta had arguments with Gabriel over musical direction. Resentment was also building in Fast for what he saw as a lack of recognition for his contribution to Gabriel's records. Recognized as a world expert on the synthesizer, Fast had felt he deserved a co-production credit on the third album, and thought after three months' work he deserved the same credit for the fourth album. "There are things that he absolutely wants to hear and he will pipe up about it and get it. It is his career, so for the most part there is no fighting about that."

After Fast finished in the studio, Gabriel and Lord continued for several more months to refine the sound. When the final selection of songs was edited down, Gabriel added his vocals, remixing, rewriting and revising many times before reaching the final version. Lord's views of working with Gabriel echo those of Fast. "I like the way he really perseveres and struggles through things that you might not think would work. I could be sure he wouldn't get a song out of this idea, sure that he was going round in circles and not getting anywhere – he always knew at the end of it he would, he always had to prove that he was right. He doesn't like being proved wrong, though he is not dogmatic.

"Most of the people I think are interesting musically would regard Peter as being influential, though I don't know how much effect he has had on the mainstream hit parade stuff." Lord and Gabriel developed an easy working relationship.

In contrast to the previous album and the intrusions of John Kolodner and his Doobie Brothers suggestions, Peter was now being visited by executives from his new American record company, Geffen, who supported what he was attempting, despite the delays. "We established a relationship with Peter," said Ed Rosenblatt. "And when Peter went into the studio to make the album I said, 'Look, I know how you feel. But if you want another ear to listen to this record while you are in a formative stage, we have somebody who is a great fan here, Gary Gersh, our A&R director, and you can either listen to what he says, or don't listen to what he says, put out whatever you want to put out.' So I'm sure Peter had a certain sense of confidence that we were going to put out whatever he gave us, regardless."

Geffen kept to their word and did not interfere creatively. But there was disagreement over Gabriel's continued insistence that his albums should have no title other than his name. Gabriel finally agreed Geffen could put a sticker on the American cover and call the album *Security*. "I think he was thinking that it would make the record company feel secure," said Rosenblatt.

The fourth album was not as well received or as commercially successful as the previous album. It went straight into the UK charts at Number 6, but quickly slipped out again. The third album had benefited from the success of the single 'Games Without Frontiers'. But there was nothing commercially accessible on the fourth album to chart. The single 'Shock the Monkey' made it to Number 58, while 'I Have the Touch' did not even make the Top 75.

The album suffered from an over-long gestation period, and the mood was one of unrelenting intensity. Yet it contains some of Gabriel's strongest and most popular live songs. 'Rhythm of the Heat' is Gabriel's most powerful expression of rhythmic power and explores his perennial obsession with spiritual transformation, in this case using Jung's experiences in Africa. 'Wallflower' is an inspiring gentle hymn of hope.

'Shock the Monkey' is as close as he gets on the album to being playful, a satire on sexuality and jealousy and how it makes monkeys of us all. Musically it was a signpost to his future direction as he tried to capture the sound of early Tamla Motown. By the time the song was finished not much of that influence was obvious, but it was a pointer to his desire to further explore sixties soul and rhythm and blues.

The song alluded to sex more obviously than he had previously done in lyrics. Influenced by the use of innuendo growing up on a farm, he drew on one agricultural term for sexual coupling – cover me – for 'Shock The Monkey'.

> *Cover me, when I sleep*
> *Cover me, when I breathe*
> *You throw your pearls before the swine*
> *Make the monkey blind*
> *Cover me, darling please . . .*

'Lay Your Hands On Me', like 'I Have The Touch', reveals aspects of Gabriel's own personality, and in particular upbringing, where touch was taboo. 'Lay Your Hands' explores the emotional extremes of alienation and belonging and the need for trust.

> *Sat in the corner of the Garden Grill, with the plastic*
> *Flowers on the window sill*
> *No more miracles, loaves and fishes, been so busy with the*
>   *Washing of the dishes . . .*
>
> *But still the warmth flows through me*
> *And I sense you know me well . . .*
>
> *I am willing – lay your hands on me . . .*

'I Have The Touch' takes the need for physical contact to a pathological extreme. The character is outwardly a complete opposite to Gabriel.

> *Any social occasion, it's hello, how do you do*
> *All those introductions, I never miss my cue . . .*

160

But inwardly he is not so different to Gabriel, or any of us, in our more manic moments.

Pull my chin, stroke my hair, scratch my nose, hug my knees
Try drink, food, cigarette, tension will not ease
I tap my fingers, fold my arms, breathe in deep, cross my legs
Shrug my shoulders, stretch my back – but nothing seems to please

I need contact . . .

Gabriel explained, "I think I'm pulled in both directions, wanting to put a distance between myself and some things or people, and then wanting to break through and make contact. When I'm writing lyrics I'm not conscious of that, I'm just really following subjects that interest me."

That included books on body language, on how brain stimulation is dependent on touch, and on how race determines how frequently we touch. "There was this experiment carried out in restaurants in different capital cities around the world. In Puerto Rico they noted one table with about 250 body contacts within an hour and in Paris it was down to about thirty while in London it was down to two – the hello and goodbye – so I think this is pertinent for an English person.

" 'I Have The Touch' is made almost humorous with this alien English person who is really getting off on any skin contact because he's so deprived of it. So in formal situations where he's shaking hands it's an amazing turn-on for him. Whereas the other person thinks he can retain his distance and formality and hold the status quo."

'The Family and the Fishing Net' is lyrically one of the most extraordinary songs that Gabriel has written. It is an impressionistic view of the ritual of marriage. "I was looking at the undercurrent of symbolism within a normal everyday Western wedding in a church. The territorial battles between fathers' daughters and mothers' sons, the ring, all sorts of sexual undertones."

Gabriel said it was written "under the influence of Dylan Thomas". Like Dylan Thomas, Gabriel has an interest in often surreal images, unexpected rhythms and rhymes, and tightly compressed imagery which sometimes seems, superficially at least, confusing. Dylan Thomas urged his readers not to "understand" his poetry, and in so doing gave a clue to what Gabriel aspires to. "I can give you a rough idea of the 'plot'," Thomas wrote. "But of course it's bound to be most superficial

161

and a perhaps misleading idea, because the 'plot' is told in images, and images are what they say, not what they stand for."

'The Family and the Fishing Net' has many images in common with Thomas' poetry and prose: images of the sea and shores and the people who live off them, and much Christian symbolism. Rarely are Gabriel's images more potent than in this song.

> *Silence falls the guillotine*
> *All the doors are shut*
> *Nervous hands grip tight the knife*
> *In the darkness, till the cake is cut*
> *Passed around, in little pieces*
> *The body and the flesh*
> *The family and the fishing net*
> *Another in the mesh*
>
> *The body and the flesh.*

Because the recording of the fourth album coincided exactly with the organizing of the WOMAD festival, Gabriel was constantly getting fed new sounds from around the world. Ethiopian pipes formed the harmonies around which 'The Family and the Fishing Net' was written. The surdo drum and Brazilian rhythms inspired 'Kiss Of Life'. Gabriel said the song was about "a large Brazilian woman with abundant lifeforce raising a man from the dead". The surdo is also used on 'Rhythm of the Heat', along with Ghanaian drums banged by the Ekome Dance Company, an Afro-Caribbean performance group from Bristol.

'San Jacinto' expressed his long-standing fascination with American Indians. He described it as a "mixture of American Indian culture and Palm Springs – Sinatra golf and pool images." San Jacinto is a mountain in California, overlooking Palm Springs and some Indian reservations.

The song evolved out of an encounter between Gabriel and an Apache brave who worked as a porter in a Cleveland hotel. Returning from a gig, Gabriel spotted the Indian looking agitated and wandering around looking for a taxi. "He'd heard that his flat was burning down and he was trying to get in from this fairly remote hotel to where his flat was, so I gave him a lift back that night and got talking to him afterwards, for most of the night, and he was describing how he was initiated to becoming a brave.

"He was taken up into the mountains with this sort of shaman character, a medicine man, and he was carrying a rattlesnake in his bag, and the medicine man took it out and held it to the boy's arm and the snake bit him. And if he came down again from the mountain after fourteen days he was a brave, and if he didn't he was dead. Apparently nearly all of them got through it, and he was describing the way they hallucinate really strongly for that period. I think there are hallucinatory materials in the poison of the snake."

Gabriel received some scathing reviews. The single 'Shock the Monkey', released at the same time as the album, was too much for Dave McCullough in *Sounds*, who equated Gabriel's innovations with Genesis' traditional melodic approach. For McCullough Gabriel epitomized wealth, greed and shallow sentiment. "Forget heavy metal, punk, the Rolling Stones, forget the most horrendous musical niche you can think of – because the most horrendous of the lot is the Comfortably Middle Aged Set at which Genesis and associates sit at the head of the (leather-bound) table.

"Genesis, Roxy Music, Gabriel – all comfortably well-off, middle-aged and classed, cheapies who are characterized by a smugness, a fascismo organisation around them as big as a multi-national, and a music as predictably fascismo-bland to match. These are the people we really ought to go for, in a sense there is so much ill-used wealth here that the multinational tag is really apposite . . .

" 'Shock the Monkey' is so middling in every respect, middling white harmless reggae trash – geared for the charts with a slide rule and a snide smile . . . In a context where Genesis can cruise comfortably, the more arseholes, gutter-snipes, piss artists and madmen around to match the extremes of contradiction that are inherent in music, the very much the better."

Gavin Martin's album review in the *NME* was equally unforgiving. "Gabriel is a far more influential character (more's the pity) than he's been given credit for. Hardly a day goes past without another sweatshop independent outfit sending me a single that bears a sizeable trace of Gabriel's theoretical over-wrought hollow sorrow. The image that this LP throws up is that of an alienated artist trapped in Bath (Bath!) struggling with the contradictions of civilization, the soul, our very existence . . . Gabriel seems entrenched in white liberal guilt, working from the premise that for truly great art to be created torment and suffering must be encountered at every turn. It's also echoed

163

in the music, an endless barrage of stilted electronic devices, feebly constructed dire attempts to produce dynamics and atmospherics . . ."

More vitriol follows including "half-assed posturing and nebulous conceits", "stagnating in dank, painful introspection", "the incredibly selfish notion that we must look to tribal civilizations to understand ourselves (as if they'd been created specifically for the purpose)", "bland, wet condescension" and "what are we going to do with these arthouse bores?"

Chris May in *Black Music and Jazz Review* did not agree, harking back to his own review of *Music and Rhythm*, the WOMAD album. "I observed that Gabriel brought a guileless honesty and wit to his music which kept it entirely in character with his source material. The same is true of his latest release. Sadly, the honkie poseurs of the rock press don't agree, so Gabriel has been crucified in their weeklies for 'cultural imperialism'. Which mainly serves to illustrate the double irrelevance of half-understood Spartist concepts once they're applied to an area as intangible and human as music."

Not all the music press were dismissive. "Gabriel walks a fine line between brilliance and churning out a load of old cobblers," was the *Record Mirror* verdict. And in the end of year album roundup in *Melody Maker*, Simon Scott wrote, "With this album, Peter Gabriel continues to extend the barriers of rock music, and furthers the realization of his ideas totally unhampered by traditional restrictions. His preoccupation with primitive rhythms is explored with stunning results, and although this is not an easy album, the patience needed to enjoy it is well rewarded. Gabriel's skill in pursuit of his visions make this one of the most innovative albums of the year, and sets a standard that other rock artists have only hinted at."

Gabriel gave his views on the criticism to the *South Bank Show*. "Part of it is straight reaction to the music and I'm not dodging that, but I think a lot of it has to do with fashion. One of the real satisfactions with me with this record is that I'm played on black stations in America, and even though in the white press I had some fair slagging this time, I had some very good reviews in black magazines. Even though I don't think my music has much in common with black music, for me it's great to feel that the rhythm is strong enough to get through to black people. There are definitely elements of this album which are a progression for me. I want to continue exploring this hybrid between electronic non-European influences. I think a lot more musicians are now working in this area and there will be a style of music to emerge in the eighties which I think will be very important and influential."

Early in 1981 at the same time as Peter Gabriel started work on the fourth album, the family left the cottage, their first home in the Bath area. Peter had fallen in love with a large Victorian house overlooking Solsbury Hill. But Jill found it "monstrous".

"We knew we had to move because the cottage was too small. But I was totally unhappy at the new house. It was vast, we had hardly any furniture in it, and we couldn't afford to do anything with it. Peter was hardly there at all, he was writing and then recording the album at Ashcombe."

After six months at the house Jill could take no more. The studio cook at Ashcombe was leaving and she suggested Jill take over. "She knew that the pressure on our relationship was really bad at that point, we just weren't seeing each other. But she cooked three-course Cordon Bleu meals, it was unbelievable, and she had to cook extra courses because of the vegetarians.

"Something inside me said, 'You really have to go for this.' Because I was really unhappy up there and wasn't seeing him it seemed a logical move. So I moved with the kids to Ashcombe and left the other house deserted. I told Peter he had to sell it, which he didn't want to do at all. In retrospect it was crazy, it was a good property and cost a lot of money, but I was totally emotional, I just hated it!

"All four of us slept in the same room above the kitchen because we had the whole band housed there, and I took on the cooking. When I started it had a tremendous value. I took it very seriously and learnt how to cook the way she did, she gave me the odd hint.

"I took it on to run the house, do their washing, keep it clean, and do the cooking. It was a full-time job and I was still trying to look after the kids. It was a means of getting closer to him. In fact that was the joke because of course you don't get closer at all. It was a nightmare because I was closer to him and even further away. We couldn't relate, and it would end up at two in the morning, he would come to bed and I was wrecked anyhow.

"I think that was the picture of how our lives weren't working. It intensified, it couldn't possibly work.

"The kids were definitely suffering at that point, because they couldn't get through to either of us then. I was always working, always cooking something, there were all the people around us,

165

always somebody talking, Peter was working. So it was a very difficult time for them."

In June 1982 the album was at last nearing completion. Peter and David Lord worked through a couple of nights to finish the mixing before Peter went to New York to personally deliver the master tapes to Geffen. He had to catch a 7 a.m. flight and just after dawn in the sunshine outside Crescent Studios he was seen off by the small group of people who had worked so intensively on the project. Among them were Jill and David Lord.

"I think everyone felt very lost and shattered – it had been so intense, and it was all over," Jill remembered. "We all stood there and there was a very empty feeling that it was all over. The feeling of loss for me was just enormous."

Jill felt isolated, having no one to go to who could understand her feeling of desolation. "It sounds so corny, but it is like having a baby. It was as if it were taken away and we were all just left there." Jill mentioned to David that they should all meet up. "It was an incredibly empty day, and as I drove away I thought, 'I could go and see David.' Not that we were that close, because we weren't. We hardly communicated, really. But I did think I could relate to him. There was another person I could have gone to but I made a decision to go and see David partly because I thought he was extremely safe, funny really. I drove over that evening, and we talked for ages, and we did end up sleeping together, which was very strange, but I came back to the kids.

"I probably regret nothing more in my life than that. Peter often said, 'Well you couldn't have found a better way to hurt me.' I wasn't consciously thinking, 'This is the way to hurt Peter.' Our relationship was very bad at that point. I was asking for attention he couldn't give, his work was so intense. Peter has always said, 'I will always go one better than you.' And he always has, he is always capable of that. So I managed to punish him. He managed to punish me better."

"We met at fourteen and sixteen years old, you are very different people at that age, so it's been a very bumpy ride," said Peter. "We've swopped over roles. Initially I was the good guy, she was the bad guy, and then maybe four or five years ago the roles reversed and she became the really solid one, working hard to keep the relationship going, and I was the one mucking around.

"It was partly neglect on my side, because when work becomes obsessive, as it does for me, you don't give enough time and energy to the relationship. And relationships, I have discovered, don't run on neutral, you're either working on them or they're getting worse. So I think she just felt totally ignored by me during that period and so ended up getting involved and then I got badly hurt. I think we've both been pretty hurtful to each other. I think what happens is that when things go bad you desensitize yourself, and you actually cut off from the hurt that you are causing."

Jill's and David's affair continued, at that point unknown to Peter, throughout the WOMAD débâcle. Just before WOMAD, in July 1982, Lord helped produce the German language version of the fourth album while keeping up the pretence that nothing was going on. In the end it was too much to bear, and the day before the WOMAD festival he feigned illness and let the studio engineer take over his job.

In September Peter went to the continent to promote the new album. On his return he confessed an infidelity to Jill. "That showed up the state of our relationship because Peter is tremendously loyal, but there must have been a great distance in many ways, and I must have been giving him nothing." Peter's admission prompted Jill to confess her relationship with David, which he had not suspected.

Peter felt betrayed and arrived at David's doorstep in the middle of the night. Both men are calmly spoken and slow to anger, so a lot of quiet anger was expressed.

The situation was getting too intense for Jill, and she decided to take drastic action. She saw a newspaper advertisement for a cottage to rent in the Lake District, packed the Range Rover with her own and the children's belongings, confronting Peter with the news just before making off. "That was my bid to go away and sort out my life." Though her relationship with David had started off almost casually, she was now trying to decide which man she wanted to be with.

"I knew I must be on my own with the children because they had been having a shitty time. Cumbria was wonderful because I solidified my relationship with my children, and found myself in many ways. Stupid things like being cut off without a telephone and teaching the kids every day were very important to me. We had a routine and lived on a very small amount of money."

Though desperately upset at Jill's flight with Anna and Melanie, Peter was powerless to do anything about it. Soon after he was off on a six week American tour and went up to Cumbria to say goodbye. The family kept in touch by post. Jill sent him letters and he sent cards to the girls. "Despite all the rubbish, one thing we did was that we never said a bad word against each other in front of the children. The kids knew everything, he talked to them, and then I talked to them."

Jill struggled with the elements as winter came on, for the first time in her life she was faced with having to fend for herself. "She actually did very well, she'd always had a sheltered life. And the kids liked it because they had undivided attention," said Peter. David visited on Jill's 31st birthday, 2 December, and she had pre-arranged with Peter for him to call her at a given time at the local callbox.

"In that phone call I said to him, 'Have you had other relationships?' and he said, 'Yes, five.' That was devastating. Unknown to Jill at the time, one was a serious relationship with actress Rosanna Arquette, subsequently acclaimed for her roles in *Desperately Seeking Susan* and *After Hours*.

Jill decided to return to Bath for Christmas. Peter was also back having finished touring. They were living together at Ashcombe House, but Jill was looking for a house for her and the girls.

Peter thought Jill could not have found a better person to hurt him with than David. Likewise she thought he could not have found a better person to hurt her with than a young, beautiful successful actress. "In many ways Peter holds the cards in our relationship and I actually love that about him. I am a very fiery person and I give him a hard time emotionally, but in the end he is actually more powerful. And that was the ironical thing about that time, he held me in a sense with Rosanna. It was strange, but it turned everything around and it was a good punishment for everything I had ever done from our whole past."

Jill made a befuddled attempt at suicide. She resolved to drive to nearby Solsbury Hill, made famous by Peter's song, and take an overdose.

"One of the things that I suffered from was unbelievable guilt," said Jill. "I felt incredibly bad about being unfaithful. We had just reached a pitch one night and I said to him that he should look after the children and I should just go away, and he reacted with 'Fine' and went to bed, which kind of gave me permission. It felt like he was saying, 'I agree with you'.

"I had a lot to drink, I planned to make it quite comfortable. I took with me a blanket and lots of pills and more drink. I was driving in a complete daze." Jill attempted to drive on to Solsbury Hill only to find her path blocked by an eight foot high mound of clay. It had been put there by the National Trust fearing a hippy peace festival. She felt it was an ironic omen for which Peter was responsible by drawing public attention to the hill in the first place.

"It sounds pathetic now," said Jill. "It felt like God saying 'Fuck you'. I had come to my senses in a way when I saw the mound. I drove back, it was very frightening because I felt scared of God. It was my first and last thought of suicide."

Jill eventually rented a cottage in a village several miles away and moved in with the children, while Peter stayed in residence at Ashcombe House. "I was mixing the live album and a furniture van came. I knew about it, but it was still pretty traumatic," remembered Peter.

Throughout this time Jill continued seeing David. "I think I was incidental to the whole thing. I was just one chapter in the story of their relationship," said David Lord. "I wasn't trying to split them up. Jill and I had a genuine relationship. It was actually very strong and quite rewarding, without the complications of a three-way relationship. It came to the point where I just had to leave her on her own to make up her own mind."

"I decided to go to Senegal and to Brazil," said Peter. "I thought 'It's silly to sit around, moping. Do something positive!'." He refuses to speak about Rosanna Arquette. Their relationship carried on for over a year, as much as hopping across the Atlantic would permit.

Peter and Jill's contact revolved around his visits to the children. "We would meet up to take the kids out and we would talk, and sometimes there were quite good, positive sessions. I think what has sustained our marriage has basically been a great friendship, a great sense of companionship. So though we often have periods when we don't talk, when we do get into deep talk it's great."

In the spring of 1983 Peter and Jill were recommended a visit to Robin and Prue Skynner's Institute of Family Therapy in London. Robin Skynner and comedian John Cleese, a former client, wrote the bestselling *Families and How To Survive Them*, which illustrates some unnerving characteristics of all relationships. Perhaps the most remarkable being "that people unconsciously choose each other because of similarities in the way their families functioned". The book gives plausible proof of this hypothesis.

Skynner is particularly illuminating on how we all screen off emotions that make us feel bad. The act of screening-off is an approximation of repression, while the screen itself is the unconscious. Skynner explains: "Although we all want to be loved by our families and not display feelings that upset them, we also have a keen hunger to be whole, to be complete. When we sense, and are drawn to, the denied parts behind the screen in our partner, we're really hoping, deep down, to get back the missing parts of ourselves again . . . The extraordinary paradox is that your partner is exactly the one you can best grow with . . . but also the one you can get most stuck with. Even . . . the one you can end up hating most of all."

Peter was sceptical. "I thought 'Shrinks! Who needs it?' It struck me as a lot of Californian nonsense that I'd never been attracted to." But his opinion soon changed. "The Skynners are wonderful people. They would do it together so you have the male and female sides presented. They wouldn't really take sides, but they both had their independent opinions. There would be three or four other couples, many of whom were breaking up. It wasn't an attempt to get couples to stay together, it was an attempt to get people to communicate well, and to handle whatever was going on.

"Doors began to open in the relationship and some of the hurt slowly healed. I had a real sense of emptiness without them. I think it is a sense of self you get through the family unit, having had it and being so really proud of my kids. I love both of my kids, I loved that part of the family life, even though I didn't give it enough time. It was very important to me, so there was a real sense of mourning and loss, and I think once we had got through several layers of pain, both Jill and I, we began to feel there was still a really strong bond."

Peter was unable to commit himself to regular marital therapy sessions because of his work schedule. "I actually finished us going to the thing. Sometimes I think that is a pity because we could have done with longer."

In May 1983 Peter combined a trip to Brazil with a visit to Disney's Epcot Centre in Florida and a holiday with Rosanna in Antigua. Peter spent the autumn of 1983 touring Europe, and for much of 1984 became involved in writing music for films. He stayed in close contact with Jill and the children, but neither Jill or Peter could contemplate divorce.

No one was happy with the unsettled situation. "It had gone on so long, we were all fed up thinking about it to any degree," said David Lord. "I felt I should leave them to it. And if she decided she was going to split up with him then whether I did anything with her was another question. But I don't think it was a situation where she might leave him for me. They were two different things."

In August 1984 Jill went with the girls to join her parents at Balmoral. Peter went to see Rosanna in New York to resolve the situation. "When I got back he came over and I asked if he had decided, and he said, 'I have, I have decided I will stay with you.' And then we attempted to start up again."

Peter's love for Anna and Melanie was a major factor in his reuniting with Jill. "He's terribly in love with his daughters, and they with him," said Jill.

His daughters still have to put up with their father's absence through work. Despite a strong affectionate bond he has tried to make their lives less sheltered than his own upbringing. "I believe in discipline, in giving a strong wall for kids to bounce off," said Peter. "I was a sixties liberal, but now I'm more realistic. We still have the teenage years ahead, but I think you do children a greater service by being yourself and giving them something to push against. They want a battle, that's what they need."

Eighteen months after Jill moved into her own cottage Peter reunited with the family. They stayed there until they bought a new house nearer Bath in 1985.

Peter felt it was important that the conflicting people in his life should meet to try and dissolve any enmity that might remain and allow him to stay friends with Rosanna. Jill agreed and went with him to New York for two days. "I thought I would survive. You know, the age, the extra years, I thought I would be able to hold my own and feel better for what I did. She was very young and bouncy and full of energy." Jill was intimidated and did not feel the encounter was a success.

The situation was finally concluded when Rosanna visited London in early 1987 with a new boyfriend, later to become her husband. Peter asked Jill to accompany him to lunch with the couple. "The two meetings with Rosanna are an intensely hysterical memory for me." Jill was again intimidated, this time by the way Rosanna's charisma captivated not only her luncheon companions, but also the other men in the restaurant. "I can see the value if I had been a strong enough person, if I had more belief in myself like I have now. At the time I didn't feel I had anything compared to what she had to offer."

David Lord has had no contact with Jill since she and Peter got back together in 1984 and has only exchanged pleasantries with Peter when they have bumped into each other.

171

The separation was a major catalyst for change in both Peter's and Jill's lives. She became more assertive and began looking for a career role for herself. Jill applied to become a marriage guidance counseller, but was turned down because separated couples are not allowed to counsel, only married or divorced people. She did start training as a counsellor for the Samaritans, but that was halted when she went to Cumbria. She explains her desire to counsel others despite her own traumas as a way of being liked by someone. Subsequently Jill trained as a counsellor primarly involved with couples. She is also in a group with Robin Skynner training to become a psychoanalyst. "I leave all that open because I stopped doing anything with my life because I thought I was too stupid to. But I have ambition for the first time. It has taken me so long because I lived through Peter initially. It was my way of avoiding taking hold of myself."

HUMAN RIGHTS

In 1980 Miami Steve Van Zandt, still guitarist in The E Street Band, was in Los Angeles mixing Bruce Springsteen's album *The River*. While taking time off he came across an art-house theatre showing old movies. Waiting for the film to start, he was struck by the interval music.

"The projectionist put this tape in, and it was this most extraordinary thing. I had no idea who it was or what he was singing about, but it was very, very moving. I went upstairs and said to the projectionist, 'What was that?' It turned out to be Peter Gabriel singing 'Biko' and I went out and got it. I got such an emotion from that song I had to find out what it was all about. That's the ultimate musical accomplishment, I guess, to move you to do something. And then I began to look at US foreign policy in general. It had always been in the back of my mind to find out more about South Africa."

In the summer of 1984 Little Steven, as he liked to be known after leaving Springsteen's band, visited South Africa twice, including the Sun City resort in the tribal 'homeland' of Bophuthatswana. Initially he set out to do research on his next album. But he put that on hold, deciding instead to organize what was to become the Sun City Project.

Gabriel heard of Biko's death the day it was announced in September 1977. "I made a note of it in my diary. When I started getting into African rhythms on the album it seemed appropriate and I began buying books about him and researching as much as I could."

Stephen Biko, a Bantu medical student, was founder of the South African Students Organization and was a leading figure in the South African Black Consciousness Movement. He became a banned person in 1973, and was put under house arrest at his home in the Eastern Cape. He had been detained several times before his final arrest at a roadblock. A month later he sustained

173

brain damage after a "scuffle" with his police interrogators. He was then transported naked 600 miles in the back of a police van from Port Elizabeth to the prison hospital in Pretoria. He died aged thirty on 12 September 1977 on a mat in the corner of a cell.

> *You can blow out a candle*
> *But you can't blow out a fire*
> *Once the flame begins to catch*
> *The wind will blow it higher*
> *Oh Biko, Biko, because Biko . . .*

'Biko'; Gabriel, 1979

Biko's friend Donald Woods, editor of the *East London Daily Dispatch* at the time of his death, wrote, "Steve Biko represented, in my opinion, the last hope for a peaceful accommodation to resolve the growing South African race crisis." Woods was himself detained when his articles condemning the South African Government became too controversial. He secretly wrote his biography of Biko in jail, eventually escaping disguised as a priest.

Gabriel met Woods in July 1983 when he performed at a concert in aid of the Lincoln Trust, founded by Woods to counteract censorship and South African Government propaganda throughout the world. Gabriel topped the bill in front of 20,000 people at Crystal Palace Football Club's ground in south London, helped by Phil Collins on drums, who had been brought in to help Gabriel's regular drummer, Jerry Marotta, who was suffering from back pains.

"I think Biko was a key youth leader, and had he lived, he would have emerged as a world figure for young people, rather than as just a black South African leader," said Gabriel. "If one reads any of his writing he seems in many ways a well-reasoned and sensitive leader."

The song appeared on record three years after Biko's death. 'Biko' has become one of the most moving moments in Gabriel's shows. It is Gabriel's most effective 'message' song, and has become a virtual anthem for Amnesty International. But Gabriel was disappointed when 'Biko' failed to reach the Top 30 on its release as a single in August 1980.

Even so, it earned over £50,000 in royalties. Gabriel sought to donate the royalties from the song to the Black Consciousness Movement of Azania, which Biko founded. The movement embraced the Black Peoples' Convention, set up in London just before Biko's death to co-ordinate the activities of South African exiles in the UK, which received all the proceeds from the record. The money was used partly to find better premises for the movement in Gower Street, Bloomsbury, and kept it running for three years. The rest of the money was apparently sent to help refugees in Botswana, Lesotho and Swaziland, to the Black Consciousness Movement within South Africa, and used for medical equipment at the Impelweni Clinic in the Eastern Cape, founded by Biko under the Black Community Programme. The Black Peoples' Convention closed its London office in 1983 through a lack of funds and its activities have been absorbed by the refugee committee of the Pan African Congress.

In October 1987 Gabriel got the chance to re-release a live version of 'Biko' as a single to promote *Cry Freedom*, Sir Richard Attenborough's biopic on Biko. Though the song was not a part of the movie soundtrack, its accompanying video included clips from the film as well as live footage of Gabriel performing the song. The royalties again were to be donated to the anti-apartheid cause.

In September 1985, five years after first hearing 'Biko', Van Zandt recorded the *Sun City* single and album, raising over $500,000 for the Anti-Apartheid Movement, a school, and the families of political prisoners. "We had this list of people we were trying to find to record with. Peter's name was on the top of the list because of 'Biko' with Gil Scott-Heron because of his song 'Johannesburg'."

By coincidence, Gabriel was at the Power Station studios in New York at the time recording for the *So* album. Van Zandt and producer Arthur Baker visited Gabriel and recorded a vocal segment for the 'Sun City' single. He can just about be heard in the chorus of the title track, and can be seen momentarily in the video singing "I" in the studio in between shots of Bruce Springsteen's "I" for the chorus "I ain't gonna play Sun City". What started out for Van Zandt as a single ended up as an album because of the wealth of material he was left with once everybody from Bob Dylan and Jackson Browne to Bob Geldof and Run DMC had made their contributions.

"Peter just began to improvise. In the end I am listening to this thing, I love it so much, I thought, 'My God, I can't use five seconds of this in a single, this thing is a total song.' I brought in some musicians and put some more chords into it, and wrote

175

some lyrics around it, and that became 'No More Apartheid'," said Little Steven.

At the session Gabriel explained, "Our music is based on a black heritage. That has now become absorbed, and generated a huge income for white people. So it's about time some of us paid some homage to our sources."

On the album Van Zandt wrote, "I would like to especially thank Peter Gabriel for the profound inspiration of his song 'Biko' which is where my journey to Africa began."

Van Zandt is forthright in his praise of Gabriel. "I think Peter's one of the most important artists of our time and I don't say that lightly. I would have said that even before he became a good friend of mine because he communicates so well and so purely. It seems to come right from his soul to yours, soul to soul, rather than the other things that get between.

"Everybody knows he is wonderfully innovative, but it's the emotional side that really gets to me more than the technical side. He is just a great, great singer, which sometimes is forgotten. I love the way he combines different kinds of music. I do the same thing, so I can appreciate how good he is at it. I think he is the best at that, combining things in a very natural way."

Except for the righteous condemnation of the British music press, Gabriel only gained in credibility through 'Biko'. He was then in a unique position to view the criticism thrown at Paul Simon over the recording of the *Graceland* album in South Africa.

Both men got a chance to discuss the issue in San Francisco in February 1987 on the first leg of Simon's *Graceland* tour of America. They met backstage after the show and Simon went back with Gabriel to his friend Peter Schwarz's home in Berkeley. Several other people were present, including Jon Mcintire, manager of the Grateful Dead, a close friend of Schwarz. They all stayed up engrossed in conversation until 4.30 a.m.

"I liked the *Graceland* album but felt that he had handled it wrong, and had maybe been a little naïve," said Gabriel. "He was arguing and said, 'Did anyone think I was for apartheid?' and he said, 'Have you tried to get approval from the ANC?' The musicians he wanted to work with weren't being allowed to leave the country. So the only way he could work with those musicians was to go in there. At that time he asked about the UN ban. He was advised the ban meant live performances as opposed to studio performances. So I think he was quite shaken by the uproar that emerged.

"He was then advised, when he had finished the recordings,

176

that the ban did apply to studio work. I think he was genuinely innocent of that, but I think he could have had a little more foresight of the possible consequences, and also made a strong declaration earlier on. If you worked with a group of, say, Jewish musicians in Germany just before the Second World War you were bound to know something was going on. And not to make reference to it is, I think, strange. I don't think you can take the role, 'Oh, we are just musicians, I don't want to get involved.' "

Simon's riposte to that simile later appeared in *Rolling Stone* magazine. "To go over and play Sun City would be like going over to do a concert in Nazi Germany at the height of the Holocaust. But what I did was to go over essentially and play to the Jews. That distinction was never made."

"I think *Graceland* has done an enormous amount for South African music," said Gabriel. "What really pisses me off about the bans are that I support the prevention of rich white musicians, or Westerners, going to South Africa and taking a lot of money out and supporting the goverment in that way. However, there are many black artists, writers, painters, musicians, that need to get heard, and that are really talking about their experience in that country at this time. The Musicians Union ban and the Equity ban can forbid their voice being heard. And that must be counterproductive."

The charge of cultural imperialism has frequently been thrown at Gabriel, and it is one he readily refutes. "I think there is a lot of bullshit talked about it. Show me an artist who is pure and doesn't feed off other people. Show me a musician who is pure and particularly show me a rock musician who doesn't feed off other people and other styles and other traditions.

"I think what Paul Simon does is healthy, he has a tradition of doing this. He was the first white musician with any measure of success to take reggae music seriously. Reggae wasn't hip at the time he was working with it. He helped get an interest in South American music and folk music, and that definitely helped musicians trying to get work in Europe and America. And he has definitely increased the stature of South African music with this album.

"The problem occurs when all the money goes in one direction. 'Soweto', the Malcolm McLaren track, is one of my favourite records of 1983. And I gather that was pretty much intact before McLaren stuck his name on top of someone else's song." McLaren and producer Trevor Horn visited the Soweto township in South Africa as part of a trip around the world. The

177

single 'Soweto' reached the UK Top 40. For Gabriel, McLaren was a plunderer because he blatantly passed off other people's tunes as his own. Paul Simon was the opposite, painstakingly acknowledging his sources.

"I think I can hear Paul Simon's digestive system, if you like, the music going in and coming out, it's not just imitative," said Gabriel. "Personally I would probably try to remove it a little further from the source music. I feel more comfortable doing that, but I don't think what he did was wrong. And if you go to Africa you hear the influence of the West is just as strong there as the influence of Africa is in the West. It's always been that way."

Gabriel first made contact with Amnesty when he visited their London offices to get some books and brochures for his research into 'Biko'. His first personal involvement came around 1981 through a friend who suggested he join the Amnesty scheme whereby individuals adopt certain political prisoners and write on their behalf to the presidents, prime ministers and gaolers who are holding them.

"I think it has practical and achievable goals and the prisoners are continuously being released and got out of torture as a result of Amnesty's efforts. And I think quite often now, when I sit down with my benefit priority list, which numbers many hundreds, it has to be related to how I respond emotionally to the subject, and also to how practical and effective the work is."

He maintained a low profile allowing his name to be used on leaflets handed out by Amnesty. Then in June 1986, when Amnesty celebrated its twenty-fifth anniversary, Gabriel became one of their major public supporters. He cancelled a planned promotional tour of Spain, Portugal and Japan to join the Conspiracy of Hope Tour across the United States after an invitation from Bono of U2.

The bill included U2, Sting and the Police, Lou Reed, and Bryan Adams and along the way Bob Dylan, Tom Petty, Jackson Browne, Joan Baez, Joni Mitchell, Little Steven and Miles Davis. At first Gabriel met resistance from Geffen. The *So* album was just about to be released and they wanted him to tour soon after, not before. In the end he placated them by doing his own tour of the States in November and December 1986. Gabriel took a new band out with him, as well as Tony Levin and David Rhodes, he now had Frenchman Manu Katche on drums, with Larry Klein, Joni Mitchell's husband, on bass, and Ian Stanley of Tears For Fears on keyboards. During their half hour set they played two songs off the *So* album for the first time in public, 'Red Rain' and 'Sledgehammer'.

The tour was conceived by Jack Healey, executive director of Amnesty USA. "In many ways Peter was the heart of the Conspiracy of Hope tour," said Healey. "I remember the first night we were out in San Francisco and I was very worried about how it would go. As soon as we heard Peter we knew we were OK. We were in the hands of a master and we were cooking. It was the first time he had played 'Sledgehammer'. His set was overpowering."

Gabriel was not the headline act, going on before The Police and U2. "They were all different things to the tour. I don't want to sound silly, but Sting's music is more intellectual, U2 are the explosive part of the tour, they were the power, and Peter was the heart of it.

"The tour was bigger, better and more powerful than anything we thought it could be. We were hoping to get six prisoners out, we got two out, one in the Soviet Union and one in South Africa. We said we would like to raise between two and three million dollars, we raised $2.6 million. We wanted 25,000 new members and got 40,000. We wanted to leave the music industry happy and we have. Everyone on the tour ended up selling more records. We played to a total of 150,000 people.

"Artistically all the equipment worked perfectly. We had eleven hours on MTV live from Giants Stadium, East Rutherford, across the river from New York City, and it came within ten seconds of schedule. There was a three hour Amnesty radio show. For the bands themselves they all liked one another and they all got to be friends. It was a gigantic success, it's becoming legendary, bigger than it actually was.

"What Amnesty had to worry about was the interfacing with human rights. And that's where Peter was the keystone because 'Biko' held it all together in a human rights manner. You could feel it in every one of those six shows.

"There were about forty prisoners of conscience at the Giants Stadium. They were all personally touched by Peter and wanted to meet him and shake his hand. 'Biko' blows them all away because they feel he is singing about them. Biko was killed the day I arrived in South Africa as a peace worker on my way to Lesotho. Having been an observer, knowing the agony of South Africa, remembering Steve Biko and his approach to nonviolence, the beauty of that song was overpowering, I was deeply touched by that song.

179

"I grabbed one of the prisoners of conscience who had been imprisoned on Robben Island in South Africa and went backstage with him. The song gave him hope of one day overcoming apartheid. We thanked Peter, there were tears on our faces, we all cried like big babies, it was wonderful."

Gabriel mentioned two incidents from the shows. "After the show in San Francisco, a South African who had been imprisoned with Stephen Biko came backstage with tears in his eyes. 'I didn't know there were people who cared.'

"In New York, there was a brave Chilean woman that we met. She was talking to the press conference about the torture she had received. Three days later her son was murdered."

"I don't know how to tell you how much respect I have for Peter as a professional singer and as a person, knowing Jill and his kids," said Healey. "I have the deepest respect for him in every way. I think he is one of the forces in the world able to communicate to people what human rights means. He is somehow bigger than life that way.

"He is a very rare and exceptional, dedicated person to our cause. He is very rare because he is deeply interested in issues of human rights. He wants to meet prisoners of conscience. There is a driving force behind him which is admirable and at the same time very serious. He is just a damn good person, there are not many. He is always available as a friend and adviser. I think to a great extent Amnesty represents his own intellect and his own mind. He is basically shy, very bright and very determined to get things done in a reasonable way. I think Peter has his own shyness about being famous and powerful. Peter is better at causes than he is at his own material, it frees him up working for a cause than for himself. He is very shy singing for himself."

On the Amnesty leaflets given out at his shows, Gabriel states:

The work that I have done with Amnesty is very important to me. I was very moved to meet some of the people that had been rescued from torture and unjust imprisonment, for whom Amnesty had been the only line of hope.

Although there is still so much that needs changing, there is no doubt that Amnesty, in its twenty-five years, has changed the attitudes of governments on human rights all around the world. Through the simple tools of letter writing and the embarrassment of publicity, Amnesty has been surprisingly effective.

180

It is part of a process that is making ordinary people aware of the power and responsibility they have in improving our world.

I ask you to get involved.

Gabriel says it is only in Britain that his middle class background is constantly used against him, along with being ex-public school and ex-Genesis. Being a white liberal is another common, if not strictly accurate, term of abuse. In 1982 'Wallflower', on the fourth album, a song that has become closely identified with Amnesty, came in for criticism because of its theme.

Hold on, you have gambled with your own life,
And you face the night alone
While the builders of the cages
Sleep with bullets, bars and stone
They do not see your road to freedom
That you build with flesh and bone

Though you may disappear, you're not forgotten here
And I will say to you, I will do what I can do

Gabriel aired his doubts to Tom Robinson after recording 'Biko'. "He said it didn't matter if you were exploiting this position for entirely the wrong reasons," Gabriel told Adam Sweeting in *Melody Maker*. "If what is achieved is that attention and money get directed in the right direction, you can be as much of a hypocrite as you like, it doesn't matter. So that helped quieten any doubts."

"I think that has to be the criterion for anything that happens in the pop world or anywhere else. By their fruits shall ye know them," Tom Robinson said. "Motives are so questionable, particularly in the pop business, that you'd go bonkers trying to work out what the true motives were for anything and whether or not they were valid. It's really the results, and the massive classic example that's come up since then, of course, is Live Aid, where you can say so what if Bob was trying to save a desperately sinking career, who gives a shit, it was Adolf Hitler in reverse. And by the same token, if 'Biko' raised consciousness about the South African problem, even for totally wrong reasons, what the hell? Peter was saying to me, 'I don't know whether I wrote that for the right reasons, whether it was actually my concern or whether I just wanted to establish some credibility, I'm not sure, sometimes I lie awake and worry about it.'"

Robinson continued, "The conversation came up because he was asking me, 'How do you get over it, you must get accused of it and you must wonder yourself.' And I said, 'Well, of course I do, I will never know whether 'Glad To Be Gay' helped the gay movement or whether the gay movement helped my career.'

"Peter is certainly given to racking himself with questions. But it may be that he needs to question it that much in order to be Peter Gabriel. That if he didn't go into things in that fine, nitpicking toothcombing detail, then the quality of his work would not be such as it is."

Ready to support the causes of human rights and world peace, Gabriel pointedly steers clear of supporting any political parties. His sentiments are left of centre, but his beliefs cross party barriers. He dislikes Margaret Thatcher, opposes nuclear power, and believes in enterprise and competitiveness running hand in hand with co-ownership. He argues that the enormous social change that will be created by the information revolution will necessitate a new ideology.

"Marxism/socialism was a response to physical exploitation. It assumes work is available to all people. If you start going at it from another point of view, that there isn't work for all people because machines and computers can do most jobs better than we can, then how do you sort out income and employment, and what do people do with their time?

"I think there needs to be some sort of restructuring that means people's rights are established without reference to work. I don't know how it will come, but it will have to come because there has to be somewhere a response to the selfishness of the Thatcherites, and yet I don't see that coming out of British or Labour thinking."

He believes the computer and emerging technologies will forge an answer. "One of the most exciting ideas about the information revolution is that it decentralizes power." Theoretically, the remotest of villages around the world could tap into computer information systems. "I think it has enormous consequences because information is going to be quite hard to contain, as the Russians are beginning to understand with both satellite broadcasting and personal computers.

"I don't say that it will make it a safer or happier world, but it will give people more power. How they choose to use it is another question."

His Amnesty appearances are the latest in a line of benefits he has played since he started performing as a solo artist. In August 1977 he performed for the International Youth Festival of Hope for Mankind in Ockenden near Haslemere, Surrey, organized by the Ockenden Venture. He was impressed with the work of Joyce Pearce who set up the venture after the war to help refugees settling in the UK, and continued it rescuing refugees from war zones around the world, notably Vietnamese boat people. He described her as "an English Mother Teresa".

Gabriel kept in touch with Joyce Pearce over the years. "She rang me up one day and said there was a group of people who were campaigning hard to prevent war or minimize the outbreaks, and was I prepared to help. It seemed a fairly ambitious task, so I asked her a little more about it and agreed to meet up with some of the people because I had enormous respect for her. She was not someone I would say no to."

The meeting eventually led to a trip with the family to Costa Rica in August 1986 to investigate first hand the activities of the University for Peace. The university was the brainchild of Rodrigo Carazo, president of Costa Rica from 1978–82, a nation that disbanded its army in 1948. The university's charter was adopted by the General Assembly of the United Nations in 1980. It operates as a post-graduate university offering a plethora of peace studies from mediation in international disputes to foreign debt and refugees.

Gabriel was enlisted to help in the Music for Peace programme formed to raise funds for the university's Global Computer Network. "As more and more power goes into the hands of the military, the people who are working to improve this planet need to start a database information network linking the various peace groups," he declared. "The idea is that the system will halt the aggressive competition that exists between the East and West over information – the 'I-know-something-you-don't-know syndrome'."

He agreed to help with a compilation album. Various artists were approached, including Paul McCartney who made a demo of a song originally titled 'The Politics of Love' with Gabriel. The two visited each other's homes for rehearsals. Gabriel was helped by Hiroshi Kato, a London based representative of Japanese record and creative companies and adviser to the President of the Council of the University for Peace.

On 16 September 1986, nominated the International Day of Peace during the International Year of Peace, Gabriel performed four numbers on the North Lawn outside the UN building in New York. His band included Steven Van Zandt and Youssou N'Dour. Gabriel got hold of N'Dour at short notice. He was so keen to have him he flew him from Senegal to Paris and then on by Concorde to New York where N'Dour arrived an hour and a half before the performance, flying back the next day.

On the day of the concert Gabriel met Hiroshi Kato, Van Zandt and officials from the University for Peace to discuss a proposal from the UN Secretariat. They wanted, rather belatedly, to hold a concert to round off the Year of Peace. "I suggested Japan because they are the leading economic power, they have too much money and they do not contribute enough to other societies," said Kato.

The money raised would go towards the Global Computer Network. Kato believed it would not be too cold to hold the concert outdoors. The plan for a compilation record was postponed.

The Hurricane Irene concerts were held in Japan on 20 and 21 December 1986. As well as Gabriel and his band the line-up again included Van Zandt and Youssou N'Dour, as well as Howard Jones, Lou Reed, Jackson Browne and Nona Hendryx, all of whom had appeared on the Conspiracy of Hope tour, plus musicians from Japan and the USSR. The concert was a joint venture between the University for Peace, Japanese Red Cross and Japan Aid.

The concerts, held during the afternoon at the 30,000-capacity Jingu baseball stadium in Tokyo, were well below capacity, with a combined attendance for both nights of 32,000. The temperature was mild, but a cold wind forced the audience to wrap up. The promoters obligingly provided everyone with instant chemical heat pads. Despite such setbacks, the University for Peace raised approximately $200,000 from the event, with a further $100,000 expected through sales of a concert video released in December 1987.

Gabriel returned to Central America in May 1987, ostensibly to discuss a film project with director Alex Cox. He admired Cox's film *Repo Man*. Cox was in Nicaragua on his biggest project to date, filming *Walker*, a historical drama about American adventurer William Walker, who became president of Nicaragua from 1856–7.

While in Nicaragua Gabriel had an unscheduled hour-and-a-half meeting with President Daniel Ortega. He travelled with Matt Mahurin, an illustrator and video director, and Marina Kaufman from the University for Peace. There they met Bary Roberts, executive assistant to the President of the University for Peace. Though a Costa Rican and cousin to former President Carazo, Roberts, ironically, was a key figure in the overthrow of Nicaraguan President Somoza.

During the revolution Roberts commandeered crop spraying planes to form the Sandinista Air Force. "They would tie themselves with rope to the side of the plane and take the doors off the hinges and have home-made bombs which the guy with the rope tied round him would then drop out of the aeroplane," said Gabriel. Roberts was one of those who tied himself to the plane.

Through his exploits Roberts had become a personal friend of Ortega's and he was able to introduce Gabriel to him. By chance they also met Tomas Borge, the Minister of the Interior, in a hotel lobby.

"He's a national hero, a small Napoleonic character, quite jocular, but a little scary. He was curious to find out who we were. Bary introduced us, and said we were going down to the Alex Cox film set. Borge hadn't heard about the film and wanted to go down and see it.

"He spent fourteen years in gaol under Somoza and one year of that he was wearing a bag over his head, a method of torture, so he has reason to be a little bitter, and he is bitter. Unfortunately there are now some human rights abuses committed under the Sandinistas, under his jurisdiction.

"He was making eyes at this English girl, who was nicknamed by one of our party the 'Purple Peril' because she looked like an extra from a James Bond film. She spoke many languages, was very bright and not backward in coming forward. She was in the hotel lobby, and El Commandante's eyes remained glued to her. She somewhat brazenly came up and started chatting to him, and within two minutes had given him her phone number. El Commandante invited her to come and visit the film and then I think he had qualms of conscience and decided he should be going with his wife, so he rang up his wife, who arrived in a Jeep-type vehicle loaded with guns in the back. There were two army Jeeps at the front and the back, each with four guards with machine guns, with the wife plumped in the middle.

"He invited me to travel with him rather than in the bus the Sandinistas had made available for us. And you don't refuse your Commandante. So I got in there and I was a little surprised to see the Purple Peril approaching us, walking through the guards, and come up to the window. She picked up that I was a rock singer and started beaming at me as well as El Commandante, and then quick as a flash the Commandante, sitting in the driver's seat with his wife next door to him, turned round to me and said with a wink, 'You are doing all right tonight, Peter,' and invited her in the back of the car.

"Each time the car stopped or turned round all the guards with machine guns would jump out to the four points around the car. We went right through red traffic lights. It was scary."

Gabriel was sceptical at first when Bary Roberts told him he could arrange a meeting with Ortega. "Cox had told us he had been trying to arrange it since he was down there to meet up with some of the ministers, let alone the president. And there were lots of journalists we met in the Inter-Continental who couldn't get an interview with him. So I was a little dubious it would come off.

"We were told, 'OK, it's going to happen today sometime,' but we were never told when. Then suddenly we were driving along in the bus and were told, 'OK, we are here.' We were at the Nicaraguan equivalent of the Pentagon. It is a pretty small building with a six-foot concrete wall outside and four guards on the way in."

Gabriel, Roberts, Kaufman, and Mahurin faced Ortega and two ministers. Ortega, not surprisingly, was not familiar with Gabriel's records. But no doubt he was briefed he was important enough to meet. "Apparently they used me a little bit. The front page of their daily newspaper wrote of the 'short three-day visit of international singer Peter Gabriel, here to see all the US atrocities'. I guess it's wartime." Gabriel was moved by his visit, and despite reservations on the Sandinista human rights record, supported the regime.

"It's really the first government to reach power mainly from the Beatles generation, so there is an open-mindedness that goes with sixties children reaching political power. And the other aspect is the Christian side which I discussed with Ortega in some depth. It is a Christian country first and a communist country second, and you don't normally hear about that, particularly in America where it's reds under the bed.

"Ortega told some stories about religion and how the Catholics were trying to use the faith of the people against the government. There had been this old man who had had a vision

186

of Christ in the mountains, and Christ had said that communism was bringing evil into the church and they should burn all the Sandinista books.

"And then Ortega said the church realized this wasn't having enough effect. So they called up the old man and asked him to have another vision on the first hill outside Managua, which he duly did. Only this time he saw the baby Christ with his mother Mary, and the baby had these two tooth marks in his backside. These were symbolic of the influence of the Sandinistas on the purity of the Church.

"The second half of this vision was to say that people of Managua could also be privileged to see the vision if they stared at electric light bulbs. And most of the population, including Ortega's mother, were then spending the next couple of weeks staring at electric light bulbs. This was not long before I went there.

"And he was trying to tell her, 'Mum, this is crazy! This is just propaganda on behalf of the Church.' And she was slapping him and telling him not to be so disrespectful. And sure enough she saw something in the light bulb, as did many others.

"Ortega was full of good-humoured anecdotes and at other times his face would be close to tears as he was talking about the war and the killing. I was quite moved. I think he has a lot of personal charm and charisma, and a gentle strength."

Gabriel also met Cardinal Miguel Obando y Bravo, Archbishop of Managua, who is pro-American and anti-Sandinista, in an attempt to get a balanced view.

Gabriel's meeting with Cox seemed secondary after that. He talked to Cox about filming the last leg of the 1987 European tour in the autumn.

Though Cox left the chance of working on the film open when Gabriel left, he subsequently ran out of time and was too involved in the Walker project to direct Gabriel in concert.

187

CONTACT

Leaping helter-skelter into the audience had proved a disaster when Peter Gabriel first tried it in 1971, and broke his leg. Such a violent outcome had, of course, not been planned, but it left him wary of similar exploits as a member of Genesis, preferring to vent his dramatic urges on stage in a theatrical setting.

Though he could summon a wildly enthusiastic response from Genesis audiences, it was nothing compared to the mania of The Osmonds concerts. In 1974, an intrigued Gabriel went to see them at Madison Square Gardens in New York.

"It was not that he really cared for my music, but he wanted to see what all the hysteria was about," said Donny Osmond. "For us a lot of it was timing, and a lot of it sex appeal. A lot of it had to do with a young kid singing 'Puppy Love'. It was all very innocent. We didn't have any problems with parents because we were clean cut."

Gabriel made his admission to Osmond when they met in August 1986, a meeting that led directly to Osmond recording his album at Ashcombe House, making him the last person to record there in 1987. It was unlikely Gabriel was hoping to emulate the then teen star.

When Gabriel returned to performance as a solo artist in 1977, after two years off the stage, his simpler show was a deliberate attempt to distance himself from Genesis and its associations. He did not dispense with all theatricality. Stark pool room lights dangled over the stage, and the grey track suit he wore was more of an anti-costume.

Forever idealistic, Gabriel was looking for a new form of direct contact with the audience that was dramatic but also personal. His initial faltering steps were made on his first solo tour which started in the USA and Canada in the spring of 1977, helped by the new innovation of the radio microphone. As the introduction started for 'Waiting For The Big One' Gabriel would disappear off the stage, and accompanied by the tour manager make for the back of the hall or any other vantage point like a box. A spotlight operator would wait for a flash from the tour manager's torch to pinpoint where Gabriel had got to. The song has a long bluesy introduction, and he would then start singing in the darkness. The audience would assume he was on stage only to realize they had been fooled when the spotlight turned on him in the auditorium.

"It was always a nice feeling because people seated furthest away from the stage are always feeling a bit miffed; if you then shift the performance to where they are it's a good moment."

Chris Welch described Gabriel's voyage into the audience at the Palladium in New York in 1977. "Suddenly he disappeared, only to reappear lying like a Cheshire cat on one of the theatre's balconies, singing through a radio microphone.

"Then he pranced into the audience, hotly pursued by fearful security guards, still singing and occasionally disappearing under a sea of clutching hands."

During that first tour Gabriel played to one of his biggest crowds at the 12,000-seater Montreal Forum. Gabriel and the road crew, then headed by road manager Norman Perry, decided to vary the theme, and came up with the idea of lifting Gabriel on a sheet of plywood about three feet wide and six feet long.

"The road crew looked like they were four pall-bearers and carried him out into the crowd. Peter was very agile and managed to hold on very well. It was the first version of what eventually became throwing himself into the crowd and having the crowd pass him around. It was very spontaneous and the crowd went wild," remembered Perry, who is now one of Gabriel's Canadian promoters.

"Those first concerts were brilliant. I think Peter has always been an excellent performer and what he was doing was stepping out of the preconceived anticipation of the audience. It was very stark and the emphasis was on Peter as a performer as opposed to the props and slides and theatricals that people associated with Peter and Genesis."

But it was not always straightforward. "It was funny the first night I went running out into the audience," he told Chris Welch. "Our roadie, Chip, was sent out to look after me and make sure I got back onto the stage, and one of the house security men saw this guy following me and thought he was trouble.

"They bopped him. There was our security man, being beaten

up by the house security man, while I was poncing away, totally unaware of what was going on. A few nights I didn't think I'd get back on stage, and I've doubled my life insurance. At some places the audiences have been very polite, stayed in their seats and shook my hand. At other places they mobbed me. But I think if you stay on stage and seem to be above the audience, that invites much more aggressive tendencies. But if you walk around being vulnerable, then people are very friendly. I'm not putting over any big superstar thing so there's nothing to hit out at. At least that's what I tell myself as I go in wearing my bullet-proof vest!"

The next tour in 1978 was labelled the 'Fluorescent Tour' by the band because Gabriel made everyone wear uncomfortable bright plastic orange vests as worn by traffic wardens or police on traffic duty. Members of the band would rebel and take them off soon after the performance started, complaining the plastic made them perspire. But as they went along on the tour they picked up anything fluorescent they could find including hats and collars which would then be worn on stage. Gabriel wanted the look more unified to make it look more like a band than a collection of session musicians as it had originally been on the first tour.

During 1978, touring Europe and America from August to December, Gabriel carried on his experiment of going into the audience, varying it between 'Solsbury Hill', 'On The Air' and 'I Go Swimming'.

The Dive, as it became known, did not start until the next tour, the 1984 Tour of China, which started in February 1980. For the encore he would perform 'On The Air' from his Mozo repertoire. Larry Fast remembered having to improvise on the synthesizer. "When Peter got stuck in the audience we had to keep the song going for a long time, it was something that could be extended or contracted." Gabriel experimented using different numbers for the Dive, including, again, 'Solsbury Hill' and the apt 'I Go Swimming' where he would mimic an Edwardian bather on stage and then fall face down onto the awaiting outstretched arms.

The three-and-a-half-week US leg ended in New York where the band played two medium-sized open air concerts in Central Park. But the crew were unable to use their elaborate lighting because of the daylight. Wanting to treat New York to his lights Gabriel arranged an extra gig at the Diplomat Hotel, a club venue.

But there were hitches here too, and it was feared the hotel's power system could not drive the sound and the lights. Gabriel was also worried that the stage was so weak it would collapse under all the activity. One way to avoid that was for everyone to leave the stage. As the Diplomat was the final date, Gabriel decided he would share his experiences of audience contact with the rest of the band. With some trepidation they all lined up on the edge of the stage. Jerry Marotta, the most strapping member of the band, was also the most apprehensive about falling off the stage. "The crowd opened up in front of him," said Larry Fast. "He had a big beard and looked like a mountain, it was like watching the waters part. I was standing next to Jerry and he did hit the floor. He was not hurt, they just lowered him to the floor. If you see someone like me coming it's not going to be any problem.

"We had seen Peter doing it for God knows how many shows and he had come back and said, 'It feels great! It's like a big moving mattress that holds you above.' It sounded kind of interesting. Normally there wouldn't have been an opportunity for the rest of us to do it. I felt good about it, so we all dived in. I had a great time, it was almost like defying gravity. There was a little bit of movement, it was like waves on the ocean that don't really carry you out, but don't carry you back in.

"The problem was that normally the front rows are made up of, say, smaller girls who are a little shorter and they don't block the views of the slightly taller people behind them, and that is who you are falling on, although Peter will sometimes take a dive and end up a few rows back."

Towards the end of the 1980 European tour one crowd was far too hostile to even contemplate The Dive. Gabriel was booed off stage, an experience he had always dreaded, supporting Frank Zappa in Berlin. The audience were older and more impatient than usual. "I think they thought who is this arrogant little shit getting up and doing these stunts? But I made myself vulnerable, too, to see if there was any possibility that it would allow a change of mood. It didn't work," he told Timothy White of *Spin* magazine.

"People were throwing stuff at me, wanted to punch me. There was a guy yelling, 'English Pig, Go Home!' I crawled back up on stage and started to do 'Here Comes The Flood', which was literally the quietest number I had at that point, and that didn't work either. I walked off.

"It was my worst night ever as a performer. Up until then I'd always been afraid of it happening. Now it had happened. Once the hurt and the shock wore off, I began to adopt a different

191

frame of mind. After a day's break, the next show was in Bremen with Zappa, and even though it wasn't going over again, I felt relaxed, intact. I began laughing and feeling at home, and the crowd responded. In the end, we did much better – it still wasn't fantastic – but I'd overcome my fear of being challenged, of being rejected by an audience."

The following tour of North America, titled Playtime 1988, ran from October 1981 through to December 1982, coinciding with the release of his fourth album dubbed *Security*, which included 'Lay Your Hands On Me'.

Gabriel attempted to shift audience complacency right from the start. The band were dressed in black Japanese martial arts type outfits with white knee pads. They entered from the back of the auditorium pounding out the beat of 'Rhythm of the Heat' on big marching drums while powerful hand-held torch beams combed the auditorium. "It was great because people didn't expect it, they thought it was police or security guys coming in," said Gabriel.

Later in the set he would alternate between walking back into the audience, scurrying over their seats clutching their hands, gripping their heads with his hands, or diving in for the aptly titled 'Lay Your Hands On Me'.

I walk away from light and sound, down stairways
Leading underground

But still the warmth flows through me
And I sense you know me well
It's only common sense
There are no accidents around here

I am willing – lay your hands on me
I am ready – lay your hands on me
I believe – lay your hands on me, over me

'Lay Your Hands On Me'; Gabriel, 1981

"The song was about trust, about healing and sacrifice. It's been misconstrued, with reviews saying that I'm acting like Jesus Christ, and that's not what I'm trying to do with that at all. I feel I am trying to gradually involve the audience emotionally with what we are doing with the music. I feel it's an offering of trust to the audience. Clearly it is a dramatic moment which is contrived, in a way; I am not denying that. But I think the effect

192

is strong because really what an artist is trying to do is engage the viewer, the audience, the listener in what they are doing and get them to feel and become part of the experience and not separated from it. I think it really works like that, it does help bring people in. Because most concerts are a part of long tours, people think, well, this is going to be the same if I see it in ten days' time or two months' time. And as soon as you involve the audience you introduce the unpredictable. You cannot know for certain when I am going to get back to the stage, what's going to happen to me down there, and so I think it keeps things interesting."

On his first dives into the audience Gabriel went forwards, face down, but he would frequently be turned over. Then more recently he began falling backwards, so he could not see immediately where he was going. "Falling backwards is a real show of faith," he said.

Gabriel, not alone in the rock firmament, can inspire quasi-religious fervour. He probably takes more time and care in replying to fans than most stars and in one instance met a woman to break her out of her obsession for him, hoping she would realize he was a fairly regular guy; it apparently worked. Some fans like to call themselves Gabriel's Angels. In 1977 one shouted to him on stage in Hollywood, "You are God!" "No, we are just good friends," came the reply.

A review of Gabriel's USA tour of 1982 in *The Northern Star of Illinois* newspaper did not please Mr Mark Kinsella. He wrote to the editor, "In the Dec. 7 *Star*, Sharyl Holtzman's 'Peter Gabriel: Command Performance,' deeply saddened me. After reading about Gabriel climbing a 'tower-like stand', demonstrating his incredible hold over a crowd, being 'clapped and chanted to' and finally being 'swept up by the crowd and passed over-head', I have to ask Miss Holtzman to come out of her Gabriel fervor and remind her Mr Gabriel is only a man. I don't see a man who should be worshipped, chanted to or clapped to. I see a man who may gain the whole world but lose his soul. I see a man who hasn't realized that the humble will be exalted and the exalted humbled." Mr Kinsella gave his address as "Northern Lights, College Ministry of Glad Tidings, Assembly of God".

Gabriel made various efforts to improve his movement on stage. In 1982 he spent three or four days with choreographer Laura Dean to enlarge what he called his vocabulary of movements. Gabriel, Rhodes and Levin would stretch and warm up before the gig, and incorporated some of Dean's ideas on 'Shock the Monkey' where Gabriel bounded across stage bent like an ape with dangling arms and jumped up and down crazily with Rhodes. Gabriel has subsequently used other choreographers to help iron out awkward movements, notably Charles Molton, who helped him in 1986 with the silly walk on 'Big Time', and on 'No Self Control'.

Much of Gabriel's movement is taken from the rituals of other cultures. Michael Argyle's book *Bodily Communication* was a source of inspiration. One gesture, the outstretched hand with the palm facing out used while performing 'In Your Eyes' from the *So* album looks deceptively like Gabriel is giving a blessing.

"I watch some of the Indian and Pakistani singers and they have this gestural language too, and there is definitely a sense there of energy exchange, which sounds like a post-sixties term. But for me there is a real joy with 'In Your Eyes', and I think some of that comes through to the audience. If you really want to beam in anyone, who they are or what they are, you can do so through their eyes, and so that is acknowledging that. But I am not trying to put myself over as the preacher."

Gabriel has an unnerving gaze off as well as on the stage, his eyes relentlessly stare directly into your own almost as if there is a contest as to who can stare the longest. "I never used to do that but I know I can look into people if I want to now. It's something that happens if you start allowing yourself to be looked into. You get what you give. I used to do some sort of eye meditation. A Japanese meditation which you do with a mirror, where you look at your own image until it disappears. You try and put your consciousness into the mirror image, rather than where you are. What happened for me was that I would get a flash, I would lose myself, effectively.

"I think if you want to talk to someone and get close to them you can just look into each other's eyes, as lovers do, and find out a lot about what's happening – the old thing about mirror of the soul.

"I feel that at times I should be of use to people. What I like in other people's work is things that make me think about what I am doing – gives me an awareness of something I didn't know about before, activates my conscience, my imagination, or my spirit, and I think when what I do is working well and is pure, then other people can use it in that way. So partly that is what I am trying to do with 'Lay Your Hands'. I really do try and get a picture before I go into the audience of the circle

194

around all the people. So there are images going through my head at that point, some of which I feel happy to talk about, others I don't. I am not trying to dominate that moment, I am trying to serve it.

"I think partly what is interesting for people that are into what I do, is that they see me going through the struggles, and representing their own struggle. I feel all right about it when I feel there is some strength in it and some commitment in it. But when I feel I'm floundering, as I do occasionally, then I don't like it."

Gabriel is notorious for forgetting the lines of even his most well-known songs when he is on stage. It was more understandable with Genesis who specialized in contorted lyrics. More recently, an over-long introduction and Gabriel shuffling over to Tony Levin on stage are signs that he has forgotten his lines.

In his earlier solo shows the lack of lyrics was occasionally intentional. At Stony Brook, Long Island in New York State in October 1978, Gabriel introduced a song called 'The New New One'. He told the audience, "When you sit down there and you watch some shows you get the feeling that you are watching a very rehearsed band who know exactly what they are doing. Well, our policy is to provide the opposite of that. And to that effect there are a few new numbers which as yet have no words and no melody and a few loose ends and we are playing these in slowly. This is one of those and it may give you an opportunity to watch us mess up. I hope you enjoy it."

The words appeared to be the stream of consciousness variety with little meaning, most of them could well have been gibberish. 'The New New One' was a bouncy up-tempo rock tune. There were other songs that were played a few times on stage, but never appeared on record, including 'Why Don't We' and 'John Has A Headache'.

The lyrics always come last for Gabriel, but that has not stopped him trying out unfinished songs on audiences. At the Reading Festival in August 1979 he had written the music for 'Biko', but was still forming the lyrics. The only identifiable word at that performance was Biko. The improvised sounds he makes are referred to by his fans as 'Gabrielese'.

Ever since he has performed as a solo artist, Gabriel has wanted to incorporate different multi-media elements into his shows. But his ambition ran ahead of available time and finance. "I would try and integrate the *Birdy* type of music with the song

195

albums, so that it was a mixture of songs and atmosphere," he said.

In the Playtime 1988 programme for the 1982/3 tour there is a mock-up picture of Gabriel in a space suit, another mock-up of him at what could either be a space mission control or a TV control room, and a picture of a modern airship. The copy reads:

Peter has been toying with a number of playful and inventive ideas for future stage shows. Perhaps the most ambitious of these is to suspend a full stage set from a helium-filled airship and to sail the thing slowly around the world. This idea is reported to be popular with overworked roadies, but so far lack of necessary cash – not to mention airship – has relegated the notion to pipe-dream status.

This comes after a 1980 attempt to convert a train into a mobile stage.

Also on the drawing board, and far more feasible, is a project being researched in America to create a multi-media show using the latest development in video and 3D, some of which can be seen at the Epcot Centre in Florida and the New York Institute of Technology.

It mirrored Gabriel's ideas well, based half on fact, and half fantasy.

Gabriel saw the value of video long before pop promos became essential tools for record companies to sell records. When he signed his new solo contract with Tony Stratton Smith in 1978 he insisted his video work should be excluded. "In other words, by selling or contracting my records, I do not accept I have contracted my video performances, or video work. And at the time no one would argue that case at all. I remember Strat thinking I was just off my rocker. But it turned out to be extremely useful."

His first solo single, 'Solsbury Hill', released in March 1977, had an accompanying video directed by Peter Campus, a video artist with the prestigious Leo Castelli Gallery in New York. "It was a little conceptual, dealing mainly with close-ups of my shoulder. And it was not greeted with enthusiasm by the record company first of all." The video was made in a small town north of Boston using personnel from the pioneering Boston TV station WGBH.

Three months later 'Modern Love' was released. Gabriel was photographed spreadeagled in the nude intending the picture to be put on the record label. But Charisma Records thought it improper. "The idea was when you put the record on the turntable the little thing in the centre sort of gave me generous endowments. I was quite pleased with the idea at the time but it didn't go down very well. I think it joined the long list of misses from my single releases, of which there have been many."

For the video Gabriel dressed up in an American football outfit and wore a fencing mask. He was filmed on the escalators at the Shepherds Bush Green Shopping Centre surrounded by model girls. The modest video was made by Peter Medak who directed the 1971 film *The Ruling Class*.

He ran into trouble again with the next video for 'Games Without Frontiers', in February 1980, directed by David Mallet who did David Bowie's *Ashes To Ashes* later in the year. *Top of the Pops* objected to the way children were used in the video. The children are dressed as adults and seated round a banqueting table, mimicking their self-important seniors. Gabriel, with short hair, is seen in various guises in front of blown-up images of bald naked dolls, and crawls around invisible to the arguing children, peering at them. A segment with a newsreel film of a girl saluting Hitler at the 1936 Olympic Games was taken out and replaced with custard pie throwing before it even went to the BBC for approval.

"The idea of the song was countries behaving like playground kids," said Gabriel. "It's against nationalism, but they had seen me moving around the table with the kids and thought that I was leering at them like a dirty old man. At the end there was a whole series of children's toys, and they thought that the Jack in the Box was an obvious reference to masturbation. So it says a lot more about the minds of the people who ran *Top of the Pops* than it did about my video."

Gabriel sought out the latest video innovations and experimental artists in the USA during his 1982 tour. He planned to use video inventively on his next tour. In Washington DC he visited a video festival run by the American Film Institute. He investigated the video synthesizer and a company attempting to make 3D TVs.

In Los Angeles he saw videos by Laurie Anderson and the Residents. In Hollywood he met a special effects designer on *Star Wars* and *Close Encounters of the Third Kind* who was pioneering work on holograms. And in New York he met the curator of the Video Section of the Museum of Modern Art, who introduced him to experimental video-makers. He was most amused by the work of William Wegman, one of whose pieces featured him crawling on the floor spitting a mouthful of milk into a thin white line. His dog then went in the opposite direction licking up the line of milk that his master has spat on the floor. As well as the planned stage uses of video, Gabriel wanted to fulfil a long held ambition to make a long form video.

Gabriel's first big production video came in September 1982 for 'Shock the Monkey', directed by Brian Grant, part of probably the first big video promo company, MGMM – Millaney Grant Mallett Mulcahy.

Gabriel was depicted alternately as a businessman in a dark suit, and then a shaman with elaborate face paint and a shaved head in a white suit. The exterior normality was contrasted with the primitive man inside, the monkey hurt by jealousy. It did not make easy viewing with scenes of Gabriel running in the forest as if he were being hunted, imprisoned in a cell, and then being captured by dwarves.

The next video, for the live version of 'I Don't Remember' was even more disturbing. Gabriel was surrounded by the nearly naked white painted bodies of the Rational Theatre Company. Inspired by Malcolm Poynter's uncompromising sculptures, it was directed in July 1983 by Marcello Anciano, and looked like it was filmed in Bedlam.

It was a journey through the unconscious, exploring an amnesiac's memory. It opens with Gabriel's death mask lying on a rubbish-strewn floor, outside the window all is red, inside there is dripping water. Gabriel metamorphoses into an old man with a hideous grin, then he is back to normal, he lies down, then wakes up in a sweat. Eventually appearing to overcome his memory loss, he walks across the room to find a framed picture on the floor. He picks it up and wipes the dust off to show a picture of Gabriel as a young boy with his parents gazing at his baby sister Anne in her mother's arms. He then goes to lie down on a couch with a beautiful woman, and they both turn into screaming, agonized, ghost-like figures and then back to normal. The journey continues with the caressing woman, gangsters with poisonous blow darts, and South American Indians. He appears to escape from the cell, only to find himself locked up again. Not surprisingly, regardless of artistic merit, it did not receive much TV airtime.

Gabriel planned to make a 3D video that autumn, but the project never came off. He was impressed with some of the 3D images he had seen. "Some of the most haunting images in 3D for me are not those using gimmicks or with things jumping out of the screen, but landscapes, full of texture and detail which really provide one with the experience of being in another situation and not merely observing it. It's like being in a dream," he said.

Gabriel discussed a video collaboration with Laurie Anderson after being impressed with her show 'United States' in London in spring 1983. He wanted to produce as well as appear in a thirty minute programme with different artists.

That idea never came off, but in December 1983 he and Anderson were invited by Vietnamese director Nam June Paik, a veteran of the sixties American multi-media scene, to appear in *Good Morning Mr Orwell* broadcast by the Public Service Broadcasting network on 1 January 1984. Gabriel and Anderson performed 'Excellent Birds', a song they composed together over twenty-four hours in New York. They were filmed seated looking at animated storm clouds rushing by, animated birds, and snow and computer images are also incorporated in the video. Gabriel and Anderson are finally depicted suspended, treading the air.

'Excellent Birds' appeared on Anderson's 1984 album *Mister Heartbreak*. Gabriel's more dance-oriented version 'This Is The Picture', subtitled 'Excellent Birds', appeared on the *So* cassette and CD, though not on the album. There was a gap of nearly three years from his last solo video 'I Don't Remember' until the next video, 'Sledgehammer', in April 1986.

SO

The big time beckoned in 1986. Peter Gabriel was now ready to embrace the success he had forsaken eleven years earlier.

"I'm on my way, I'm making it," he predicted on 'Big Time' for the *So* album released in May 1986. Within three months his singles and albums had topped the charts on both sides of the Atlantic.

A few die-hard fans argued he had lost some of his spirit; for them *So* stood for sell-out. But Gabriel was never more spirited, self-confident and playful. He even looked different with a trendy new haircut from Knightsbridge and a wardrobe of fashionable clothes from New York.

'Big Time' is as much a piece of self-mockery as a comment on the success ethic. "It is a satirical story about a basic human urge. A small man from a small town achieves all his ambitions, with all parts of his life, personality and anatomy growing larger than life, and consequently very heavy.

"In America, which is still a vigorous and enthusiastic nation, success has reached religious significance. This drive for success is a basic part of human nature and my nature."

Gabriel shunned stardom in 1975, leaving Genesis for his family, his sanity and creative freedom. The situation was inverted in 1983 when his family left him through neglect caused by work. Freed from the constraints of family life Gabriel underwent a personal transformation, similar to the transformations referred to in his own songs. It helped clear away some doubts.

"At the time of coming back he had tremendous determination," said Jill. "He said, 'I do want to make it! I do want to succeed!' The album came out of it. Instead of going along with the idea he is different, special, unique, precious, behind a wall, this last album was about him saying, 'Fuck that! I am going to come through, I'm going to allow myself to succeed'. This period has been a big change for him, it puts him on the line far more. He could go along with being a respected artist and not going for big success, but the challenge is breaking through."

"He loves success," said David Rhodes. "After working for a long time, to get recognition is good. He enjoys it and it has made him more confident in trying to achieve all the other things he wanted to do. The success he's had with this record has given him much better opportunities of contacting people, speaking to people, he's not just treated as a reasonably well-known English artist who used to be in Genesis."

Success is a theme that Tony Banks pursued. "He would probably disagree with this, but I think he has always wanted to be famous. I think with this last record he compromised just enough to get it. To take the most obvious example, the cover has his face. Obviously he's good-looking and he has never really let that come through before by shaving his head and appearing on all those covers with squiggly lines through them. Finally he has a cover with a title even, marvellous, and a good-looking portrait of the guy. The songs are shorter, more direct and simpler lyrics." If this is a contrivance of Gabriel's then Genesis clearly learnt the lesson a lot earlier and better.

"Compromise is a bad word," continued Banks, "because it implies that it's a very conscious thing. I think it came naturally, but there's no doubt it's an easier album. I think it's a very good album, but I personally like the ones that came before it because I prefer the more difficult albums."

For the first time Gabriel allowed himself to get caught up in the awards circus. He was the only artist to receive two awards from the British Record Industry in February 1987, as Best British Male Artist and for Best British Music Promo Video. On receiving his second statuette at the Grosvenor House in London in front of an estimated TV audience of 400 million, Gabriel noted, "Now I have two of these, I'll investigate the mating potential."

He was nominated for four American Grammy Awards, and attended the ceremony in Los Angeles in April 1987, but came away with nothing. He was willing to be identified with wanting success. "It's a very painful process, but he had to put himself on the line to actually be there," said Jill.

Gabriel was nominated for eleven MTV Awards and on 11 September 1987 the 'Sledgehammer' video won an unprecedented nine out of the sixteen categories. The headline in *Variety* declared "Gabriel Pulverizes Field . . ." In addition Gabriel was inducted into MTV's *Video Vanguard*, a video hall of fame. It was ironic that this time Gabriel was unable to attend. Instead he sent a video message of thanks from Stockholm where he was appearing on the night of the awards.

The 'Sledgehammer' video won a clutch of other awards and Gabriel won a host of polls in music papers, becoming the first artist to win three sections in the *Rolling Stone* magazine poll.

The *So* album elevated Gabriel into the bottom of the first division of superstars. If Live Aid had been held in 1987 instead of 1985 it would have been unthinkable not to include Gabriel in the line-up.

The personal turmoil in Peter Gabriel's life had peaked and appeared to be on its way to a resolution as the musical and lyrical direction for the *So* album started to gel during late 1984. One song on *So*, 'Don't Give Up', has strong associations for Jill Gabriel. To such an extent that she finds it hard to watch Kate Bush held in Peter's arms on the video. 'Don't Give Up' was inspired by a TV programme on the effects of unemployment on relationships and home life, and by a photograph by Dorothea Lange – 'In This Proud Land' – showing dust-bowl conditions in America during the Great Depression. But it was the parallel with his own family life that so moved Jill.

> *No fight left or so it seems*
> *I am a man whose dreams have all deserted*
> *I've changed my face, I've changed my name*
> *But no one wants you when you lose*

Doubt is replaced by hope based on self-respect in Gabriel's lyrics. The pain can be soothed by the succour of loved ones. One-liners in the lyric could almost be aide-memoires from Peter Gabriel to himself: 'you worry too much', 'you're not the only one', 'you still have us', 'you know it's never been easy', all interspersed by 'don't give up'.

"When he gets into very deep depressions, I am always saying don't give up," said Jill. "I think that song is very much about us."

The separation gave Peter the chance to live out his stud fantasies. Though he had expressed sexuality on stage throughout his career, he had never openly celebrated sex through music as much as he was to on *So*.

Having resolved not to sit around and mope during the separation, he paid two visits each to Brazil and Senegal in 1983 and 1984, which brought in fresh rhythmic and melodic influences. He had for a long time harboured ambitions to make a rhythm and blues album, and also at one time had wanted to put out an album of cover versions of his favourite soul music. Unlikely ever to find the time to indulge in these projects, he decided to incorporate all those influences on the new album.

He started preparing the rhythm tracks for the *So* album early in 1984 after a three-week holiday over Christmas and New Year with the family in Australia and Singapore.

Peter made slow progress in 1984 on the new album, sidetracked by writing 'Walk Through The Fire' for *Against All Odds*, 'Out Out' for *Gremlins* and, in autumn 1984, the sound-track to *Birdy*. But he did make one crucial move forward. His search for a new co-producer was over having found Daniel Lanois, co-producer of *Birdy*. Work on *So* started in earnest in February 1985 at Ashcombe House.

Gabriel wanted to get back to more traditional forms of songwriting after the instrumental atmospheric moods of *Birdy*. He was aiming for more intimacy with his listener. "I wanted to be more playful, a bit more open, less mystery . . ." he said. The moods were less sinister, the music more accessible and his spirit stronger. It was ironic that the music was more 'up' considering the emotional pain that preceded the album's composition. "It was a dark period for me and one in which I had to become a little more open to the world," said Gabriel.

"One of the contributing factors to the album was that Peter was not into darkness like he once might have been," said Lanois. "I like the darker side, but I wouldn't say I gravitate towards heaviness, certainly not on *So*. I think Peter was heading that way already and he saw that in me and thought this is going to work. As a personality I tend to be of the soulful category, meaning that I am not the sort who would lean on technology, I would lean on feelings, emotions and mood. I knew that Peter was interested in being more focused and having a song record."

"Six months of the record was pre-production preparation," Lanois continued. "Most of the ideas were formed to a certain degree." He was only booked for six months, but was forced to postpone subsequent commitments to complete the album. "We had to screen the many ideas that Peter had, which were maybe twenty foundations for songs, and narrow that down to twelve of our favourites. Having done that we had to come up with arrangements."

Larry Fast, for the first time in Gabriel's solo career, did not appear on any of the final recordings. He is credited on the album sleeve with 'thanks for additional work' having helped with treatments on completed tracks, but Gabriel himself took over most of the keyboard work.

Jerry Marrota's influence on the drums was also starting to wane. None of Gabriel's backing band ever gets formal contracts, their loyalty has always been enough to guarantee commitment. They all fix their other considerable session or production schedules so as not to conflict with Gabriel's plans. But that is not helped by Gabriel being prone to delays.

Marotta, who joined Gabriel on his first tour in 1977, was an antidote in those days to the likes of Genesis and Robert Fripp. "They would butt heads with one another in what I think is a very English way, as opposed to the way I would butt heads with Peter, which is to start yelling at him, and somehow force some sort of reaction out of him.

"I was working with Hall and Oates after I did the first tour. After that Peter called me up and said 'I'm going to be doing another album and I don't have any money, I can't afford to pay a lot of money'. I said, 'Don't even talk to me about money, I'm just going to do it. If you want me to do it I'll be there, and whatever you can pay me, pay me'. That was always my feeling with Peter. For the first few years of working with him, there wasn't a single person from the road crew that wouldn't have gone out on tour for no money at all, just to be involved with this guy and his calibre of music and professionalism."

Marotta was convinced Gabriel was displeased with him for missing one session on *So* because he was drumming for Paul McCartney's album. Stewart Copeland, who had worked with Gabriel on the fourth album and played with him at the first Womad in 1982, filled in. Eventually Marotta did a seven-day week taking time away from McCartney to play with Gabriel. But Marotta's harder rock approach was increasingly at odds with Gabriel's sparser, more direct approach. One track on *So* Marotta was convinced would be put out with his drumming was 'Big Time', but Copeland's session was used instead.

"It was one of the best things I have ever participated in," said Marotta. "We had cut this very powerful, traditional sort of Gabriel track. I literally had goosebumps. I said, 'Peter, look they don't go away, I can't get rid of them'. I had them for days. And what ended up on the record was this kind of funky, pop version of the powerhouse we had cut. It was more conventional, more commercial sounding than our original idea."

Marotta's favourite Gabriel album was the first. "I get the feeling that back then he wasn't concerned with being successful.

Nowadays, I get the feeling that that's more of a concern with him – being successful and selling records."

In early 1986, before the release of *So*, Gabriel selected his new touring band, and the line-up did not include Fast and Marotta. "He picked me up at a coffee shop in Notting Hill Gate," said Marotta. "I was hitching a ride to Bath with him and he could hardly talk, he was so flustered. I'm sure he felt terrible. I spent most of the time calming him down, telling him it's OK. It's all right, you know, no problem.

"But I'd like to be working with Peter. I don't know what to say, it's one of those things. I guess if Peter had asked me to do the tour I probably would have done it. We're still friends, but our friendship was based on working together.

"He said we're trying to go for a different vibe, a different feel. The drums were a very prominent part of the shows I did. Everyone was just blown away by the power coming from the drums. Maybe he wanted to back off from that a bit and focus on some other aspect.

"My only funny feeling about that is working with somebody for nine years, I would have thought he could have sat down with me and said, 'I want to move into this, can you do it?' It's hard to say anything nasty about Peter, we all like one another. There's no real reason for what happened except for me to say it's his perogative, he's the boss, and he just decided he wanted some new people.

"It's really funny because one weekend when I was in Bath working on the album with Peter he made a big point of saying, 'I want you to know that you are definitely doing the tour', and I'm learning at my age that you really start worrying when people start reassuring you."

Larry Fast had a similar experience. "He gets very shy and awkward and makes an awkward face and mumbles an awful lot. There wasn't a tour, but he thought it best to let me know he was thinking of trying other musicians. I felt crestfallen, but then that is natural when you have put over a decade into it. But it isn't as though it is the only thing that I do. It's just the way this business works, there are no guarantees. It is inherent in what Peter does that things are going to change.

"With Peter you know that nothing is permanent, things change, it isn't a democracy. That doesn't change my respect for him musically and liking what he does. As to whether the changes were successful, you would have to ask someone else. I had seen it with guitarists, there were five different guitarists."

205

Richard Macphail confirmed: "He agonized over it for a long time."

By the summer of 1985 most of the rhythm tracks for the album had been laid, though the lyrics were more behind than usual. Recording was originally scheduled to finish on 31 July 1985, but it was a hopelessly optimistic date.

In early September, Gabriel and Daniel Lanois spent five days at the Power Station in New York, recording with a horn section that included Wayne Jackson of the Memphis Horns, the original trumpet player for Otis Redding, for the funkiest numbers on the record, 'Sledgehammer' and 'Big Time'. Jim Kerr of Simple Minds and Michael Been of the Call also sang backing vocals for 'In Your Eyes'. It was during those sessions that Gabriel was tracked down by Steve Van Zandt to sing on the 'Sun City' single.

The backing vocals for 'In Your Eyes' also included Sengalese singer Youssou N'Dour, who Gabriel had invited to Ashcombe House in June 1985. Gabriel had first seen N'Dour exactly a year before, performing during his first visit to England at the now defunct Venue in London. Ten days later Gabriel was in Paris and went to see N'Dour again. This time Gabriel went backstage and introduced himself to N'Dour, then aged twenty-four who had never heard of Gabriel. They agreed to meet later that night at Phil One, an African club, but missed each other. A month later Gabriel, accompanied by George Acogny, a Senegalese who lives in Bath, and later producer of Donny Osmond, turned up unannounced at N'Dour's home in Dakar, Senegal.

Anyone in town who wanted Youssou, a Bob Marley figure in his homeland, had to turn up at his home since he had no telephone. Gabriel and Acogny were invited to see N'Dour perform at his own club, the Sahel, that night. N'Dour is a devout moslem and member of the Mouride sect. His lyrics are coloured by religious sentiments as well as social comment.

N'Dour's background is explained in the Peter Gabriel tour programme. "His mother was a Gawlo who sang in the tradition of praise singers and story-tellers bringing the history and myths of ancient empires and ancestors right down to our own times. Youssou stepped into that line as if to a vocation and he first came to the attention of the Senegalese public at the age of fourteen, with his homage to a great Senegalese saxophonist – MBA. His voice quickly captured the mood of a nation anxious to re-find its national and cultural identity after years of colonialism. He knew how to use the traditional dance rhythms and percussion of his country and match them with more modern flexible instruments to create a new popular music which he calls Mbalax."

N'Dour's appearance on 'In Your Eyes' was unscheduled. He was playing with his band The Super Etoile De Dakar at the Town and Country Club in London. His friend Jenny Cathcart, a researcher at the BBC who had met him while working on the TV series *The Africans*, phoned Gabriel to invite him to the concert. Gabriel was unable to attend, but invited Youssou to lunch in Bath that weekend. The 'In Your Eyes' session followed that afternoon.

"It was one of the most incredible days I can ever remember," said Jenny who accompanied and translated for Youssou. "He said to Youssou I want you to listen to this. He attempted to get him to sing in English, but Youssou translated 'In your eyes, the light the heat, in your eyes, I am complete' into Wolof, and stood up and sang to this track, improvising all the way like the Gawlo that he is. Peter joined in and everybody was incredibly uplifted that afternoon. Youssou didn't even know he was going to do this, it was as if it was meant to be."

"It was really the beginning of my awakening to Peter's music and to modern music in general," said N'Dour. "To me Peter is like a true moslem brother."

N'Dour returned for more concerts in England in July 1986, playing again at the Town and Country Club, and a few days later at the WOMAD festival in Clevedon, near Bristol. Gabriel agreed to appear on BBC TV *Breakfast Time* with N'Dour on condition that he only talked about N'Dour and the WOMAD festival. Gabriel then invited N'Dour back into the studio to add more vocals to a remix of the US single 'In Your Eyes' released in October 1986, and also put on the B-side of the UK single 'Don't Give Up' released in November 1986. The result was one of the most enchanting moments on any Peter Gabriel record.

In September 1986 N'Dour joined Gabriel on the North Lawn of the United Nations building in New York for the International Day of Peace concert. In November he joined the Peter Gabriel world tour, accompanying him over eleven months.

"What was really touching was that Peter came out on stage and said, 'I want you to listen to these marvellous musicians, they make the best music coming out of Africa', which was very humble of him, he didn't need to do it," said N'Dour.

"People said what's this, but when we finished our thirty minutes I felt they were thinking, let's see some more of this. By the time we got back on for 'In Your Eyes' there was a very strong feeling." Gabriel also brought African dancers on stage for the joyous 'In Your Eyes' and danced with N'Dour, who stayed for the 'Biko' finale.

"I thought about Peter producing my next record, but Peter said no, he was not a producer. He said he would sing on it if I wanted him to, that would make him very happy as he felt very close." N'Dour's association with Gabriel led to him singing on the Paul Simon hit 'Diamonds On the Soles Of Her Shoes' from the *Graceland* album and has opened up a wide audience for his music in the west.

Another completion date was set for the *So* album, 14 December 1985. But, like the 31 July date, that passed with still more work to do. The major delay was now caused by Gabriel's lack of lyrics. Daniel Lanois was so frustrated he resorted to drastic, supposedly playful, action. He locked Peter Gabriel in a back room in the studio, nailing up a sliding door, and said he would not be let out until some lyrics had been completed. "It was meant to be a joke, but he didn't take it as a joke. He did a few hours later," said Lanois.

"I think it is the most upset I've seen him at the studio," said David Rhodes. "One of the technicians let him out after about twenty minutes." Throughout the recording of the album, Gabriel would frequently interrupt the sessions in the evening to maintain his tradition of 'kissing time', leaving the studio to wish Melanie and Anna goodnight, before carrying on recording. He would also try to drive the girls to school in the mornings.

"I always think that the way Peter works makes the studio very much a natural part of his life," said David Rhodes. "If he's not in a great mood then that sometimes spills over. I think albums three and four are darker, but that was him not letting his more playful spirits out. I don't know whether he would agree with that."

The final touches were made to the album in January 1986. On Saturday, 8 February, Ed Rosenblatt and Gary Gersh from Geffen Records arrived with Gail Colson to hear the album. The following Tuesday, 11 February pressing of the *So* album started. It was exactly a year and £200,000 after the first sessions.

Ten days later the album artwork was finished. Gabriel had decided on an unadulterated picture of himself for the cover for the first time and went with pictures by Trevor Key.

An ordinary, quite flattering, moody picture would not be noteworthy for most other artists. But for Gabriel it was a departure not to deface himself. His previous excuse had been that he did it to annoy his mother. The *So* photograph represented the final casting off of his mask, it betrayed a greater self-confidence and pride. It was also a good move commercially, as Phil Collins had found with *Face Value*. He succumbed to record company pressure and gave the album a proper title. But *So* is about as close as one could get to not having a title. "It has a nice shape but very little meaning," said Gabriel.

The single 'Sledgehammer' was released on 24 April 1986, one month before the album's release. It was a new and unexpected departure for Gabriel. Upbeat, up mood, and rude. Gabriel thought up the funky groove and the title long before the rest of the lyrics followed.

In notes about the album, Gabriel wrote: "This is an attempt to recreate some of the spirit and style of the music that most excited me as a teenager – sixties soul. The lyrics of many of these songs were full of playful, sexual innuendo and this is my contribution to that songwriting tradition." He told one interviewer: "Part of what I was trying to say was that sometimes sex can break through barriers when other forms of communication are not working too well." The sledgehammer was the physical means of breaking through. "There is a phrase by Nietzsche about what constitutes a good book, which he said should be 'Like an axe in a frozen sea'. That triggered me off to think of tools, not to put too fine a point on the word. Obviously there was a lot of sexual metaphor there. I was trying to write in the old blues' tradition, much of which is preoccupied with mating activities. The idea was the sledgehammer would bring about a mini-harvest festival."

Gabriel had been sent a showreel of fledgling American video director Stephen R. Johnson, by Tessa Watts, then Director of Video at Virgin Records. She had met Johnson through top video director Steve Barron who recruited Johnson to his Limelight Productions company.

Watts was intrigued by Johnson's technique of pixellation on a showreel he showed her which included a college film called *Homebody*. This was first spotted by David Byrne of Talking Heads who used Johnson's technique on the award winning video 'Road to Nowhere'. Pixellation is a technique of shooting movement frame by frame to give the illusion of human animation. Johnson had perfected the technique through a method of synchronizing the mouth with the soundtrack.

As Watts expected, Gabriel was intrigued by Johnson's showreel. "He called me up out of the blue," said Johnson. "I was fearful of doing something with Peter Gabriel because I had such a high respect for his past work like *Shock The Monkey*. I enjoyed his stuff, I didn't want to do something with such high stakes." But Gabriel persisted and suggested a meeting. They met in

London and then Johnson went to visit Gabriel in Bath where they spent three days talking about the meaning of life over the occasional glass of wine. "He endeared himself to me," said Johnson who tried to convince him he should do a simple performance video, but Gabriel wanted animation.

Once the direction the video should take was settled, Johnson and Gabriel worked on the storyboard. They brought in Aardman Animations of Bristol, known for their TV-animated plasti-man Morph and Scotch Videotape advertisement skeleton. Stephen Johnson was impressed with the special-effects work of Stephen and Tim Quay, known as the Brothers Quay, who animated the fruit, fish, fowl and model-train effects on the video. "The first idea that I had for the video before I involved The Brothers Quay was the fruit theme, which set the style for the rest of it. I took it as a purely sexual metaphor," said Johnson.

The day before shooting began on 7 April, 1986, Johnson had last-minute doubts about the effects working. "Steve was saying, 'We will never do it, I think we should cancel it', because everything was so wild and undecided," said Gail Colson. But everyone held their nerve. It took 100 hours of shooting over eight days at the Aardman Studio and Bristol University's Glynne Wickham studio theatre. Gabriel posed twenty-five times for every second of final film, once for each frame.

He had to suffer for his art. "At some points I was in agony," Gabriel said. "For the train sequence, which lasts ten seconds, I had to be in the same position for six hours – the track had to be built up a little bit each time and the smoke had to be moved round as the train moved along. The fruit smelt all right after a few hours under the studio lights, but the fish stank."

The video starts with a constellation changing into a field of plasticine sperm, which appears at various points later on. A series of surreal scenes follow including the model steam-train going round his head, to match the opening line of 'Sledgehammer', 'You could have a steam train'. Then comes a paper plane and clouds cover his made-up face. It took six hours of shooting to get the effect of the sky covering Gabriel's face suspended in the clouds, which was used only for a few seconds in the final edit.

Countless images make up the video, the visuals are as densely packed as some of his lyrics. The big dipper and bumper cars, the fish around his head, the fruit-cage and the face made up of fruit, the plasticine model head of Gabriel that metamorphoses into sledgehammers, limbs and naked figures, and the head which finally disintegrates. Almost imperceptible are the quail and pheasant used to give the illusion of growth after hatching from the dancing egg, all before the headless plucked cabaret chickens, bought from Sainsbury's, start to strut.

Gabriel dances with animated wallpaper as a backdrop with black soul sisters in formation behind him. He sits on a stool and then makes way for momentary cameos from his daughters Anna and Melanie, followed by some schoolfriends who dance around their father.

The final sequence is of a constellation of stars, in reality Christmas-tree lights, against a black backdrop. Starman Gabriel is swathed in lights and walks off into the universe, ending as he began. The final scene, a last-minute addition after filming had finished and already gone over budget, was important to complete what he saw as the circle of life and death implied in the higher interpretation of the song. "I was so happy because it made the video work on a different level," said Johnson.

Johnson is ecstatic in his praise. "Peter is a wonderful human being, he is a good soul. I have never seen him raise his voice at anyone in anger, all the people that worked around him, his janitor even, he treats with dignity, respect and human decency. It is a rare thing, there is no streak of 'I am a big rock star'. He is a sensitive, intelligent, humane person. He is not telling me to say this."

The video cost £120,000, though not in the *Thriller* or *Bad* budget range, it was still a vast financial gamble for an artist who had not exactly stormed the singles charts in eighteen years of recording. But the investment clearly paid off, propelling the single to Number Four in the UK in May 1986, and to Number One in the USA in July where it ironically dislodged Genesis' single 'Invisible Touch'. The album topped the charts on both sides of the Atlantic, going straight to Number One on release in the UK on 19 May. By the summer of 1987 the *So* album had sold 5 million copies worldwide, having gone double platinum in America with 2 million copies and double platinum in the UK with 600,000 copies.

Gabriel sent a copy of the new album to Alan Parker, then in Los Angeles working on the film *Angel Heart*. The day he received the album Parker was working with Mickey Rourke and Lisa Bonet, on what would become the film's most controversial scene, earning it an X-rating normally reserved for near-pornographic films. "The scene is two people making love," said Parker. "It is a nightmare sequence and the ceiling is leaking. The rain is coming through and this changes to blood.

They drink the blood as they are making love. This caused me terrible problems and I had to trim ten seconds off the scene.

"The irony is that the first track on *So* is 'Red Rain'. I thought 'Oh God', and I wrote Peter a little card immediately and said, 'How astonishing that we are thousands of miles apart and I was about to do a scene that was a song you'd already done'."

The red rain Gabriel alludes to is blood. It is an emotive ballad based around a Brazilian rhythm. "Years ago I had a recurring dream. I was swimming in a swirling sea of red and black. I remember a tremendous turmoil as the sea was parted by two white walls. A series of bottles, of human shape, were carrying the red water from one wall to another, then dropping down to smash into little pieces at the bottom of the second wall," Gabriel explained. "I used this for a scene in a story in which the red sea and red rain from which it was formed represented thoughts and feelings that were being denied.

"I believe that if feelings or pain do not get brought out, not only do they fester and grow stronger but they manifest themselves in the external world. For example, if a personal storm cannot be outwardly expressed it will appear in life in events with other people or in this case in a cloudburst."

> red rain is pouring down
> pouring down all over me
> and I can't watch anymore
> no more denial
> it's so hard to lay down in all of this

'Don't Give Up' was a stylistic departure, in the main a country ballad, but also inspired by gospel, and with a lyric in the style of those traditions. Gabriel originally wanted a country singer to accompany him, but instead asked his friend and previous collaborator Kate Bush.

The twelve-string guitar, in the style of the Byrds, found its way back on to vinyl for 'That Voice Again', ten years after having been abandoned along with other Genesis musical associations. Like 'Red Rain', 'That Voice Again' was a reworking of songs written with the Mozo project in mind several years previously.

'In Your Eyes' is a gentle, soulful ballad which underwent a major lyrical change during the recording. The song contains much of Gabriel's own personal realizations resulting from his separation from Jill. For the lyrics Gabriel transplanted ideas

212

from another as yet unrecorded song, 'Sagrada'. "It's a love song. There is a tradition in Africa that intrigued me; that of writing love songs so they can be heard as love of God or the love between men and women. No one seems to do that in western lyrics so I thought I would try mixing images. The eyes are clearly a focus point for the soul." In the chorus the imagery is at its most ambiguous.

> . . . in your eyes
> I see the doorway to a thousand churches
> in your eyes
> the resolution of all the fruitless searches
> in your eyes
> I see the light and the heat
> in your eyes
> oh, I want to be that complete . .

The most melancholic song on *So* is 'Mercy Street', Gabriel's tribute to poet Anne Sexton. He dedicated three pages in his 1986/7 tour programme to her, including printing in full her poem 'In The Beach House'.

The tour programme explained: "Peter Gabriel's song 'Mercy Street' is based upon the life and work of the American poet Anne Sexton (1928–1974), with whom Peter has long been fascinated. Anne married early, and following the birth of her first child in 1953 she suffered her first breakdown, one of many that she was to have during her lifetime . . ." Sexton was encouraged to enrol in a poetry workshop by a psychiatrist after her first suicide attempt in 1956 and published her first book in 1960. According to Sexton's friend and colleague Maxine Kumin, "No other American poet in our time has cried aloud publicly so many private details."

The poem 'In The Beach House', quoted in the programme, is rich in imagery, feelings and sounds, but it is difficult to understand literally, like many Gabriel lyrics. Her poem '45 Mercy Street' was part of an unpublished collection she was still revising at the time of her death. Some of the poems were omitted by her daughter when the work was published, as she deemed them too personal and likely to cause pain to those still living. "I don't reveal skeletons that would hurt anyone. They may hurt the dead, but the dead belong to me. Only once in a while do they talk back," is a quote from Sexton used in Gabriel's tour programme. It mirrors his own reluctance to be obviously biographical or condemn in song anyone close to him. It is the spirit of Sexton, and Gabriel's empathy for solitary figures and those who have known suffering, that endears her to him.

Unlike 'The Family And The Fishing Net', Gabriel's homage to Dylan Thomas on the fourth album, Gabriel has not mimicked Sexton's style in Mercy Street. Instead he has borrowed the title and a few phrases.

> I hold matches at the street signs
> for it is dark,
> as dark as the leathery dead
> and I have lost my green Ford,
> my house in the suburbs,
> two little kids
> sucked up like pollen by the bee in me
> and a husband
> who has wiped off his eyes
> in order not to see my inside out . . .

(Anne Sexton, '45 Mercy Street', 1971–74)

> 'all of the buildings, all of those cars
> were once just a dream
> in somebody's head . . .
>
> dreaming of mercy st
> wear your inside out
> dreaming of mercy
> in your daddy's arms again . . .'

(Peter Gabriel, 'Mercy Street', 1986)

"When I discovered her work by chance in a bookstore I was struck that, unlike most writers who are conscious of their peers or their audience, she was writing entirely for herself," said Gabriel. "'Mercy Street' is filled with messages and imagery of dreams, and a constant search for a suitable father figure, whether it be a doctor, a priest, or God. That search kept her alive longer than many around her perhaps thought she could bear, gave her life meaning, and now her work gives hope to others. That's a kind of magic, I think. Creation as therapy, both the fact and the gentle endorsement of that, is a thread in the material on *So*."

During the recording of the album, the song's working title was 'Forro', based on a Brazilian rhythm Gabriel discovered while visiting the country. The 'Mercy Street' lyrics originally went with another tune, while the 'Forro' rhythm itself already had two previous sets of lyrics. Gabriel explained the derivation of Forro. "While the English and Irish workers were building the railways in Brazil they used to throw wild parties to which the Brazilians were invited with the invitation 'For All'. The Brazilians assumed that the 'For All', or 'Forro' as it later became, was the name for the event and originated the rhythm on which this track is written."

If 'Mercy Street' is melancholic, the mood is immediately altered with the next album track, 'Big Time'. It is a brash, funk number with bluesy organ based on a pattern derived, says Gabriel, from a Nigerian groove.

The press reviews for *So* were split as usual between the openly hostile and enthusiastic. "Brilliant," said the *Guardian*; "Universal message that hope springs eternal," ran the *Times* headline; "The music is studied to death," said *Sounds*; "I love it," said *Smash Hits*. "The music which Peter Gabriel makes is terrifically uninteresting. It says nothing, being merely an ordering of sounds, mostly artificial," said John McKenna in Eire's *Hot Press*. And Johnny Black in *The Beat*: "Here, if you dare let it in, dare to listen closer, is music as exorcism, music to tear your fears out, music to drown inside and still come up feeling better for it."

One unexpected outcome of his new stature was the request by Placido Domingo for Gabriel to perform on his album *España: The Passion of Goya*. Gabriel was asked to sing the tracks 'Picture it' and 'Viva España.' The record's composer Maury Yeston felt Gabriel was in tune with Goya's work, but Gabriel, although flattered, declined the chance to sing with the world's leading operatic star.

Gabriel interrupted his international promotion of 'Sledgehammer' and *So* at the end of May 1986 to join the Conspiracy of Hope caravan tour across the United States for two weeks. He returned to the United States in November to start his first solo tour in the wake of *So*'s success. Half the band were stalwarts Tony Levin and David Rhodes, and joining them, Manu Katche, who had been on the Amnesty tour, and for the first time David Sancious on keyboards, a veteran of Bruce Springsteen's early E Street Band.

The tour was called 'This Way Up' though the title was rarely referred to. The first USA and Canadian leg of the eleven month on/off tour started on 7 November 1986 in Rochester, Illinois,

215

and finished nearly six weeks later in Los Angeles. It was Gabriel's first solo shows for just over three years. The success of the singles, albums and videos had broadened the audiences. The denim-clad, earnest intellectuals were now overtaken by fans of all social types and age groups, many unfamiliar with anything but *So* material.

Seven out of *So*'s eight tracks were performed at the first shows, not including 'This Is The Picture'. The rest of the set was made up of tracks from the previous four studio albums. The critics seemed to approve. "There is – frequent press carping to the contrary – no art/rock pretence in Gabriel's ethno-treasure hunt . . . ," wrote David Fricke for *Melody Maker* after seeing the Madison Square Gardens show in New York. "In embracing diversity Gabriel has in fact created a resonant pop sound beholden to no fad yet socially responsive and emotionally direct in its lyric address . . . Gabriel's rousing encore duet with Youssou N'Dour on 'In Your Eyes' was an exhilarating demonstration of how easily two cultures can come together in a common inspirational sound. This, indeed, was the world calling – and 20,000 people answered with a hardy hello."

Even the *NME*'s Los Angeles correspondent was complimentary. "With his dramatic lyricism, good old-fashioned barnstormers like 'Sledgehammer' and the glorious 'Solsbury Hill', and his oft-quoted commitment to Amnesty International, Peter Gabriel has achieved the perfect potpourri of poetry, pop and politics, a performance artist in the true sense," wrote Jane Garcia.

Gabriel discarded the 'monkey' face make-up of the 1982/3 tour for the merest facial highlights. He used hexagonal building blocks for leaping on and off, remnants from the 1982/3 tour. Together with lighting engineer Jonathan Smeeton he devised the preying-mantis mobile lighting cranes, which were at their most menacing when they ensnared him crouching foetus-like on the floor for 'Mercy Street'. Gabriel continued with his backwards leap into the vast crowd for 'Lay Your Hands On Me'. The largest crowds of the tour were on his return to the United States to play the Giants Stadium at Meadowlands, New Jersey, in July 1987 when there were over 50,000 people for each of the two nights.

Rehearsals for the tour had taken place at Gabriel's new studio complex, christened 'Real World', in the village of Box just outside Bath, five miles from Ashcombe House. It is an attractive set of mainly Victorian buildings including a house and converted barns, with a central moat.

It was still a building site in October 1986 when the band went in to clear a space where they could practise. Faced with little choice but to leave Ashcombe at the end of his lease, he decided to invest in a state-of-the-art audio-video studio. Box embodies many of Gabriel's long-term plans. "He's not going to be trying to play rock and roll for the next ten years," commented David Rhodes.

Box would not have been possible without the increased financial success. Throughout 1988 the studio was expected to continue eating up the bulk of his royalty cheques.

By autumn 1987 some of his investment plans had to be curtailed as the budget got close to £2 million. If all Gabriel's plans materialize, it could eventually cost up to £5 million. As opposed to Ashcombe House, which was essentially his private facility occasionally leased out to other artists, Real World at Box is a full-blown commercial enterprise which will subsidize Gabriel's hunger for the latest technological hardware.

"I wanted to create another new way of recording and have a sort of cellular structure around some shared facilities and shared intelligence, so I have one large acoustic studio, then a lot of control ones around the outside. Instead of having a Fairlight, Synclaviers and all the rest in each studio, you can share some of the intelligence and access it by computer from any point on the site. We would like to have five or six other artists on the site, each with a room so that it can be a functioning community." He also planned it to have a public café and facilities that visiting artists and musicians could afford to use, as well as being a facility for technological research and development.

In February 1987 Gabriel went on a technology tour of the United States. He visited the Media Lab at the Massachusetts Institute of Technology guided by Stewart Brand, founder of the *Whole Earth Catalogue*, who has written a book about the research centre. Gabriel then went to the West Coast and toured the Silicon Valley high-technology sites outside San Francisco with Peter Schwarz, his friend from the days of the space film project. It was an excuse to find out the latest developments in computers and videos, as well as seeing what he could use for Real World.

He saw computer graphics, sound technology, and speech-recognition computers. He visited Sun Computers and Apple Computers. At Apple the engineers had digitized 'Red Rain' from the *So* album and played it to him. That spring Apple used 'Red Rain' as the theme music for the launch of their advanced new Macintosh II computer in Los Angeles.

Gabriel and Schwarz also visited Industrial Light and Magic, film director George Lucas' studio in San Rafael, California. They saw the Pixar, a 3-D digitizer, capable of tracing an image and then reproducing it with the appearance of depth on a screen. Gabriel planned to buy one for Box at a cost of $70,000. "I would like to get Box set up to be ready for developing long-form video which I think will become a really exciting medium." At the moment long-form video is in its infancy and mainly comprises several videos strung together. Gabriel envisages a new art-form where film or video directors could work in parallel with musicians in the creation of the work, and Real World is set up specifically to do that.

Gabriel planned to set up a company jointly with David Gardener, who edited his *Games Without Frontiers* video in 1980. (Gardener has the distinction of turning down the edit of the *Sledgehammer* video because he was too busy working on the Channel 4 Chart Show.) Gardener and Gabriel found they were thinking along parallel lines, trying to use the advanced semi-intelligent transputer microchip linked to a conventional computer creating digital effects. They plan to use the Real World Studios and a facility in London to house their advanced technology post-production company. Gabriel wants Real World to have a library of video effects for use on video synthesizers, equivalent to the library of audio effects used on the Fairlight CMI and other audio synthesizers.

A long-standing ambition of Gabriel's, dating back ten years, has been to have a video tour. It would combine live performance with a combination of giant video screens and banks of smaller screens that instead of just giving close-ups of him on stage would complement the show with various images. "The possibilities are enormous, but so are the costs," he said. He tried to get sponsorship from Sony and other major consumer electronics manufacturers, but none was forthcoming. His plan is to experiment initially at small venues.

This project was resurrected at the same time as the video album. He had intended making a video of every track on *So*. "We worked out the budget. If I do all of the tracks, it will cost something like $1.5 million. And the possible income, even if it's very successful, will be something like $750,000. So I have either to trim my ideas or trim the number of tracks. I don't mind not making a profit on it, but I do mind losing money, because the studio itself is about three times as expensive as we were planning." Gabriel did not film all the tracks, but compensated by adding the best of his previous video promos on the video album due for release in spring 1988.

As well as *Sledgehammer*, the videos include *Big Time*, also directed by Steve Johnson. The animated plasticine sperm of *Sledgehammer* make another appearance in this video. Gabriel is dressed in a loud evening jacket and bow tie. His big head is superimposed on a tiny body. Johnson again literally translated the lyrics and we see the big house, the bed and some phallic symbolism.

The promo video for *Don't Give Up* has been haunted by its own title. Gabriel did give up with Jim O'Brien, director of acclaimed TV series *The Monocled Mutineer* and part of *The Jewel In The Crown*. "We had this dramatic script and I suddenly panicked at the eleventh hour and pulled out of it, which I found difficult as I had developed a lot of respect for Jim," said Gabriel.

He then called in Kevin Godley and Lol Creme, who had an unshaven Gabriel trying to look like a Depression-era proletarian clasping Kate Bush to his breast. Gabriel and Bush slowly rotate on the spot while the giant flaming sun goes in and out of eclipse behind them. "I wasn't that happy with the way it came out, but it was getting late and the single needed a video," said Gabriel.

He then hired American Jim Blashfield, who directed *The Boy In The Bubble* for Paul Simon and *And She Was* for Talking Heads. But because of his commitments Gabriel, for the first time with a video, was unable to oversee the production. He got back a kitchen-sink drama of doleful husband and long-suffering wife played by actors.

Refusing to give up, Gabriel asked Blashfield to try again, this time making minimal use of the actors. "That song has to be 100 per cent convincing, it's quite personal, and it can easily fall into sentimentality or kitsch," said Gabriel. "It was redone at extra cost, but it had all been a bit of a disaster."

It is a clear example of how fastidious Gabriel is with his work. He cannot possibly hope to recoup the expenses of remaking *Don't Give Up*. The single was released with the Godley and Creme version, and Blashfield's promo is unlikely to add significantly to sales of the video album.

Gabriel hired illustrator and photographer Matt Mahurin, who accompanied him to Nicaragua, to shoot videos for 'Mercy Street' and 'Red Rain'. Both are high on atmosphere and low on action. *Mercy Street*, in black and white, has bleak images of a boat being pushed out on smooth sand, a woman's face in shadow. Gabriel appears wearing a raincoat pushing out the boat. *Red Rain* has Gabriel appearing in shadow and images of a dancer with a veil, a glow on the horizon that could be a nuclear bomb exploding, a woman's petticoats lifting to reveal a crying baby, and the cracked scorched earth bursting into flames.

Gabriel was also collaborating with artist Graham Dean for the first time since the experimental *Undercurrents* in 1981. They were planning to co-direct *In Your Eyes,* which would be Gabriel's first attempt, albeit in partnership, at direction. They made use of the video facilities at Box.

The video album was planned in tandem with a feature-length film for cinema release of Gabriel in concert. Gabriel's visit to Nicaragua in May 1987 was to see if he and Alex Cox could work together. He also met up with David Lynch, director of *The Elephant Man, Eraserhead* and *Blue Velvet* and Bernardo Bertolucci, director of *Last Tango in Paris, Lunar* and *1900.* He also talked to Wollker Schlondorf, director of *Tin Drum,* but all had other commitments.

"Live shows can be pretty boring by the time they get to film," said Gabriel. "I would like to try and somehow get to represent what it is like to be in my position. Normally you have the concert as seen from the audience, it would be nice to cut away and treat the music as raw material so if you want to stop in the middle of a number and cut away to silence you can do that rather than saying the music has to stay intact." Gabriel wanted to satisfy the demand for performance footage while escaping the tedium and clichés associated with concert films and videos.

While Gabriel was on the last European leg of the tour that had begun in November 1986 the plan for a concert film finally fell into place. He had been seen by over one million people by the time he played in Budapest, Hungary, on 15 September 1987, his first time behind the Iron Curtain.

Martin Scorsese, a friend for the past few years, came to the rescue of the concert film. Though Scorsese was unable to direct it, he sent instead his cinematographer Mike Chapman who worked with him on *The Last Waltz* concert film of The Band and Bob Dylan, Michael Jackson's *Bad* video as well as *New York, New York, Raging Bull* and *Taxi Driver.*

Jackman filmed Gabriel at extra dates in Athens in October 1987, setting up on Scorsese's instructions the set, lighting and camera angles for Scorsese to edit. The film may have fantasy sequences written by Gabriel with playwright Dennis Potter whom Gabriel had met before going on the final European leg.

One song that did not make it on to the *So* album was

'Sagrada', "named after the Church of the Sagrada Familia, which Gaudi, the visionary architect, began building in Barcelona in 1884 and was obsessed with until his death in 1926," said Gabriel. "The song was an interplay between his way of building and that of a lady named Sarah Winchester. She was the heir to the Winchester rifle fortune who, in San Jose, California, started building this enormous home because she believed she was haunted by the ghosts of all the people who had been killed by the rifle. By her death in 1922, she'd added 160 rooms."

After fifteen years of talking about it in public, Gabriel set about planning in earnest his own visionary building scheme in 1986. He found he had to redefine his original concept of the Real World theme park and make it less a park and more a functional building, albeit a massive one.

Gabriel was an old friend of Neville Quarry, a well-known Australian architect who presented a TV show called *The Inventors*. Quarry thought of Gabriel when the New South Wales Ministry of Works asked for submissions for the Darling Harbour leisure development in Sydney in 1986. He suggested Gabriel hired imaginative London architect Will Alsop of the Alsop and Lyall partnership. The firm is known internationally for its non-conformist inner-city designs. In the profession they like to use words like 'responsive' and 'structurally expressive' to describe their work.

Over the years Gabriel had tried to interest painters, psychologists, architects, musicians and film-makers in the new art of 'Experience Design'. By the time he finally commissioned Alsop to design a Real World scheme for Darling Harbour in May 1986 there were just two and a half weeks left before the closing date for submissions. Gabriel had envisaged an underground park on a wilderness site, preferably close to the sea. The relatively small two-acre Sydney site was by the sea, but in the middle of the city. Even so the invitation was too good to pass up.

Gabriel wanted a theme park that was opposite in philosophy to the passive consumerism of Disneyland. "It would have to be a place where you had fun because you couldn't survive without it. If it was just serious and a place where you were challenged then it would be too much. Maybe you would involve a regular funfair in it as well.

"I picture a lot of places in the future that are a combination of holiday camp, university and art gallery. It's the way things must go. With mass unemployment, it seems there are only three solutions to the prospect of massive riots – education, entertainment, or warfare. And the first two are preferable to conscription."

Gabriel wanted to extend the notion of transformation and make it a practical outcome of visiting the park. He talked with psychologist R. D. Laing about his idea for a Ride of Fears where you confront your phobias and are awarded bravery tokens if you come through them without pressing the panic button. He wanted a Big Dipper simulator. He was interested in a device where you could place Walkman-style TV screens over the eyes to give a 3-D effect for computer-linked interactive video. The participant creates his own characters and travels through an adventure like Jason and The Argonauts or The Pilgrim's Progress.

Gabriel also envisaged using Magic Motion Machines, a theatrical flight simulator for 40 people that simulates space flight. There would be computer-controlled spaces where the walls changed, video games that groups of people could play at the same time, pressure-sensitive floors that could activate patterns on giant video screens. Music would also play a vital role, and Gabriel talked to David Byrne about ideas for aural environments.

The Sydney Darling Harbour plan was based on a 250-metre-long crescented building that would include the world's longest swimming pool. It would be raised like a bridge, giving swimmers a view. The pool was to go the entire length of the building but would be only three metres wide, forcing people to keep moving. And, fittingly for Australia, the building would also house the world's longest bar, again the entire length of the building.

Alsop's task was to interpret Gabriel's frequently vague ideas. "It seemed to me much more interesting to have something like that in the middle of a city," said Alsop. "To have something that is free to walk through and see what is going on and then pay to experience what you want. I was interested in the idea of mixing these experiences with prosaic parts of everyday life." He wanted that to include supermarkets, launderettes and hairdressers for example so the mundane could be enjoyed in a new context, as well as providing the opportunity to have a go at state-of-the-art 'rides'.

Gabriel and Alsop met Richard Branson to see if the Virgin Group were interested in investing in the £30 million Sydney project. Branson was interested in principle.

The plans were submitted and the results announced a month later. Gabriel and Alsop's theme park was rejected in favour of a more traditional funfair.

Gabriel had taken on the role of developer of the Sydney

project, so he had to pay Alsop's undisclosed fees. "The return is that it actually gave physical presence to some very vague ideas," said Alsop. "At least it shifted the Real World project, which was in Peter's head, to a description of just what it should be, therefore it is money well spent, and it gives you good grounds on which to continue with the conversation."

The plans were resurrected a year later, in May 1987, after Alsop was invited by the city of Cologne to submit designs for a media park on disused railway sidings near the city centre, for a space four or five times the size of the Sydney site.

It would be like a giant version of Gabriel's Box studios, to include auditoria, recording, video, film and TV studios. But it would also incorporate the Sydney idea of a long, adaptable building. The swimming pool was to be included, shops, other commercial activity, private apartments, and the 'rides'.

Central to Alsop's ideas is the flexibility of buildings, able to expand to meet changing needs, with glass floors that can move. "I like the analogy of the glass floor being a glass table. The nice thing about tables is the way you can reset them to suit different occasions."

The Cologne scheme is planned to cost £150 million. The Real World theme 'park' would take up just part of the structure, probably costing just £2 million to £3 million. Added to that would be the cost of the 'rides', at least a few more million. Private investors like Branson would again be needed to back the project. Alsop's models, drawings and report, based on Gabriel's ideas, were submitted in August 1987.

Alsop is convinced Real World, or what he once called Gabrieland, will become a reality. "The difficult task is that though we know what it could be, we have to be aware of the commercial reality, and if we let Peter go off on his own it could be a wonderful place, but a financial disaster.

"Involved in the business he is, and he is a lot more intelligent than a lot of people in that business, Peter knows it is not a very real world that he occupies. He needs to place his involvement with music in a broader cultural context and Real World is a way of grounding it. Real World gives him the opportunity to talk to people in different disciplines, and takes him away from music a little bit, but it can also feed back into the music in other ways.

"Architecture in the end is all about delight. Which is why Real World is a wonderful thing for us to begin to think about, it is also about delight."

EPILOGUE

As this book was going to press Peter Gabriel's personal life was in a state of flux. In October 1987 he again separated from Jill and once again made contact with Rosanna Arquette, who by then had separated from her husband, record producer and film score composer James Newton-Howard.

As always in Peter Gabriel's life his current state of mind was hard to ascertain. What he was certain of was that although he loved both Jill and his daughters Anna and Melanie, his love for Rosanna had created impossible conflicts. The separation he and Jill had worked so long to avoid had become inevitable.

He will not sever contacts with his family. After the separation he slept on the floor of his office at the Real World Studios in Box, but intended to find a new home in the Bath area.

Discussing these matters is difficult for all parties. Their concern is to give an honest account of their lives. In so doing it is hard to know where the boundaries of privacy and personal conflict lie in relation to the interests of the reader seeking to understand the emotional and intellectual dilemmas that have gone into shaping Peter Gabriel's work.

PETER GABRIEL
DISCOGRAPHY
1968–1988

This definitive discography includes all Peter Gabriel's recordings. I have not catalogued cassette and compact disc releases where they do not differ from the original albums. The release of the first albums on compact disc in May 1987 completed the CD catalogue of all Peter Gabriel's albums.

The recordings are all UK releases with the exception of the two German version albums recorded by Gabriel with German lyrics.

I am indebted to Sinclair Salisbury for his work on this discography.

ALBUMS

Genesis:

From Genesis to Revelation *(March 1969)*
'Where the Sour Turns to Sweet'; 'In the Beginning'; 'Fireside Song'; 'The Serpent'; 'Am I Very Wrong?'; 'In the Wilderness'; 'The Conqueror'; 'In Hiding'; 'One Day'; 'Window'; 'In Limbo'; 'Silent Sun'; 'A Place to Call My Own'.
(Decca SKL 4990)

Trespass *(October 1970)*
'Looking for Someone'; 'White Mountain'; 'Visions of Angels'; 'Stagnation'; 'Dusk'; 'The Knife'.
(Charisma CAS 1020)

Nursery Cryme *(November 1971)*
'The Musical Box': 'For Absent Friends'; 'The Return of the Giant Hogweed'; 'Seven Stones'; Harold The Barrel'; 'Harlequin'; 'The Fountain of Salmacis'.
(Charisma CAS 1052)

Foxtrot *(October 1972)*
'Watcher of the Skies'; 'Time Table'; 'Get 'Em Out by Friday'; 'Can-Utility and the Coastliners'; 'Horizons'; 'Supper's Ready': 'i. Lover's Leap, ii. The Guaranteed Eternal Sanctuary Man, iii. Ikhnaton and Itsacon and Their Band of Merry Men, iv. How Dare I Be So Beautiful?, v. Willow Farm, vi. Apocalypse in 9/8 (Co-Starring the Delicious Talents of Gabble Ratchet, vii. As Sure As Eggs Is Eggs (Aching Men's Feet)'.
(Charisma CAS 1058)

Genesis Live *(August 1973)*
'Watcher of the Skies'; 'Get 'Em Out By Friday'; 'The Return of the Giant Hogweed'; 'The Musical Box'; 'The Knife'.
(Charisma CLASS 1)

Selling England by the Pound *(September 1973)*
'Dancing With the Moonlit Knight'; 'I Know What I Like (In Your Wardrobe)'; 'Firth of Fifth'; 'More Fool Me'; 'The Battle of Epping Forest'; 'After the Ordeal'; 'The Cinema Show'; 'Aisle of Plenty'.
(Charisma CAS 1074)

The Lamb Lies Down on Broadway *(November 1974)*
'The Lamb Lies Down on Broadway'; 'Fly on a Windshield'; 'Broadway Melody of 1974'; 'Cuckoo Cocoon'; 'In the Cage'; 'The Grand Parade of Lifeless Packaging'; 'Back in NYC'; 'Hairless Heart'; 'Counting Out Time'; 'The Carpet Crawlers'; 'The Chamber of 32 Doors'; 'Lillywhite Lilith'; 'The Waiting Room'; 'Anyway'; 'Here Comes the Supernatural Anaesthetist'; 'The Lamia'; 'Silent Sorrow in Empty Boats'; 'The Colony of Slippermen (The Arrival, A Visit to the Doktor, The Raven)'; 'Ravine'; 'The Light Dies Down on Broadway'; 'Riding the Scree'; 'In the Rapids'; 'It'.
(Charisma CGS 101)

Solo:

Peter Gabriel *(February 1977)*
'Moribund the Burgermeister'; 'Solsbury Hill'; 'Modern Love'; 'Excuse Me'; 'Humdrum'; 'Slowburn'; 'Waiting for the Big One'; 'Down the Dolce Vita'; 'Here Comes The Flood'.
(Charisma, CDS 4006)

Peter Gabriel *(June 1978)*
'On The Air'; 'Do It Yourself'; 'Mother of Violence'; 'A Wonderful Day in a One Way World'; 'White Shadow'; 'Indigo'; 'Animal Magic'; 'Exposure'; 'Flotsam & Jetsam'; 'Perspective'; 'Home Sweet Home'.
(Charisma, CDS 4013)

Peter Gabriel *(May 1980)*
'Intruder'; 'No Self Control'; 'The Start'; 'I Don't Remember'; 'Family Snapshot'; 'And Through the Wire'; 'Games Without Frontiers'; 'Not One of Us'; 'Lead a Normal Life'; 'Biko'.
(Charisma CDS 4019)

Peter Gabriel *(September 1982)*
'The Rhythm of the Heat'; 'San Jacinto'; 'I Have the Touch'; 'The Family and the Fishing Net'; 'Shock the Monkey'; 'Lay Your Hands on Me'; 'Wallflower'; 'Kiss of Life'.
(Charisma PG4)

Peter Gabriel Plays Live *(June 1983)*
'The Rhythm of the Heat'; 'I Have the Touch'; 'Not One of Us'; 'Family Snapshot'; 'DIY'; 'The Family and the Fishing Net'; 'Intruder'; 'I Go Swimming'; 'San Jacinto'; 'Solsbury Hill'; 'No Self Control'; 'I Don't Remember'; 'Shock the Monkey'; 'Humdrum'; 'On the Air'; 'Biko'.
(Charisma PGDL 1)

Birdy – music from the film, by Peter Gabriel *(March 1985)*
'At Night'; 'Floating Dogs'; 'Quiet and Alone'; 'Close Up' (from 'Family Snapshot'); 'Slow Water'; 'Dressing the Wound'; 'Birdy's Flight' (from 'Not One of Us'); 'Slow Marimbas'; 'The Heat' (from 'The Rhythm of the Heat'); 'Sketchpad with Trumpet and Voice'; 'Under Lock and Key' (from 'Wallflower'); 'Powerhouse at the Foot of the Mountain' (from 'San Jacinto').
(Charisma/Virgin CAS 1167)

So *(May 1986)*
'Red Rain'; 'Sledgehammer'; 'Don't Give Up'; 'That Voice Again'; 'In Your Eyes'; 'Mercy Street (for Anne Sexton)'; 'Big Time (suc cess)'; 'We Do What We're Told (Milgram's 37)'.
(Charisma/Virgin PG 5)
So cassette and CD include extra track 'This is the Picture (Excellent Birds)'.

MISCELLANEOUS

Genesis:

Genesis Collection Volume One and Volume Two *(April 1975)*
Boxed set One includes 'Trespass' and 'Nursery Cryme'; Boxed set Two includes 'Foxtrot' and 'Selling England by the Pound'.
(CGS 102/CGS 103)

Genesis R-O-C-K Roots *(May 1976)*
Re-issue of 'From Genesis to Revelation' plus early singles 'Silent Sun'/'That's Me' and 'A Winter's Tale'/'One-Eyed Hound'.
(Decca ROOTS 1)

Several compilations of little note have included Genesis and Peter Gabriel tracks through the years. A sample are *Wowie Zowie – The World of Progressive Music*, released in 1969, which includes 'In The Beginning'; *Charisma Disturbance*, released in 1973, which includes 'The Return of The Giant Hogweed'; *The Old Grey Whistle Test – Take Two*, released in 1976, which includes Genesis' 'Ripples'; *An Hour of Pop Hits – Reels on Wheels*, released in 1979, with Gabriel's 'Solsbury Hill'; and *Hot Wax*, a K-Tel album released in 1980, which includes 'No Self Control'.

Solo Albums:

Ein Deutsches Album *(July 1980)*
'Eindringling'; 'Keine Selbstkontrolle'; 'Frag Mich Nicht Immer'; 'Schnappschuss (Ein Familienfoto)'; 'Und Durch Den Draht'; 'Spiel Ohne Grenzen'; 'Du Bist Nicht Wie Wir'; 'Ein Normales Leben'; 'Biko'.
(Charisma 6302 035)
German language version of third album.

Deutsches Album *(September 1982)*
'Der Rhythmus Der Hitze'; 'Das Fischernetz'; 'Kon-takt'; 'San Jacinto'; 'Schock Den Affen'; 'Handauflegen'; 'Nicht Die Erde Hat Dich Vershcluckt'; 'Mundzumundbeatmung'.
(Charisma 6302 221)
German language version of fourth album.

Peter Gabriel Plays Live *(June 1985)*
Single compact disc selection of 13 of the 16 *Plays Live* double album tracks – 'I Have the Touch'; 'Family Snapshot'; 'D.I.Y.'; 'The Family and the Fishing Net'; 'I Go Swimming'; 'San Jacinto'; 'Solsbury Hill'; 'No Self Control'; 'I Don't Remember'; 'Shock the Monkey'; 'Humdrum'; 'Biko'. In October 1987 full double CD released.
(Virgin PGDLCD1 and CDPGD100 [double])

SINGLES – SEVEN INCH

Genesis:

'The Silent Sun'/'That's Me'
(Decca F12735. February 1968)

'A Winter's Tale'/'One Eyed Hound'
(Decca F12775. May 1969)

'Where the Sour Turns to Sweet'/'In Hiding'
(Decca F12949. June 1969)

'Looking for Someone'/'Visions of Angels'
(Charisma GS1. 1970)
Promotional single for DJs.

'The Knife' Part I/'The Knife' Part II
(Charisma CB152. 1971)

'Happy the Man'/'Seven Stones'
(Charisma CB181. October 1972)

'Twilight Alehouse'
(October 1973)
One-sided flexidisc issued free with *Zig Zag* magazine.

'I Know What I Like'/'Twilight Alehouse'
(Charisma CB224. February 1974)

'Counting Out Time'/'Riding the Scree'
(Charisma CB238. November 1974)

'The Carpet Crawlers'/'Evil Jam' (live version of The Waiting Room recorded at Los Angeles Forum).
(Charisma CB251. April 1975)

Solo:

'Solsbury Hill'/Moribund the Burgermeister'
(Charisma CB301. February 1977)
A live recording of 'Solsbury Hill' from The Bottom Line, New York City on 4 October 1978, was released as a flexidisc and given away at the Hammersmith Odeon concerts in London between 20 and 24 December 1978.

'Modern Love'/'Slowburn'
(Charisma CB302. June 1977)

'D.I.Y.'/'Perspective'
(Charisma CB311. May 1978)

'D.I.Y.'/'Mother of Violence'; 'Me and My Teddy Bear'
(Charisma CB319. September 1978)
Gabriel re-arranged the Coots/Winters childrens' song.

'Games Without Frontiers'/'Start'; 'I Don't Remember'
(Charisma CB354. February 1980)

'No Self Control'/'Lead A Normal Life'
(Charisma CB360. May 1980)

'Biko'/'Shosholoza'; 'Jetzt Kommt Die Flut'
(Charisma CB370. August 1980)
33rpm 7" with full length version of Biko.

'Biko'/'Shosholoza'.
(Charisma CBD1370. August 1980)
Edited version of Biko.

'Shock the Monkey'/'Soft Dog'
(Charisma Shock 12. September 1982)
Small number of copies issued with B-side instrumental version of 'Shock the Monkey'.

'I Have the Touch'/'Across the River'
(Charisma CB405. December 1982)

'I Don't Remember'/'Solsbury Hill' (live)
(Charisma GAB 1. July 1983)

'Solsbury Hill'/'Games Without Frontiers'
(Old Gold Series 9265. July 1983)

'Walk Through The Fire'/B-side 'The Race' by Larry Carlton.
(Virgin VS689. May 1984)

'Sledgehammer'/'Don't Break This Rhythm'
(Virgin PGS 1. April 1986)

'Don't Give Up' [Duet with Kate Bush]/'In Your Eyes'
(Virgin PGS 2. October 1986)

'Don't Give Up'/'In Your Eyes'
(Virgin PGSP-2. October 1986)
Issued with limited edition video-still poster.

'Big Time'/'Curtains'
(Virgin PGS 3. March 1987)

'Red Rain'/'Ga Ga'
(Virgin PGS 4. June 1987)
'Ga Ga' is an instrumental version of 'I Go Swimming'.

SINGLES – TWELVE INCH

'Biko'/'Shosholoza', 'Jetzt Kommt Die Flut'
(Charisma CB37012. August 1980)

'Shock the Monkey'/'Soft Dog'
(Charisma Shock 12. September 1982)

'Shock the Monkey'/'Shock the Monkey' [vocal/instrumental]
(Charisma Shock 343. September 1982)

'I Go Swimming'/'Solsbury Hill'/'Shock the Monkey'
(Charisma REP1 420. May 1983)
'Limited Edition Sampler Album' for shops to promote the *Plays Live* album.

'I Don't Remember'/'Solsbury Hill'/'Humdrum', 'On The Air'
(Charisma RAD 10. May 1983)
'Special DJ Selection From Peter Gabriel Plays Live' for club and radio DJs.

'I Don't Remember'/'Solsbury Hill'; 'Kiss of Life'
(Charisma GAB 12. July 1983)

'Walk Thorugh The Fire'/'The Race', 'I Have the Touch'
(Virgin VS68912. May 1984)

'Out Out'/'Gizmo'
(Geffen A12-4953. December 1984)

'Sledgehammer'/'Don't Break This Rhythm'; 'I Have the Touch'
(Virgin PGS 112. April 1986)

'Sledgehammer' (dance mix); 'Don't Break the Rhythm'/'Biko'; 'I Have the Touch'
(Virgin PGS 113. April 1986)

'Don't Give Up'/'In Your Eyes' (special mix); 'This is the Picture'
(Virgin PGS 212. October 1986)
Duet with Kate Bush.

'Big Time' (dance mix)/'Big Time'; 'Curtains'
(Virgin PGS 312. March 1987)

'Red Rain'/'Ga Ga'; 'Walk Through the Fire'
(Virgin PGS 4. June 1987)

'Biko'/'No More Apartheid'
(Virgin PGS612. November 1987)
Only 12 inch and cassette singles issued. Live version of Biko recorded at Blossom Music Center, Cleveland, Ohio, on 27 July 1987. Single used to promote Cry Freedom, Sir Richard Attenborough's film on Biko.

Cassette singles

'Sledgehammer' dance mix; 'Don't Break This Rhythm'; 'Sledgehammer' album version; 'Biko'.
(Virgin PGSC112. April 1986)
Also released in limited edition of 2,000 flip top cigarette style silver boxes.

'Big Time' extended version; 'Curtains'; 'No Self Control' live version; 'Across the River'.
(Virgin PGSC312. March 1987)
Also released in limited edition gold box.

'Red Rain'; 'Ga Ga'; 'Walk Through the Fire'.
(Virgin PGSC412. June 1987)

'Biko'; 'No More Apartheid'.
(Virgin PGSC612. November 1987)

CD single

'Big Time' extended version; 'Curtains'; 'No Self Control'; 'Across the River'; 'Big Time' seven inch version.
(Virgin GAIL312. March 1987)

VARIOUS ARTISTS' ALBUMS

All This and World War II, released 1977.
A film soundtrack of World War II film footage, linked to Beatles' songs, performed by various artists. Includes 'Strawberry Fields Forever' by Peter Gabriel.
(Riva RVLP2)

The Bristol Recorder. Volume 2, released January 1981. Peter Gabriel contributed three tracks to the 'Talking Magazine'. 'Humdrum' (live at Diplomat Hotel, New York, 12 July 1980); 'Not One of Us' (live at De Montford Hall, Leicester, 24 February 1980); 'Ain;t That Peculiar' (live at Uptown Theatre, Chicago, 11 March 1977).
(Bristol Recorder BR002)

Music and Rhythm, released July 1982.
The WOMAD benefit album, with Gabriel's contribution 'Across the River'.
(WEA K68045)

Against All Odds, released April 1984.
Gabriel's contribution to the movie soundtrack was 'Walk Through the Fire'.
(Virgin V2313).

Let the Children Play, released April 1984.
A charity double album in aid of the British Peace Camps, the most prominent being the women of Greenham Common. Gabriel contributed 'Exposure'.
(Panic Peace 1)

Raindrops Pattering on Banana Leaves, released June 1984.
A benefit album for WOMAD that includes 'Lead A Normal Life' – a live version recorded in Normal, Illinois on 3 December 1982.
(WOMAD 001)

Gremlins – Original Soundtrack, released October 1984.
Gabriel contributed 'Out Out'.
(Geffen GHSP 24044Y)

Sometimes a Great Notion, released November 1984.
A charity album for the British Deaf Association. Gabriel contributed 'I Have the Touch'.
(EMI Topcat 1)

Greenpeace, released April 1985.
Gabriel contributed 'Shock the Monkey'.
(Towerbell EMI Fund 1)

Sun City – Artists United Against Apartheid, released November 1985.
As well as his brief vocal appearance in the 'Sun City' theme song, Gabriel's voice was used more extensively on 'No More Apartheid'.
(EMI Manhattan MTL 1001)

Conspiracy of Hope, released November 1986.
Commemorating the worldwide Conspiracy of Hope campaign. Gabriel contributes the studio version of 'Biko'.
(Mercury MERH 99)

The Secret Policeman's Third Ball – The Music, released September 1987.
Live recording of Amnesty benefit with Gabriel performing 'Biko' at London Palladium, 29 May 1987. Line-up includes Lou Reed and Youssou N'Dour.
(Virgin V2458)

GUEST APPEARANCES/SESSION AND PRODUCTION WORK

Cat Stevens.
Mona Bone Jackon (LP), released 1970.
Peter Gabriel plays flute.

Colin Scot.
Colin Scot (LP), released 1971.
Credits with thinly disguised names for contractual reasons include 'P. Angel Gabriel', 'P. C. Genesis' (Phil Collins) and 'Van der Hammill' (Peter Hammill). Album produced by John Anthony; three songs were written by Martin Hall, later to collaborate with Gabriel; other session musicians included Jon Anderson and Robert Fripp.

Charlie Drake.
You Never Know (7"), released November 1975.
Written by Martin Hall and Peter Gabriel, produced by Gabriel, credited on the label as 'Gabriel Ear Wax'.

Robert Fripp.
Exposure (LP), released April 1979.
Gabriel sings and plays on 'Exposure', with added scream vocals from Terre Roche. The album includes what Gabriel calls the "quiet version" of 'Here Comes The Flood'. This track was digitally remixed for Network, a Fripp compilation album released in 1985.

Johnny Warman.
Walking Into Mirrors (LP), released June 1979.
Warman was a friend of Jerry Marotta. Gabriel contributes accompanying vocals, chants, screaming and effects on 'Screaming Jets'.

Jimmy Pursey.
Animals Have More Fun/SUS (7"), June 1981.
Both tracks credited Gabriel/Ellis/Pursey. Produced by Peter Gabriel.

Laurie Anderson.
Mister Heartbreak (LP), released February 1984.
'Excellent Birds' written by Gabriel and Anderson. He plays Synclavier, Linn drum, vocals and co-produces with Anderson. Also backing vocals on 'Langue D'Amour' and 'Gravity's Angel'.

Phil Collins.
No Jacket Required (LP), released February 1985.
Backing vocals on 'Take Me Home', also released as 7" and 12".

The Call.
Reconciled (LP), released May 1986.
Backing vocals on 'Everywhere I Go', also released as a remixed single.

Nona Hendryx.
Female Trouble (LP), released June 1987.
Backing vocals on 'Winds of Change (Mandela to Mandela)'.

Robbie Robertson.
Robbie Robertson (LP), released October 1987.
The former guitarist with The Band, co-produced by Daniel Lanois. Gabriel's backing vocals on 'Fallen Angel', also released as a single in November 1987. Song includes the line, "Come down Gabriel, blow your horn." Also vocals on 'Broken Arrow'.

Joni Mitchell.
Chalk Marks in a Rainstorm (LP), due for release in February 1988.
Vocals on 'My Secret Place' recorded at Ashcombe House, autumn 1986.

Cover Versions:

Alan Ross.
Are You Free On Saturday (LP), released in October 1977.
Martin Hall and Peter Gabriel wrote 'Get The Guns', released as a single in June 1977.

Tom Robinson Band.
TRB Two (LP), released January 1979.
'Bully For You' was co-written by Gabriel and Robinson, and was also released as a single.

Tom Robinson.
North By Northwest (LP), released August 1982.
Gabriel and Robinson co-wrote 'Merrily Up On High', and 'Atmospherics (Listen to the Radio)'.

Peter Gabriel also wrote the music for a 'Dans Le Creux De Ta Nuit' on the album *Soleil Dans L'Ombre* by Catherine Ribeiro. His songs have also been covered by two artists who could hardly be more diverse, James Last who did a version of 'Games Without Frontiers' on his album *Magic Hits From 1980* and put the same track on his album *Hamsamania*; and Robert Wyatt who covered 'Biko' on his 12" EP 'Work In Progress'.

232